GUARDIAN ANGEL

JACK OF ALL TRADES...

GUARDIAN ANGEL

*Life and Death Adventures with
Pararescue, the World's Most
Powerful Commando Rescue Force*

WILLIAM F. SINE

Senior Master Sergeant, USAF (Ret.)

CASEMATE

Philadelphia & Oxford

Published in the United States of America and Great Britain in 2012 by
CASEMATE PUBLISHERS
908 Darby Road, Havertown, PA 19083
and
10 Hythe Bridge Street, Oxford, OX1 2EW

ISBN 978-1-61200-122-7
Digital Edition: ISBN 978-1-61200-134-0

Cataloging-in-publication data is available from the Library of Congress and
the British Library.

10 9 8 7 6 5 4 3 2 1

Printed and bound in the United States of America.

For a complete list of Casemate titles please contact:

CASEMATE PUBLISHERS (US)
Telephone (610) 853-9131, Fax (610) 853-9146
E-mail: casemate@casematepublishing.com

CASEMATE PUBLISHERS (UK)
Telephone (01865) 241249, Fax (01865) 794449
E-mail: casemate-uk@casematepublishing.co.uk

Front cover photo: An Alaska Air National Guard pararescueman performs a high-altitude
jump from a Coast Guard C-130 Hercules during a training mission above Joint Base
Elmendorf-Richardson, Alaska.—*Airman 1st Class Jack Sanders (USAF), af.mil*

Frontispiece: "Jack of All Trades" by legendary PJ Udo Fischer.

All photos are from author's collection unless otherwise noted.

MIX
Paper from
responsible sources
FSC® C011935

CONTENTS

INTRODUCTION

Angel of God, my guardian dear
To whom His love entrusts me here
Ever this day be at my side
To light and guard, to rule and guide
Amen
—*traditional Catholic prayer to one's Guardian Angel*

THE WORLD'S MOST POWERFUL AND ACCOMPLISHED RESCUE FORCE IS U.S. Air Force Pararescue. Military leaders rely on pararescue forces to accomplish the most difficult and dangerous national priority rescue missions such as recovering American jet pilots who are shot down and stranded deep behind enemy lines. Pararescuemen, also known as PJs for pararescue jumpers, are ultra-elite commandos whose training is on par with that of U.S. Navy SEALs, U.S. Army special forces (Green Berets) and rangers, and Marine Corps amphibious reconnaissance. A PJ's mission is unique among U.S. unconventional warfare operators. PJs and their Combat Rescue Officers, called CROs and pronounced crow, are masters of all things rescue, but they remain little known outside the close knit and secretive special operations community.

PJs routinely take on harrowing missions that are beyond the capabilities of other rescue organizations. They can operate in the depths of the sea or at the roof of the world. They have braved withering Iraqi machine-gun fire to scuba dive in filthy canals, searching for casualties, and have saved hundreds of injured climbers on the treacherous slopes of Mt. McKinley. PJs also provide worldwide humanitarian aid after natural disasters. In the fourteen days immediately following Hurricane Katrina, PJs rescued four thousand victims. Pararescue has always been cutting-edge and has supported America's space program from the beginning. For decades NASA used PJs to support capsule splashdowns and space shuttle operations. In their humanitarian role, PJs rescue civilians of all nationalities, especially distressed sailors isolated far out at sea. Since USAF Pararescue's founding in 1947, PJs have saved almost forty thousand lives. The pararescue motto succinctly explains a PJ's willingness to sacrifice all in the performance of his duties: *These things we do, that others may live.*

The lifesaving mission of pararescue and the selfless sentiment embodied in the PJ motto represents a noble calling that is worthy of a divine benefactor. Many PJs believe this patronage takes the form of a guardian angel who nurtures and protects the pararescue profession and its endeavors. Like many PJs, I believe I have a guardian angel. Looking back on my career and the many close calls I had, I think my angel must be unusually powerful! A "Rescue Angel" is the centerpiece of the PJ emblem.

In 1966 the air force chief of staff authorized PJs to wear a distinctive maroon beret adorned with a metal badge depicting the PJ emblem. The maroon beret is a tangible symbol that acknowledges the extremely hazardous duties of pararescuemen and pays homage to the blood they shed in the line of duty. Historically, pararescue is only the second specialty in the American armed forces, and the first in the U.S. Air Force, authorized to wear a distinctive beret.

Pararescue is not only the most capable humanitarian rescue organization in existence; it's also the world's most effective combat search and rescue force. To a greater extent than any other country in history, America takes care of its men and women in uniform who serve and sacrifice for their country: it's a national core value. American civilians around the world and U.S. military personnel serving overseas know with certainty that their country will go to incredible lengths to rescue them. The Department of Defense places the highest priority and value on personnel recovery (PR) and views it as a military and moral imperative. PR consists of the ability to quickly and accurately report an incident, locate the isolated personnel, support the rescue operation with the full might of our nation, recover the person using combat search and rescue forces, and reintegrate the rescued personnel back into their unit or society and care for their long-term physical and mental wellbeing. The rescue mission is so important that air force leaders decided there should be an elite force exclusively dedicated to PR. The U.S. Air Force calls that force the Guardian Angel Weapon System. Guardian Angel is made up of the trio of pararescuemen, combat rescue officers, and SERE specialists (experts in survival, evasion, resistance, and escape). Guardian Angel is the only Department of Defense asset that provides the full spectrum of personnel recovery services. Air force brass usually reserve weapon system status for war-fighting hardware such as jet aircraft. It is a singular honor for the human components of Guardian Angel—PJs, CROs and SERE—to be acclaimed as a high-priority weapon system.

Pararescue has a remarkable and storied past. PJs have played a prominent role in every armed conflict since World War II. The pararescue profession can trace its beginnings to 1943 when Lt. Col. Donald Flickinger, a flight surgeon, and two enlisted medics parachuted into the Burmese jungle to rescue twenty-one allied crew and passengers who had bailed-out of their damaged airplane over Japanese-occupied territory. The mission turned into a month-long ordeal in which both survivors and rescuers struggled against man-eating tigers, bloodthirsty leaches, fierce head-hunters, and Japanese soldiers. Famous war correspondent and television journalist Eric Sevareid, a was among those stranded in the jungle. He later wrote of Lieutenant Colonel Flickinger and his two medics, "Gallant is a precious word. They deserve it." This amazing rescue mission helped inspire the creation of USAF Pararescue in 1947.

Surprisingly, pararescue is little known outside military circles. PJs are combat rescue and recovery specialists second to none. During the Korean War PJs rescued nearly a thousand men from behind enemy lines and helped establish the helicopter as the iconic rescue aircraft. During the Vietnam War PJs were credited with nearly twenty-eight hundred combat saves and were the most decorated enlisted warriors in the air force. PJ heroes earned a Medal of Honor, a dozen Air Force Crosses, one hundred and five Silver Stars, and hundreds of Distinguished Flying Crosses. In 1989 during Operation Just Cause, the invasion of Panama, PJs parachuted onto Rio Hata Airfield and provided exceptional medical coverage for the assault force. PJs were also a powerful presence in Haiti during Operation Uphold Democracy, but most famously PJs fought side by side with U.S. Army rangers in Somalia in 1993 during the Battle of Mogadishu. The fierce fighting and conspicuous gallantry of the American warriors inspired the book and movie *Black Hawk Down*. During the firefight, the largest since Vietnam, PJ Scott Fales earned a Silver Star and Purple Heart and PJ Tim Wilkinson earned the Air Force Cross. In 1999 PJs played a key role during NATO'S first major military engagement: Operation Allied Force in Kosovo. When enemy forces used an SA-3 antiaircraft missile to shoot down an F-117A Night Hawk stealth fighter, rescue helicopters with PJs recovered the pilot from deep in enemy Yugoslav territory. Take a moment and think about that: PJs rescued the pilot of the only stealth fighter ever to be shot down in combat, and yet most people have never heard of USAF Pararescue. PJs were also involved in the dramatic rescue of a shot-down F-16 pilot during the same conflict.

Flash forward to 2002 during Operation Enduring Freedom in Afghanistan. On his very first deployment PJ Jason Cunningham volunteered for a complex and dangerous rescue mission during Operation Anaconda. At the Battle of Takur Ghar, also known as the Battle of Roberts Ridge, his helicopter was hit by a rocket propelled grenade and crash-landed. In the chaotic aftermath of the crash and the desperate fighting that ensued, enemy fighters shot Airman Cunningham below his body armor. Despite his mortal wound, Pararescueman Cunningham continued to medically treat his injured comrades until he died from loss of blood. For his valiant and selfless efforts to save others despite his fatal wounds, our grateful nation awarded Jason Cunningham the Air Force Cross. When army Pfc. Jessica Lynch was captured in 2003 during the invasion of Iraq it was Joint Special Operations Command (JSOC) forces that rescued her. This was the first successful rescue of an American POW since World War II and the first ever rescue of a female POW. At the climax of the rescue operation a PJ was the first American to arrive at her side. Despite being unknown to most people, PJs take part in many important, but often classified, JSOC raids. True to its name and nature, JSOC missions are often conducted by composite teams peopled with the best special operators each U.S military service has to offer. PJs are frequently a key component of these teams, because they have all the basic and advanced commando skills, high levels of physical fitness, and unexcelled expertise in combat medicine. PJs and

CROs have skills and carry gear possessed by no other special operators in the world such as those needed to execute rescues from confined spaces and following structural collapses and technical rope rescues.

It's hard to become a PJ: 85 percent of PJ candidates fail to complete training. PJs attend the military's most grueling combat schools. They must graduate basic and advanced army parachuting courses. They learn to scuba dive in a combat environment and survive in the open ocean. They attend Air Force Survival School and learn to evade enemy soldiers and resist interrogation. After completing the military's toughest commando courses, they train for an additional six months to become nationally registered paramedics, and *then* they can begin actual PJ training at the Guardian Angel Training Center.

On the battlefield, PJs are jacks-of-all-trades. PJs have mastered skills that set them apart from all other special operations forces. PJs can operate seamlessly with other service's and even other country's special operations teams and often accompany them into battle as their rescue and medical experts. Despite their advanced medical skills, PJs are not considered medics. According to Chapter IV, Articles 25 and 29 of the Geneva Conventions, medics are officially noncombatants and if captured are afforded special status. Medics usually wear a clear insignia such as a white armband with a red cross to distinguish them from combat soldiers. PJs dress like the frontline fighters they are and are armed like the hero in a first-person-shooter video game. Their camouflaged battle-gear is festooned with grenades, pistols, assault rifles, and ammunition. PJs have ended the lives of many enemy soldiers. PJs are ready to fight their way in to accomplish a rescue and shoot their way out if necessary; they are war-fighters who specialize in personnel rescue.

PJs are certified experts in technical rescue, including structural collapse and vehicle extrication. When a terrorist detonates an improvised explosive device, flinging an eighteen-ton armored vehicle through the air, and the shattered convoy radios its distress call while still under fire, PJs are often the first responders. Arriving on-scene in Pave Hawk HH-60 helicopters, they use advanced pneumatic lift bags, high-powered portable saws, and other specialized devices to move the vehicle, cut into compartments and free those trapped inside, oftentimes while under enemy fire. Their tempo of operations can be astounding. During a ninety-day deployment to Afghanistan, PJs will participate in many hundreds of rescue missions. During many of these missions the rescue zone is still *hot*, requiring the PJs to play the dual role of skilled fighter *and* rescuer.

During one mission in Iraq a PJ accompanied an assault team to take down an enemy-held building. It was a trap: the structure was sabotaged with explosives. When the assault team entered, the bombs detonated and collapsed the building around them. The PJ, positioned outside, immediately leaped into action and used his specialized gear to free the assault team, rescuing everyone who had been trapped inside. As part of his rescue kit, the PJ carried lift bags and structural collapse tools and was able to free teammates trapped under rubble. Among the panoply of military commandos, only a PJ could have achieved this feat.

As you might expect of U.S. Air Force commandos, PJs are completely at home in the air. Like the flight engineers, pilots, and other aircrew members, PJs are an integral part of internal aircraft operations. Intimately familiar with the inner workings of rescue aircraft and trusted by air force pilots and crews, PJs control and direct activities in the back of the aircraft during recovery operations. On air force aircraft, all other special operators are merely passengers. In a rescue helicopter full of navy SEALs and army Delta Force, it's the CROs and PJs who are in charge.

There are fewer than six hundred PJs in the air force. Pararescue is such a gratifying career choice, that I feel like a born-again proselytizer, obligated to spread the joyous word. I've lived and breathed pararescue for more than three decades. Through my writing I hope to attract America's best and hardest young men to our ranks; young men who have the *steel* to be pararescuemen. Pararescue is an adrenaline rush experience, physically, intellectually, and emotionally. This profession is extraordinary because it combines the excitement and danger of being a prime player in impossibly difficult military missions, with the mental challenges and rewards of administering emergency lifesaving medical treatment. PJs and CROs have a patriotic and sexy mission. In this book, I focus on operations that define PJs and set them apart from all other special operators. Pararescue embodies a lifestyle filled with global adventure. For a PJ performing his duties the sacrifices are great, but the rewards are incomparable. The mission of pararescue is a arduous but noble undertaking. Within the ranks of pararescuemen we have an informal saying, absolutely *not* approved or endorsed by our higher-ups, "USAF Pararescue. Maybe you can be one of us. But we doubt it!"

CHAPTER 1

_____

INTO THE VALLEY

_____

Two roads diverged in a wood, and I,
I took the one less traveled by,
And that has made all the difference.
—*Robert Frost, "The Road Not Taken"*

HELMAND VALLEY, AFGHANISTAN, 16 FEBRUARY 2002
A HUGE MILITARY PLANE SPEEDS THROUGH THE NIGHT. I STAND INSIDE with my legs braced wide, weighed down with combat gear. My attention is laser focused on the ramp and door at the tail end of the plane. I am about to lead my pararescue team on a desperate rescue mission, a night parachute jump into enemy territory. My mouth is as dry as the desert thirty-five hundred feet below. We're wearing state-of-the-art military parachutes. Underneath our parachutes, our tactical vests contain thirty pounds of ammunition, hand grenades, and fighting gear. Massive rucksacks snap to the front of our parachute harnesses with quick-release connectors and hang almost to the ground, making it awkward to walk. Each rucksack contains eighty pounds of equipment including night vision goggles, medical supplies, and satellite radios. We have M4 assault rifles strapped to our sides, updated versions of the M16 of Vietnam War fame, fitted with powerful grenade launchers and laser sights. All told, each man is burdened with nearly one hundred and fifty pounds of parachutes and combat gear.

I am a pararescue team leader flying in an HC-130 Hercules, a large four-engine cargo plane reengineered to conduct combat rescue missions.

This unique rescue aircraft boasts sophisticated radar and communications arrays and uses cutting-edge navigation computers. HC-130s can fly through the eyes of hurricanes and refuel rescue helicopters in mid-air. But most importantly, this plane can drop paratroopers. Like my teammates I am saddled with full combat jump equipment, but with adrenaline charging my muscles, I feel like Superman; I'm ready to go.

Slowly, the back of the plane opens like a giant clamshell and cold winter air suddenly rushes around the cavernous interior. The loadmaster gives me a thumbs-up, signaling that in thirty seconds our pilot will flip a switch turning the red jump lights to green. When the lights turn green, my team is clear to jump from the plane. My two teammates follow me as I carefully shuffle to the edge of the open ramp and stand just inches away from a thirty-five hundred foot drop. *This is it!,* I think. I stare into the night, poised to dive into the cold, empty sky.

We are jumping to save a soldier who had a leg blown off by an anti-tank landmine. Once we parachute from the plane my first responsibility will be to land my team clear of the deadly minefield. When my parachute opens I'll use its steering toggles to avoid the minefield and land on safe ground marked with a strobe light. In a deadly earnest game of follow-the-leader my two teammates will chase me through the air, mimicking my every turn. I bend over and brace my hands on my knees, temporarily shifting the weight of my jump gear off my spine. Doubts and second-guessing threaten to overwhelm me, but I know that moments of greatest turmoil and stress require the greatest calm and professionalism: it's the pararescue way. I rein in my emotions, clear my mind, and focus on the task at hand.

I reflect back on the peculiar series of events that led to this moment. Only a few short months ago I was training in Florida with members of my pararescue unit. We were at Patrick Air Force Base conducting week-long parachute training, High-altitude, low-opening jumps we call HALO. HALO parachuting is a bread-and-butter pararescue skill. Gathered in front of the 39th Rescue Squadron's operations counter, we were preparing for the day's parachute training. Occasionally, we glanced at a large TV mounted on the wall. Suddenly, we were watching passenger jets crash into New York City's World Trade Center towers. Everyone crowded around the screen, mesmerized by the stunning events unfolding before us on the screen. Gradually we came to the sickening realization that terrorists were attacking our country. In short order, the president grounded all planes in the United States and ordered all military personnel to report to their units. We immediately canceled the remainder of our training, organized into vehicles, and began the four-hour drive back home to Moody Air Force Base, Georgia. My boss, Maj. Terry Johnson, rode with me in my SUV. He was the 38th Rescue Squadron's operations director and second-in-command under Maj. Vincent Savino, our commander.

I felt the 9/11 attacks in the pit of my stomach, like large angry butterflies. During the drive home I was nervous, jacked up on adrenaline. Reality felt shaky. Just as normally solid ground cannot be trusted during an earthquake, I felt as if the foundations of my world-view were shifting and unstable. I was surprised by the depth of my feelings. The 9/11 attacks had an emotional impact on par with that of the JFK assassination decades earlier. Like the Kennedy assassination, everyone remembers where they were when the Twin Towers came crashing down.

Isolated and alone in the confines of our speeding vehicle, Major Johnson and I listened to news on the radio. Except for the occasional phone call, the radio was our only link to the outside world. We listened transfixed as the drama unfolded, the radio announcers revealing the scope of the attacks one piece at a time. We learned of the kamikaze-like crash into the Pentagon and the failed attack on the capital that ended in a Pennsylvania pasture. We listened in disbelief as the announcer described the towers imploding and collapsing into colossal mounds of twisted concrete and molten steel. Our conversation was disjointed, each man absorbed by his personal worries and thoughts. We wanted to be with our families to keep them safe. The entire day was surreal. The major and I both realized, though neither of us said the words, that nothing would ever be the same. We also knew we had a lot of work to do. We were almost certain to go to war.

In the days that followed the 38th Rescue Squadron prepared to deploy overseas with our men and equipment. We just didn't know exactly when or where we would go. As the operations superintendent I had a key role in readying our PJs for war. Our unit had a lot of young inexperienced troops. Some were fresh from PJ School and had not yet had a single rescue mission. But we also had a lot of experienced men who could lead the way.

It was a hectic time. Our squadron was less than a year old. As a brand new rescue unit we had a lot to prove.

Where and when would America counterattack? We watched and waited with the rest of the nation. Eventually, our country's leaders finished plotting our nation's course of action and sent orders streaming down our chain of command. Squadrons from Air Force Special Operations Command at Hurlburt Field, Florida, deployed first. We envied those PJs and crews who would get the first opportunities to fly combat missions. But we knew that in a few months those squadrons would return to the United States and we would get our chance to serve.

From the beginning I had certain knowledge that I could have a direct role to play in the coming conflict if I wanted to. My feelings were magnitudes stronger than a vague premonition. I felt I could influence events by my sheer force of will. I had experienced this peculiar state-of-mind before, always at important crossroads in my life. I know I'm not the only person to have this experience; Robert Frost described the feeling in his poem "The Road not Taken." It's as if I am traveling towards my future when I suddenly come to a fork in the road. One path is safe; the other path fraught with risk and uncertainty. My decision to join pararescue twenty-six years earlier had been the result of choosing the risky, life changing path. In the coming days I could choose to contribute as a behind-the-scenes rescue planner, or I could get right in the middle of the combat action.

I was a forty-four-year-old senior master sergeant I was in good physical shape and was well versed in virtually every advanced PJ skill. The problem was that with my rank and experience, when I deployed my commander would almost certainly relegate me to a staff position. Normally, at this stage of a PJ's career it is time to coach, not play. I understood that rationale, but I still wanted to serve as a team leader in the thick of the action; I wanted to be in the game, not on the sidelines. Although my chances were slim, I had that premonition—that secret knowledge—so I acted as if I would deploy as an operator. While I helped ready our team I prepared myself. I sharpened my skills by flying as many helicopter training missions as I could. I did the same on the HC-130, performing night full equipment training jumps at every opportunity. I flexed my PJ skills as often as I could. Physically, I upped my training runs to five miles every other day. In between I swam fifteen hundred meters and crushed weights in the gym.

When I am in top physical shape I feel like I am invincible. I am the dominating alpha male, the pack leader with unshakable confidence. PJs are mostly always like that but the older you get, the harder it is to keep that edge and,as operators go, I was pretty old.

In early October, the United States and its allies initiated began bombing Al Qaida and Taliban strongholds in Afghanistan: Operation Enduring Freedom. We all watched the action unfold on television. We were champing at the bit to get to Afghanistan and fly combat missions. Word trickled back from the war zone about the exploits of our special-ops PJs racking up combat saves. When the initial wave special operations forces rotated back to the United States in a few months, the 38th was slated to take their place overseas. In the meantime, I had to train and help keep unit morale high. As the weeks crawled by our situation crystallized. We would deploy two PJ teams sometime in November. One PJ team would support 41st Rescue Squadron helicopter operations, deploying to Karshi-Kanabad, Uzbekistan, an old Soviet era airbase we nicknamed K2. The second element of PJs would support 71st Rescue Squadron HC-130 operations to be flown out of Jacobabad, Pakistan. A three-man PJ team would crew each of the two HC-130s. A combat rescue officer (CRO) would accompany the PJs and exercise overall command of the teams. If necessary, he could also step in as an operator. Finally, my unit was going to war, but they were going without me.

Major Terry Johnson was the CRO on the first rotation into combat and chided me about not being able to go. The unit's plan was for me to deploy on the second rotation in a staff position. My plan was to deploy as an operator and I trained harder and harder as the weeks seemed to crawl by. At Moody we received regular classified reports from the front. It was clear that our men were participating in some intense wartime missions. It was frustrating to know that our teammates were seeing action while we cooled our heels stateside, but the knowledge that we would soon join them was good for morale and kept our heads in the game. I distributed a monthly newsletter to pass on information and keep the mood loose. I filled the newsletter with *sage* advice to the PJs gleaned from my years of experience: eat power foods, like Wheaties, with Jack Daniels, and watch your drinking . . . in a small hand mirror.

First thing every morning all PJs and CROs assembled in the equipment room. Leadership passed on important information and set priorities for the day. Once I told the team, "Stop and look around at your teammates. There is a chance that not everyone in this room will return unharmed. Some of you may be killed in combat. On the other hand, you have the opportunity to save lives under such difficult conditions that no one else can pull it off. Think of all the military schools you attended, all the sweat and tears, the years of training needed to perfect your skills. Your entire life in the United States military has led you to this moment; this is the end game. I think you are all up to the challenge and will do pararescue and your country proud."

I knew everyone was stoked to go to Afghanistan, but I also wanted to steel them for the worst. "Prepare well. Your life and your teammate's life may depend on your skill and resolve." War is serious business and sometimes catastrophe is unavoidable, beyond our ability to influence the outcome. I specifically remember that talk, because it proved prophetic.

Whenever I mentioned my desire to deploy as a team leader my commander, Major Savino, would roll his eyes and chuckle. "Bill, I know you want to go as a team leader, but that's not going to happen. We need you in a staff position where we can use your experience." I knew Major Savino was right. As a leader and commander he is as good as they come. The top brass in the air force picked him to be the very first CRO commander of a rescue squadron: a singular honor. He integrated thousands of disparate pieces of information and formulated the most effective ways for our squadron to accomplish our lifesaving combat mission. It was a monumental responsibility with life and death repercussions.

As operations superintendent I ran scheduling and training and picked the PJ teams who would deploy next. It was difficult because we were experiencing serious personnel shortages. We only had half of the men we were supposed to have, barely enough to meet our basic mission responsibilities. We were especially short on recovery team leaders. A fully-qualified team leader must be an expert PJ who can lead any type of mission on helicopters or HC-130s. It takes many years to master the intricate skills required to be a team leader.

We were conducting night-jump operations a few weeks before the fresh teams were slated to replace our PJs who were returning from Afghanistan. During the jump a team leader who was scheduled to go had a hard landing and tore his knee cartilage. The injury was serious; he would not be able to deploy. I studied the list of possible replacements. There *were* no other team leaders available . . . except me. I went to Major Savino and, as I struggled to keep from grinning, explained the situation to him. Savino studied the roster of PJs looked at me, and shook his head. "Alright Sine. You can go, but this is the last time you'll ever deploy as a team leader. You understand?" "Yes sir!" I replied.

A few weeks later it was finally time for my group of PJs to deploy. After two days of flying our plane touched down, throttled back, and taxied to parking. We had finally arrived in Jacobabad. Jacobabad, also known as Jbad, is located in southern Pakistan, a short flight of three hundred miles from Kandahar, Afghanistan. Our teammates met us at the plane and helped collect our gear. Besides the runways, the base consisted mostly of a large tent city. Everything was in tents, the dining hall, latrines, even the showers. There were a few hard structures including a large camouflage hangar that sheltered the helicopters and contained offices for planning. The HC-130s were parked a mile away on a nearby taxiway. There were other aircraft on the base, including a contingent of MQ-1 Predator drones. I love it when a new tent city is first set up. It reminds me of a lawless Wild West frontier town. As time passes a tent city becomes established and military rules and bureaucracies increase exponentially. This is always the progression, but initially bare base set-ups are a lot of fun because the rules are lax.

Most Muslim men wear a beard at least one-fist long primarily because the Prophet Muhammad wore a beard. Because special operators often-times conducted their missions in the mountains and country side of Afghanistan, they let their beards grow in order to garner respect and be more effective when dealing with the tribes. The military rank and file, however, never leave the base. They are not allowed to grow beards and have to adhere to normal uniform and grooming standards. Conventional military personnel quickly figured out that Americans with beards were special operators: Green Berets, SEALs, PJs, and the like. Those with beards soon noticed the special treatment they received from their conventional military colleagues. Our bearded PJs were suddenly perceived to be as powerful as comic book super heroes. We quickly learned to exploit our new super powers. PJs used "the power of the beard" to brazenly requisition supplies and equipment, and sometimes just to have fun.

Soon after we arrived we piled into a pickup truck and our bearded PJ driver drove to the flight line where the war planes were parked. He wanted to show me the power of the beard. A security policeman stood guard at the gate. The cop stopped our vehicle and asked our business. Our driver casually replied, "We're going to drive onto the taxiway and do doughnuts with this truck." The puzzled guard scrutinized us; most of us had powerful beards. He looked hard into the eyes of our bearded driver, who returned his gaze without flinching. Finally the guard said, "OK. Go ahead." After he waved us through, we spent the next fifteen minutes, in full sight of the policeman, doing doughnuts on the taxiway. Long live the power of the beard!

Everybody lived in tent city except the PJs. We commandeered a hardened aircraft shelter we called the HAS (hardened aircraft shelter, pronounced *haz*) and made it our cozy home. Built of thick concrete reinforced with rebar steel, and normally used to shelter jets from aerial attack, a HAS makes a perfect PJ base of operations, secure and private. By the time anyone thought to question our right to the building we were already well entrenched and cited our need for secure storage for our medical narcotics and our substantial cache of weapons and explosives. We scrounged plywood and other construction materials and built private apartments along an inside wall. The average service member on J-bad shared a large canvas tent with seven other people. They slept on cots side-by-side like human sardines in a large cloth can, while each of my PJs had their own room with bookshelves and a bunk with a mattress. We walled off the front of the HAS and set up an entertainment area with DVD players, computers with internet, and air conditioning. We accomplished our renovations by making friends with key people on base: communications officers and supply specialists. We traded cool PJ gear and vodka we smuggled back from K2, and of course we used the power of the beard.

The PJs we were replacing had mastered the daily routine. Led by my good friend MSgt. Lee Shaffer, they showed us new guys the ropes. We read up on the latest intelligence and order of battle. We configured our gear and encrypted our radios. I was team leader for one team of PJs, and TSgt. Ken Fornier was the team leader for a second three-man team. Our teams took turns pulling rescue alert for three days at a time. When a mission goes down it is the alert crew who responds. We prepositioned most of our rescue equipment on the alert aircraft and the rest we stashed in a designated area in the HAS. In case of a scramble, an order to immediately launch on a mission, we could pile into a truck with our gear and load the plane within minutes. Along with the rest of the crew, we could fire up the plane and be airborne within half an hour. The cockpit crew consists of a pilot, copilot, radio operator, navigator, and flight engineer. In the cargo compartment, the crew consists of two loadmasters and a three-man PJ team. Each member of the crew has skills that are critical to the mission. The loadmasters are in charge of the plane's cargo compartment and have important duties during parachute deployments. We flew almost every night ferrying supplies, equipment, and people to Kandahar, Afghanistan. During these flights we were on airborne alert, ready at a moment's notice to divert for a rescue mission.

We flew in the dark wearing night vision goggles and body armor with titanium plates that could stop a high-powered rifle bullet. Our mechanics draped the interior walls of the plane with panels of Kevlar armor. PJs sat at lookout positions, armored seats near windows, to scan for enemy missile launches and antiaircraft ground-fire. Both PJ lookouts held a control to launch defensive flares and chaff in case of radar-guided or heat-seeking missile attacks. Hopefully, the hot flares would entice heat-seeking missiles away from our engines and the metal-confetti, radar-reflecting chaff, would fill the sky confusing radar-guided missiles. The most vulnerable phases of flight are take-offs and landings. This is when our plane is closest to the ground and most susceptible to attack. We varied takeoff times to remain unpredictable. When we landed we used a steep corkscrew approach to remain over the airfield and away from urban areas. Occasionally the enemy fired upon us, but it was from a distance and was ineffective. Flying in a combat zone is a deadly serious business.

––––––––––

On 16 February 2002 our HC-130 takes off from Jacobabad en route to Afghanistan. The mission is to transport people and equipment to Kandahar, take on another load of supplies and personnel, and fly them to K2. That night we are flying airborne alert and have a PJ from the other alert team SAmn. Jason Baird onboard. Our CRO, 1st Lt. Matt "Moose" Mc-

Guinness, is also flying with us. Moose had been an enlisted PJ before he became a CRO. In fact, I attended his PJ graduation ceremony in 1998. Moose is tall and athletic and his favorite sport is rugby. He has a shiny bald head and an infectious, gap-toothed grin. Lieutenant McGuinness made it to staff sergeant before attending Officer Training School. I occasionally poke fun at him because his college degree is in forestry management, absolutely useless knowledge for a CRO unless he's ordered to rescue seedlings. During this deployment Moose and I have been going back and forth playing practical jokes on each other. His time as an enlisted PJ gives him a good perspective as an officer.

My assistant team leader is TSgt. Rich Carroll. Sergeant Carroll had been a marine before he crossed over to the air force and became a PJ. I have great respect for The Corps; some of our best PJs are former marines. Rounding out my team is SAmn. Randall Wilkes. Randy has only been a PJ for about a year. He is inexperienced but has solid PJ skills. I assigned Randy to carry the bulk of our medical gear and manage the kit once we are on the ground. He is our primary team medic. As the highest ranking and most experienced PJ, I am the recovery team leader.

In the face of bad weather we land at Kandahar, off-load our cargo, and take on a load of supplies and personnel. I know many of the people who come onboard. They are members of the 66th Rescue Squadron, a Pave Hawk HH-60 unit at Nellis Air Force Base, Nevada. Once cargo and passengers are secure our plane takes off and sets course for K2 on the far side of the Hindu Kush Mountains. I wear a headset plugged into the plane's intercom system so I can hear conversations in the cockpit and listen to radio chatter with outside agencies. A few minutes into the flight I start hearing confused talk about a possible mission, a medical evacuation (medevac). There is no specific mission tasking, so I don't get too excited. Moose is staying on top of developments and sorting things out. Events soon gel, and the Joint Rescue Coordination Center in Saudi Arabia, orders our return to Kandahar to off-load cargo and nonessential personnel and configure for a medevac mission. A medevac operation involves setting up the inside of the plane with litters and stanchions, flying to the patient's location, and transferring them onto our plane. Our PJs will monitor the patient en route to a trauma hospital and deal with any medical emergencies that come up along the way.

Our pilot, Major Crabtree, received the order and reversed course back to the airfield. During our absence a sandstorm has moved over Kandahar. Visibility is nil, so we rely on the experience of Major Crabtree and our young navigator 1st Lt. Brian Symon to use our planes high-tech navigation aids to land us safely. As soon as we touchdown, we quickly unload our cargo and passengers. Our colleagues who were on their way to K2 will have to spend another night in Afghanistan, but they understand that rescue missions take precedence. While we clear the cargo compartment our radio operator, SSgt. Kevin Rolle, works his radios to get more detailed information on our mission. When the flight crew begins plotting the mission coordinates they discover the location is hundreds of miles away. This spot doesn't fit with the little we know of the medevac mission. Further radio inquiries confirm that the first mission had been cancelled and we are tasked with an entirely different mission.

The new mission is much more serious and complex than a routine medevac. It involves a five-man Australian Special Air Service (SAS) long-range vehicle patrol. The SAS is Australia's elite military commando force, and they are operating in the Helmand Valley near the Iranian border. One of their soldiers lost a leg when an antitank landmine destroyed his vehicle. U.S. Air Force Combat Controller Jesse Fleener is embedded with the SAS patrol. Combat controllers serve with PJs in special tactics squadrons and are very familiar with PJ skills. After the mine explosion Sergeant Fleener quickly radioed for an emergency medical evacuation. When he learned there was a PJ team flying alert on an HC-130 he quickly explained PJ capabilities to the SAS team leader who immediately requested that the PJs parachute into the SAS location to help save their teammate and friend.

Our plane takes off from Kandahar at the same time as two helicopters from the 66th Rescue Squadron. Our HC-130, with its four powerful turboprop engines, can fly almost twice as fast as the helicopters. If our plane can arrive at least a half hour before the choppers, it makes sense for us to parachute into the site, stabilize the patient, and prepare him for transport. When the helicopters arrive the patient will already be ready for evacuation. When a life hangs precariously in the balance, every second counts. The best thing we can do for our patient is to deliver him to a fully capable surgical team as quickly as possible.

These are uncharted waters. In the long and storied history of pararescue, no PJ team has ever parachuted to a patient during a combat engagement. PJs have made numerous combat jumps as part of larger joint operations involving special operators from other armed services, but an all PJ team has never jumped in combat. Over the years PJs have perfected and advertised a combat-rescue-jump capability, but the military brass is reluctant to use PJs this way. Some commanders think that parachuting PJs behind enemy lines to aid wounded soldiers is too risky, only adding to the number of people they ultimately have to recover. While understandable, PJs think this mindset is timid and seriously underestimates PJ and air force rescue capabilities. There are undeniable facts that make combat-rescue-jump missions practical: America always has air superiority and the best special operators.

I give my team a quick update on the situation and we begin to prepare for the jump. My first decision is to choose which type of parachute to use, static line or free fall. We use static line parachutes for jumps below one thousand feet, when cloud decks are low, or when it makes sense to limit hang-time and exposure to hostile small arms fire from the ground. A problematic characteristic of the round static line canopies is that they are not very maneuverable. I choose the MC-5 free-fall parachute system because of its 25 mph forward airspeed and agile maneuverability: we need to have pinpoint accuracy to avoid the mine field.

My next decision is to forgo a jumpmaster-directed drop in favor of a navigator release. As jumpmaster, I would have to throw wind-drift indicators from the plane to determine an exit point, much too time consuming in this situation. I decide to rely on the navigator and his onboard computers to calculate our exit point. I also decide to jump from thirty-five hundred feet using RAMZ procedures. RAMZ (riggable alternative method Zodiac) is the acronym describing an inflatable Zodiac boat that can be paradropped from an HC-130. For ocean rescues PJs use special techniques to parachute into the sea with a Zodiac boat. I decide to use RAMZ jump procedures, but without the boat. I will exit the plane first, followed by my teammates. We will pull our ripcords at staggered intervals. I will pull my ripcord after five seconds, the next PJ will pull after three seconds, and the last PJ out of the plane will pull almost immediately. Once my two teammate's parachutes open, they will fly through the sky mimicking my every turn and maneuver. As the first jumper out of the plane, and the low man, I will steer my parachute to land on the target. If all goes well, the rest of my team will follow me down to a safe landing.

My decision to use RAMZ is unconventional. These procedures have never been used over land and never with jumpers weighted down with so much gear. One reason I decide to use RAMZ protocols is that my team is very familiar with this routine. Our home unit is a short flight from the ocean and we practice RAMZ all the time in training for ocean rescues. I also like the low jump altitude. Normal free-fall height is thirteen thousand feet. From two miles high at night it's hard to distinguish dim lights on the ground below. From high altitude it is also possible to confuse other lights on the ground with the target light. RAMZ deployment altitude is only thirty-five hundred feet. From only a few thousand feet above the ground it will be easy to spot the strobe light marking our landing zone and avoid the minefield. Another factor I consider is our full equipment load with weapons and eighty-pound rucksacks. Sometimes during free-fall parachute jumps equipment shifts causing a jumper to enter an uncontrollable spin that can be fatal. When this happens the jumper must immediately pull his ripcord, sometimes thousands of feet above planned opening altitude. When his parachute opens it will stop his spin and save his life, but pulling high can cause the jumper to land hundreds of yards off-target—a disaster if it happens on this mission near a mine field. Jumping from only thirty-five hundred feet makes it impossible to pull too high to miss the landing area. My final reason for choosing low-altitude RAMZ procedures concerns the navigator who will compute the release point. He is inexperienced, and I think it will be easier for him to plot a low-altitude exit point.

While my team suits up the crew gets detailed medical information on the patient. I listen on my headset while I suit up and work out tactical considerations in my head. Moose monitors radios and coordinates with Major Crabtree and the flight crew. This lets me devote my full attention to my team and jump preparations. A JSTARS (joint surveillance target attack radar system mounted on a Boeing E-8) plane soon comes up radio and assumes overall command. JSTARS is a battle management aircraft with the world's most advanced command and control radars and communications gear. Major Crabtree tells Moose he's about to relay a request through the JSTARS to the Rescue Coordination Center asking clearance to jump his PJs. And then . . . a stroke of genius: my CRO, Lt. Moose McGuinness, interjects, "Major Crabtree, instead of requesting permission, *tell* the JSTARS that the SAS team requests assistance and you intend to deploy your PJs." There is a brief moment of silence as our pilot mulls over Moose's suggestion. Then Major Crabtree, an experienced and aggressive rescue pilot, contacts the JSTARS and matter-of-factly informs them he intends to deploy his PJs. The JSTARS replies, "Roger. Understand you're deploying PJs." Implicit in the wording and tone of the JSTARS's response is a clearance to drop. In an era dominated by a cover-your-ass mentality, Major Crabtree doesn't settle for the safe decision. He makes the right decision. Our parachute jump mission is a go.

Moose and I discuss various tactical options. As a result of our brainstorming, we decide to attach a single blue chemical light stick on the back of each PJ's harness to help us keep track of each other in the night sky. We also decide to ditch our body armor; it's just too restrictive and bulky. We also won't jump with night vision goggles mounted on our helmets. Although, at the time it is not approved to wear goggles during free fall, I would have ignored this directive if I thought wearing them would have conferred an advantage. We stow our goggles and body armor in our rucksacks.

As we near the SAS team's location communications become solid and we receive detailed medical information. Our patient is Sgt. Andrew Russell, a thirty-three-year-old native of Perth, Australia. His right leg was blown off above his knee, and he has other extensive injuries. This SAS team has good medics who do what they can, but it has been at least two hours since the explosion and Sergeant Russell has lost a lot of blood. The only thing we have going for us is his superb physical condition and his strong will-to-live. We later learn that his wife gave birth to a daughter only two weeks earlier. Once we reach the ground, we can give Sergeant Russell his best chance to survive. Our primary objective is to ready Sergeant Russell for transport to the trauma hospital at Kandahar as quickly as possible.

At my request, the SAS soldiers mark the near boundary of the minefield with red chemical light sticks. They drop the sticks ten feet apart in a line to the left and right of the mine crater. Next, they place a strobelight fifty meters back on their trail. Their vehicles have already driven over this ground so it should be safe for us to land our parachutes there. The strobe light marks my team's desired landing spot. We should easily see the red light sticks and flashing strobe from thirty-five hundred feet.

I have analyzed every angle of this mission and the PJs and crew are on the same page. I am standing at the edge of the ramp with my team, seconds away from jumping when the loadmaster yells "No drop!" Moose quickly informs me that our navigator is not 100 percent sure of his calculations. Given the serious ramifications of a mistake he calls a "no drop" and rechecks his data It's a good decision. What I didn't know at the time, was that Lieutenant Symon's self-contained navigation system (SCNS) has malfunctioned. SCNS, pronounced "skins," is the navigation computer that helps calculate when and where jumpers should exit the plane in order to land on their target. Senior Master Sergeant Art Millard, a very experienced flight engineer, tries to fix it, but is unable to bring the SCNS computer back on line. Lieutenant Symon manually calculates the drop parameters. I trust the crew and wait patiently for *them* to have confidence in their calculations.

The aircraft banks sharply and heads for the strobe light. The loadmaster thrusts out his forefinger and screams, "One minute!" My team lines up behind me, only ten feet from the dark void at the back of the plane. Thirty seconds before green light, the loadmaster gives a thumbs-up signal. With me in the lead we shuffle single file to within one foot of the edge of the ramp. My team presses in close behind me. The tiny red jump light seems huge, filling my entire field of vision. Our team has discussed all contingencies, adjusted gear, and performed all pre-jump safety checks. All that remains is to do the mission. The talking is done; now is the time to walk-the-walk.

The jump light flashes to green and I launch myself into thin air! I extend my arms before me, my legs bent slightly at the knees. The 130 mph slipstream whips around me as I arch my back and keep my head up. As with every jump, I feel my legs rise behind me, threatening to force my body into a forward summersault. I counter the tendency to tumble by arching hard, and suddenly I am falling flat and stable, accelerating towards the ground. I have a momentary thought, "Whatever happens now, will happen. There's no getting back on the plane." I begin to count, "One thousand one, one thousand two . . . " When I reach one thousand five, I pull my ripcord. I look overhead to see my canopy fluttering momentarily before it fully inflates, snapping into its beautiful rectangular shape. Opening shock stretches my spine and jerks the air from my lungs in a grunt. I quickly glance to each side, clearing my space, while freeing my steering toggles. Now I have complete control of my parachute. I easily spot my team, above and behind me in the night sky. I feel relieved there are no malfunctions or mishaps. My team is following me and experiencing no obvious problems. The roar of the plane is gone and I am enveloped in eerie silence.

There is still a lot to do. The pressure is on me to maneuver perfectly to the strobe and bring my team in for a landing. I steer towards the strobe light off in the distance and twenty-five hundred feet below me. I clearly see the flashing light and the crooked line of red light sticks marking the edge of the mine field. My first impression is that the target strobe light is too far away to reach. Nervously, I fly my parachute at full speed towards the flashing light. I soon realize that despite losing his navigation computer Lieutenant Symon's calculations are perfect. I am able to fly straight to the strobe without having to use S turns to bleed off altitude. I pass over the strobe while still five hundred feet above the ground. Winds are relatively calm. I fly past the strobe and, when I judge I've gone the proper distance, I hook-turn back into the wind and steer towards the strobe on my final approach to landing.

At two hundred feet I release my rucksack but don't let it fall onto its tether. I stop it from falling by balancing it on the top of my boots. If I let the rucksack fall it will hang fifteen feet below me on its lanyard; my final turns will cause the rucksack to pendulum, possibly ruining my landing. Once one of my friends fractured his femur due to the pendulum effect and another broke his back on landing when his rucksack failed to release. I will let the rucksack fall onto its line when I am closer to the ground. I control my speed and angle of descent by pulling down and braking with my steering toggles. My team is looking good behind me as I near the landing site, holding my brakes half way down at 50 percent. At the last moment I kick my rucksack free and feel a slight jolt as it reaches the end of its lanyard. Moments later I hit the desert floor and roll into a parachute-landing fall. I jump to my feet in time to see my teammates land nearby. They're quickly on their feet uninjured.

The jump portion of the mission had the most potential for mishaps: parachute malfunctions, injuries, team separation, even landing in the minefield. Now we are all safely on the ground and can concentrate on our patient. An SAS soldier approaches and we shake hands. He's very calm and professional. "We'll take care of your parachutes, you take care of our mate." The SAS has four lightly-armored vehicles equipped with heavy weaponry and communications capability; they assume responsibility for security. Sergeant Fleener handles communications with the HC-130 orbiting overhead. He relays our status and keeps us informed of the arrival time of our helicopters. We are very close to the Iranian border and in case they decide to interfere we have coalition fighter jets flying combat air patrol at high altitude above us. With others assuming responsibility for security and communications my team can devote all its efforts to keeping Sergeant Russell alive.

The SAS team leader takes us to Sergeant Russell. Close by, the front half of his mangled vehicle is tilted into the mine crater. The SAS medics did a great job of treating his injuries. It is very cold, and they placed him in a sleeping bag to keep him warm. Their splints and bandages are very professional and effective. Sergeant Russell's right leg is amputated mid-thigh. His left femur is broken, and both bones in his lower leg have splintered through his skin. His right arm has a closed fracture. The SAS administered pain medications and a small amount of fluids through veins in Russell's left arm. He has a deep laceration on his face and maybe a broken jaw. His eyes are swollen and he has multiple shrapnel wounds. There is an almost certain chance he has internal injuries. One thing is obvious; he has lost a lot of blood. Remarkably, Sergeant Russell is still semi-conscious and occasionally mumbles. One of his teammates is always present to respond and reassure him.

Sergeant Carroll applies a blood pressure cuff while Airman Wilkes measures pulse and respirations. The SAS relayed vitals before we jumped, but we need to get fresh readings to see how our patient is trending. The results are not encouraging; Sergeant Russell's last reported blood pressure (BP) was 70 over 45, which indicates severe shock and blood loss. Sergeant Carroll takes multiple BP readings, inflating and deflating the cuff while I look on. He looks up at me and shakes his head, his face grim. "I can't get a pressure," he whispers. Yet Sergeant Russell is obviously still alive. His pulse is very high and his skin is cold. We quickly examine his entire body. There is some blood pooling beneath him but no active bleeding. We need to get an intravenous line established so we can administer fluids. I assign airway management to Airman Wilkes while Sergeant Carroll and I work to start an IV. Sergeant Russell's left arm has multiple punctures from earlier IV attempts and is no longer useful. His right arm has a closed fracture and is splinted. I carefully remove some elastic bandage exposing the large vein in the crook of his right elbow. I tell Sergeant Carroll, "Inflate the BP and leave it inflated. The cuff will act as a tourniquet, and hopefully I'll be able to get a vein and start an IV."

"Helicopters will be here in fifteen minutes," someone says. We need to finish up and prepare for evacuation. I use my fingertip to feel for the slight bulge of a vein and insert a large bore catheter. We hook up the IV and get a good flow. We warm the fluids with a chemical heater that comes in our field rations: meals ready to eat or MREs. The cheap MRE heater works better than our expensive medical IV heaters. I am worried about Sergeant Russell's airway. Ideally, I would insert a tube into his trachea to establish a secure airway, but he is semiconscious and his gag reflex would probably trigger vomiting and panic that could seriously complicate matters. He has a good airway now, but I am concerned about the flight to the hospital. Sergeant Russell is in a very fragile condition.

The two Pave Hawk helicopters arrive and we guide them to the spot where we landed our parachutes earlier. The newly arrived PJs leap from the helicopter door and run over to us. They are led by a good friend of mine, TSgt. Pat Harding. While I brief Sergeant Harding, the other PJs transfer Sergeant Russell onto a litter and carry him to a helicopter. Pat Harding is an outstanding medic who has higher-level emergency-medical qualifications than I have. I assign Airman Wilkes to accompany Sergeant Harding, Amn. Mike Flores, and the patient. I will fly on the second Pave Hawk with Sergeants Rich Carroll and Bob Roberts. I warn Sergeant Harding to expect the patient to deteriorate. "Be prepared for Sergeant Russell to crash at any moment." I tell him. "He's extremely weak. Good luck man!" I barely have time to take leave of the SAS and assure them we'll do our best, when it's time to go.

Everyone boards their assigned helicopter and takes off. The pilots fly the ninety-minute route to Kandahar at only one hundred feet above the ground. They fly on night vision goggles with their aircraft blacked out to remain invisible and avoid hostile ground fire. The helicopter is far from airtight, and frigid air whistles around the cabin. It is freezing cold and pitch black. The helicopter makes sharp turns, called yanking and banking, to avoid terrain, generating heavy G forces. There is virtually no room in the back of the helicopter. The cabin is about as large as the inside of an average sized car with the seats removed. The PJs drape a poncho over themselves and the patient. The poncho blocks the cold wind and allows judicious use of a flashlight. It's hard to work in the freezing cold temperatures and jostling helicopter. During the flight the effects of his injuries finally take their toll and Sergeant Russell suddenly stops breathing. Airman Wilkes and Sergeant Harding begin CPR in the cramped confines of the chopper. They struggle to bring Russell back to life for what seems an impossibly long time. They try every lifesaving technique they know. Totally exhausted, the PJs resolutely continue CPR until they land at Kandahar and turn their patient over to army surgeons. Despite everyone's monumental efforts to save him, Sergeant Russell is dead.

Later, one of the doctors tells me that if Russell had suffered his injuries right in front of their surgical tent he would have had only a 50–50 chance of survival; his injuries were that severe. Ultimately, the effects of his many traumatic injuries and massive blood loss were too much to overcome. Despite the bad outcome of the mission, some good resulted from my after action report. Authorities started to allow PJs to carry whole blood. When a person loses a certain threshold-amount of blood, IV fluids are ineffective. IV fluids expand circulatory volume but cannot transport oxygen to tissues. Sergeant Russell needed whole blood, but all we had was IV fluids.

PJs also began to train with rapid sequence intubation. This technique uses sedatives and short acting paralytic drugs to suppress a patient's gag reflex. This allows medics to place a tube in a conscious patient's windpipe to establish a secure airway. There are many different techniques, and we were able to maintain Sergeant Russell's airway using other methods. Although I am extremely sad and disappointed that we could not save him, I am proud of the way my team performed. Like other medical professionals, PJs know they cannot save every patient. But somehow that knowledge is never very comforting in our struggle to save lives.

CHAPTER 2

PARARESCUE SELECTION

Tiger, tiger burning bright
In the forest of the night
What immortal hand or eye
Could form thy fearful symmetry
—*William Blake, "The Tiger"*

SAN ANTONIO, TEXAS 1975

I WALKED INTO THE AIR-CONDITIONED CLASSROOM, GLAD TO ESCAPE the mid-summer heat. My air force fatigue uniform was damp and clingy from sweat and the August humidity. I was here because I'd volunteered. Conventional wisdom warns that one should never volunteer for anything in the military, but I had made an exception. Earlier that morning, drill instructor Staff Sergeant Lariez, all spit-polish and intimidation, barked his commands and all of us stubble-headed basic trainees scrambled into formation to hang on his every word. He asked for volunteers to attend a briefing on USAF Pararescue. He snickered when no one stepped forward, "Just as well; that job is not for you sissies anyway." More out of spite than any real desire to learn about pararescue I immediately raised my arm to volunteer and the look of annoyance on Lariez's face was worth whatever boring lecture I would have to endure.

Now here I was, for better or worse, about to learn about pararescue. Those of us attending the lecture jumped to our feet and stood at attention as the pararescueman presenter marched into the room. He wore crisply starched jungle fatigues, bloused trousers, spit-polished Cochran jump boots, and a maroon beret sporting a gleaming metal pararescue flash. Despite my earlier disdainful attitude, I had to admit he looked sharp and professional. Technical Sergeant Trelawny "T.J." Bruce quietly introduced himself as the noncommissioned officer in charge of the Pararescue Selection Team located right there on Lackland Air Force Base, the home of Air Force Basic Training.

"Before I get started, I'd like to show a short film." Sergeant Bruce dimmed the lights and started the projector. The film was a documentary titled *All for One*. It showed the actual combat rescue of Capt. Gerald Lawrence that took place in Vietnam in 1972. After Captain Lawrence bailed out of his jet over enemy territory, a Sikorsky HH-53 Super Jolly Green Giant helicopter flew to his rescue over miles of enemy held jungle. Weapons laden A-1 Skyraiders, propeller-driven planes called Sandys, provided a rescue escort and protected the Jolly during the long flight to the downed pilot's location. As the helicopter hovered over the pilot, a pararescueman straddled a device called a forest penetrator that was designed to be able to be lowered through thick jungle treetops. He rode the penetrator down from the hovering helicopter on a thin steel cable. To protect the helicopter and PJ from enemy machine guns and antiaircraft artillery, a flight engineer and second PJ fired the helicopter's six-barreled miniguns, wicked space-age descendants of Civil War era Gatling guns. The six barrels of the miniguns whirred round in a blur, firing four thousand rounds of 7.62mm ammunition per minute. The belt-fed weapons gobbled prodigious amounts of ammo from large storage cans secured to the helicopter's floor. Every fifth round was a red tipped tracer containing a pyrotechnic compound that burned brilliant red. Even though the tracers only fired every fifth round, the guns fired so fast that the luminous red projectiles appeared to merge, resembling futuristic laser beams probing and scorching the jungle. White smoke wreathed the crouched gunners, as a torrent of hot, spent brass spewed from the gun. The Skyraiders flew round the chopper in pre-arranged attack patterns, firing rockets and ripping off long streams of explosive shells from their 20mm cannons to prevent the nearby Vietcong from interfering with the recovery. The film also included the radio chatter between the helicopter and Sandys throughout the intense action. Afterwards, the various participants in the rescue operation talked on camera about their experience. The rescued pilot's voice was choked with emotion when he talked of his rescue.

The film definitely grabbed my attention. When Sergeant Bruce went on to explain more about the history and mission of USAF Pararescue, I was hooked. In my estimation, what he described was nothing less than the perfect career. If an airman wants to be a PJ there is only one little catch; almost everyone who tries out for pararescue fails. T.J. Bruce pulled no punches as he went on to describe the difficult process of becoming a PJ. First, candidates have to pass an initial Physical Ability and Stamina Test that involves running, swimming, and calisthenics. They also have to pass an air force flight physical, the same medical exam given to prospective jet pilots. Perfect health and vision is a basic requirement, even color blindness is disqualifying. After candidates complete Air Force Basic Training and the medical exam, they enter the Pararescue Indoctrination Training Course, the hardest part of PJ training and pararescue's trial by fire.

Indoctrination is at the heart of the PJ selection process. The course is ten weeks long and consists of continuously escalating requirements of running, swimming, calisthenics, and introductory study in scuba diving physics and medical terminology. The dropout rate at the time was 92 percent and historically has hovered between 85 and 95 percent. A PJ trainee who survives indoctrination must next undergo a series of challenging prerequisite courses, known as the PJ pipeline. The pipeline consists of a series of hardcore military commando courses: the U.S. Army's basic paratrooper training (The Airborne School) and high altitude low opening (HALO) training at the army's Military Freefall School, Air Force Survival School, the USAF Combat Dive School, and a six-month-long paramedic school. Once a candidate successfully completes the pipeline schools, he enters the apprentice course at the Pararescue and Combat Rescue Officer School at Kirtland Air Force Base, New Mexico. The apprentice course consists of advanced weapons training, land navigation, combat tactics, pararescue field medicine, mountain and technical rescue, advanced parachuting, and advanced helicopter operations. The lengthy training culminates in two weeks of war games where the students work as a team, integrating all the skills they have learned in order to execute realistic mission scenarios.

In 1975, the PJ school instructors were seasoned Vietnam War veterans, many of whom were highly decorated war heroes. The cadre also included air force survival instructors who provided advanced training in the high desert spaces and forests. Future PJs were taught the core knowledge and skills they would later use to save lives. Grizzled instructors taught students mountain rescue on granite cliffs in New Mexico's Pecos Mountains, driving them hard on the sheer heights. Students also learned advanced land navigation in the pine forests that blanketed the rugged mountains. Survival instructors showed students how to use a map and compass to find their way in the wilderness and taught them how to evade enemy pursuers. Students carried fifty-pound rucksacks and walked miles and miles over steep, treacherous ground on pitch black, moonless nights. PJ candidates also learned advanced parachuting skills. They learned how to don tree suits designed by smoke jumpers and parachuted into thick forests, intentionally snagging their parachute canopies on towering treetops, then lowering themselves with special let-down rigs. They parachuted into the ocean with heavy steel scuba tanks on their backs. They became aircrew members on HH-3 Jolly Green and HH-53 Super Jolly Green helicopters and HC-130 Hercules transport aircraft that had been modified to conduct long range rescue and refuel helicopters in-flight. They learned how to use the helicopter rescue hoist in the water and on land to recover downed pilots. And they learned how to shoot the onboard miniguns to suppress enemy ground fire and protect the helicopter while in a hover.

As soon as Sergeant Bruce concluded his briefing I immediately abandoned my prior career plans and volunteered for PJ training. Pararescue seemed the ultimate profession combining athletic prowess, the excitement of extreme sports, and the mental challenge of making complex life-and-death decisions and administering medical treatment while under hostile enemy fire. Wow! When I joined the air force right out of high school I hadn't really given much thought to the type of work I wanted; frankly speaking, my primary purpose in joining the military was to get a college education while serving my country. The Vietnam War had just ended, so I never considered a wartime specialty. I planned to use the G.I. Bill to go to college and become an oceanographer. I liked academics and I wanted a profession that was mentally challenging. I also relished danger and adventure and pictured myself scuba diving and filming great white sharks like Jacques Cousteau. I liked sports and competition; I had wrestled and competed in track and field events in high school and also earned a black belt in karate before I turned seventeen. (I particularly loved karate tournaments with full-contact fighting matches.) I had never failed at anything and naively thought that pararescue training would be easy for me. The mission of pararescue was irresistible: heroically save lives and aid the injured, all the while patriotically serving the United States of America. Does it get any better than that!

By sheer chance, my upbringing seemed to have prepared me for a career in pararescue. I had a great childhood growing up in Warren, Ohio. My father was old-fashioned. He grew up in Daisy Town, Pennsylvania, a small rural coal-mining community. My grandfather, William Valentine Sine, was born in Austria, and my grandmother Elizabeth was born in West Virginia after her parents had emigrated from Hungary. My father, William "Bill" Sine, and his younger sister Marilyn grew up in a small home situated next to a gurgling creek. They hand-pumped their water from a well and used a cast iron potbelly coal stove and Heatrolla to warm the two small bedrooms and common area. Most everyone in Daisy Town had emigrant ties to Eastern Europe and observed customs from the old country. My father and most of the community spoke fluent Hungarian and there was even a church with services conducted in Hungarian.

My father was drafted and served in the army during the Korean War. After the war, he married my mother and moved to Warren, Ohio, to find work in the steel mills and eventually worked his way up to general foreman and then assistant superintendent of the blast furnace at Republic Steel. My dad was a great mechanic and could fix just about anything. He was also a scratch golfer and liked sports in general. He had definite ideas on how to raise his sons to be *real* men. When I came home from kindergarten, my dad made me do pushups, sit-ups, and pull-ups before he allowed me to watch cartoons on TV. This gave me an early foundation of physical fitness that stayed with me as I grew older. My dad was an all around outdoorsman. He taught my brother Bobby and me how to camp, hunt, and fish at an early age. I got my first shotgun when I was eleven years old and went rabbit and pheasant hunting. We also played football, wrestled, and play-fought. He was old school. He hated hippies and made us keep our hair short. Every year when school let out for the summer Dad shaved our heads. He taught us the traditional manly things that fathers taught their sons in those days: don't be a sissy, quit crying like a baby, and don't bother me unless you're bleeding. When we got out of line he would beat our asses. After he retired he moved to Melbourne, Florida, where I was stationed in the early nineties and looked after my son when I deployed to Southwest Asia for months at a time. He died of a heart attack in 1998. He was a great dad.

My mother Helen and her older brother Joe grew up in Fredericktown, Pennsylvania, a small coal-mining town on the banks of the Monongahela River. Her father Alexi Kobiloinsky immigrated to America from the Ukraine and never got further than broken English. I inherited my dark red hair from my Ukrainian great grandfather Dimitri, who was six foot seven inches tall and had red hair. Alexi was quite a man and worked forty-five years in the coalmines before retiring. As a result of his years spent laboring in mineshafts choked with coal dust he developed black lung disease, but was otherwise strong as a bull. My grandmother Anna worked hard in the home, canning and tending the garden. They also stock-piled food in the basement, a reaction to their nearly starving during the Great Depression. They lived in a two-story house perched on a hill across from a bakery, and some of my earliest and fondest memories are of eating delicious hot rolls smothered with soft butter, fresh from the baker's oven and. They had a vegetable garden and apple and pear trees grew in the yard. They also had a front porch with a swing. We would drive three hours from Warren to periodically visit my grandparents during the year, especially during summer school breaks.

My mother used to read to me when I was just a toddler. She read me fairy tales and stories like Chicken Little, The Little Red Hen, and even Gulliver's Travels. She got me hooked on books, and I credit her with cultivating the intellectual side of my personality. She also enrolled me in karate school when I was fifteen years old, because she liked the self-defense aspect of karate and somehow knew that fighting sports would be right up my alley. She was right and martial arts became a huge part of my life. For the next three decades I would live and breathe martial arts and kickboxing. During my last two years of high school I worked part time as a karate instructor at Cliff Kelly's American Karate Studio and was even Cliff's assistant on his locally broadcast karate television show. Martial arts played a central role in forming my character and remain an integral part of my self-image and identity.

When my parents divorced, my mother raised Bobby and me during our hectic high school years and did a great job as a single mother. She worked as a waitress at a local restaurant and had her hands full coping with two rambunctious teenage boys, always fighting and raising hell, like brothers always do, except we were definitely worse than normal brothers. After I joined the air force and left home, my mom married a great guy named Dom Giancarlo and has been married now for over thirty-four years. My mom is a cooking genius and is famous in our extended family for her homemade stuffed cabbages, pizza, and fruit pies made from scratch. There is nothing she can't cook better than anyone else. If I lived at home I'd weigh five hundred pounds. She is a great mom.

I was a bookworm in elementary school, reading one book after another. I liked science fiction and fantasy with over-the-top adventures and heroes saving the day. I also liked true stories of survival and adventure. The first novel I remember reading was *My Side of the Mountain* by Jean Craighead George. The book was about a boy surviving in the wilderness and it made a big impression on me. I also liked military books that recounted the patriotism and courage of soldiers. I read tons of superhero comic books. To me, Superman had it right when he fought for "Truth, Justice and the American way." I took all that sentiment seriously . . . and still do. I admired the romanticized depiction of gallant medieval knights like King Arthur and Sir Lancelot. I wanted to emulate the brave knights of old with their code of chivalry.; I wanted to rescue damsels in distress and have adventures. I thought the American values of patriotism, justice, compassion and freedom represented modern-day chivalry. When I watched the PJ briefing, it seemed as though the honor and goodness of the knights of old was embodied in modern-day pararescuemen. PJs were the "knights of new" and I wanted to be one of them. I believe God has a plan for each of us. I didn't know it at the time, but my upbringing, love for the outdoors and athletics, and patriotic, idealized mindset fit the classic physical and psychological profile of a PJ.

According to Merriam-Webster a commando is a member of "a military unit trained and organized as shock troops especially for hit-and-run raids into enemy territory." Modern day commandos are called "special operators," with "special operations forces" being the umbrella term for modern day commando units. Most of the world's militaries have their own elite special operations forces, but the American military has the most capable and renowned spec ops forces on the globe including U.S. Navy SEALs; U.S. Army Delta Force, special forces (Green Berets), and rangers; U.S. Marine Corps amphibious reconnaissance, and U.S. Air Force Pararescue and Combat Control. Compared to the large numbers of men found in conventional forces, such as, infantry and artillery, because of the hazardous nature of their missions special operations forces are composed of relatively small numbers of volunteers. There are about three hundred and thirty thousand people in the U.S. Navy, but only twenty-eight hundred SEALs. There is approximately the same number of people in the U.S. Air Force, but only six hundred are PJs and CROs, with only a few hundred more combat controllers.

Typically, special operations units are small, because their training and missions are very dangerous and the standards for membership are extremely severe: most men who tryout will fail. That's why these forces are considered elite. The armed forces pick their commandos through extremely rigorous selection processes characterized by high wash-out rates. The basic skills are universal and include super physical fitness, mental toughness, adaptability, parachuting, scuba diving, rappelling, weapons expertise, stealth, and the mastery of James Bond-like technology and ingenious gadgets. All commandos possess superior war-fighting skills. The main differences between the different special operators are their missions. PJs use parachuting skills to raid into enemy territory to rescue and save lives; army rangers parachute onto the battle field to kill enemy soldiers and capture ground, while a Green Beret will infiltrate a remote, hostile area to teach the local populace how to fight and defend themselves against an enemy. Recon marines can sneak into enemy territory and learn all their secrets. SEALs are small direct-action-oriented teams that can infiltrate areas by sea air, or land to accomplish their objectives, such as capturing or destroying high value targets. Air force combat controllers call in airstrikes, help seize enemy airfields, and use their air traffic control skills to orchestrate everything from large-scale aerial invasions to small insertions of American planes and soldiers. All of these elite units consider themselves exclusive brotherhoods. Members of these outfits live at the most dangerous extreme of human experience and entrust their lives to each other. They focus on a common mission and share unique experiences of adventure and danger.

By law, only men are eligible to participate in frontline ground combat, a requirement for all special ops units. The men who pursue this dangerous work usually share a background in sports or athletics and are very competitive and driven to succeed. They have high IQs and are instinctive survivors and innovators. They are very aggressive and love danger and the rush of adrenaline. They are drawn to anything that involves skill, speed, or danger, such as skiing, rock climbing, skydiving or fighting. They are killer savants. These guys have their own brand of humor that most others would label sick. They love to play practical jokes, especially on their buddies. Others would consider many of their pranks extreme, even appalling, but members of the brotherhood are expected to take these things in stride with good humor. When it comes to joking or pranks, nothing is sacred.

They will tape mousetraps on light switches and wrap a giant dildo in tin foil, making it resemble a gun and then sneaking it into their buddy's airport carry-on bag. Excess is hardwired into their personalities. Most work too hard and play too hard. If you're the first person to pass out at an action-guy party you will wake up the next morning with a shaved head, if you're lucky. If you are unlucky, you might wake up in a foreign country without a passport or money. It is assumed that no matter how severe the prank you'll have the resilience and fortitude to adapt and overcome.

American special operators are at the tip of the spear wielded by the most powerful nation in history. These men will experience more in the way of extreme adventure in their careers in uniforms than others will see in a lifetime at the movies. They do it for their country, for their comrades, and for the thrill of the mission itself. They do it because no one else can. The greatest honor a commando can earn is the respect and admiration of his peers and the title of "operator." Among the vast press of humanity, they are "Tigers burning bright."

This was the rarefied company I was seeking when I decided to try out for pararescue. After I passed the initial physical fitness test—one of the most demanding experiences things I of my life, up until then—I was scheduled to begin indoctrination training (Indoc) and would start the course the day after I graduated from Air Force Basic Training. Little did I realize that the easiest day at Indoc, would be much harder than the fitness test I passed to be accepted into training.

Immediately after graduating from basic training, I checked into the

PJ barracks. I was very excited to begin training the next day. The purpose of the Indoc program is to test the mettle of each candidate and weed out those who are not cut out for pararescue. The course does this by stressing the trainees until the weak voluntarily quit. They call this self-elimination. The job of the PJ instructors is to physically and mentally break you down, and they have ten weeks to do it. They pick on you and play mind games. They punish you at a whim and impose draconian penalties, sometimes hundreds of pushups and flutter kicks. To a layperson, their methods might seem cruel and unfair. If you don't like it, you can quit at any time: self-eliminate. Although the physical standards are extreme, passing the Indoc course is 90 percent mental. If you absolutely refuse to quit no matter what, you will pass. The instructors are looking for men who they would not hesitate to trust with their own lives, men who refuse to give up.

At 0430 hours an instructor threw a metal garbage can down the hallway and began screaming at the top of his lungs. Indoc had officially begun. I scrambled to my feet in panic and ran straight into a wall, nearly knocking myself out. I had a throbbing hangover, the result of some exuberant celebration after my graduation from basic training. After hurriedly dressing, our team jogged to the dining hall in the early morning darkness and ate breakfast. With my hangover, I didn't have much of an appetite. After breakfast we ran back to our barracks and our team assembled for our first session of calisthenics.

Calisthenics workouts took place downstairs in a large windowless basement we dubbed "the dungeon." The floor was covered with canvas mats, and the moist air reeked of sweat and regret. This was a Saturday, and as such it was not a normal workout day. Saturdays were designated competition days. On competition days we were ranked according to how many repetitions of each exercise we could accomplish and who showed the most improvement since the last competition. Normal training would not begin until Monday. The first week featured the easiest workouts and the beginning routines. Nonetheless, the calisthenics were grueling. Even though we were competing, we still did multiple sets of each exercise.

The most disheartening aspect of the workout was that half way through an exercise an instructor would accuse someone of improper form and make the entire class start the set over. Sometimes we started over four times just to complete one set. The instructors obsessed on trainees doing the exercises with perfect form and cadence. Sweat poured off our bodies and sounded like hail hitting the canvas mats. Soon I was desperately wishing I had not partied so hard the night before. I reeked of beer; hops and barley squeezed from my pores and fell onto the canvas. The instructors grinned at me knowingly like vengeful demons. After the dungeon session, they made me sweep the floor clean of my beer-y sweat.

A lot of my teammates were older than me and most looked like athletes. Some of the guys had been at the school for a few weeks waiting for the official start of this class and had been working out. Unlike them, I didn't have a chance to prepare or acclimate. On this first day, we met our instructors. Technical Sergeant T.J. Bruce, the school commandant, was a master of the art of inflicting mental and physical torture without raising his voice. Another instructor, Sgt. Dave Young was an all-around accomplished PJ, fresh from a tour in Southeast Asia. Staff Sergeant Mike Wagner was on the thin, smallish side. We called him, "the rabbit." His job was to run us to death during the pararescue version of cross-country runs called Fartleks. Fartlek means "speed play" in Swedish and is a type of running that stresses the aerobic and anaerobic systems of the body to their limit. The speed of the Fartlek runs varied from all out sprinting to fast jogging.

After being tortured in the dungeon, I foolishly looked forward to our swim workout. We grabbed our issued face masks and snorkels and jogged, in military formation, to the swimming pool. It was an outdoor pool and the water was cold. The pool was twenty-five meters long and our class of eighteen stood at the shallow end. Instructors assigned each of us to a swim lane. Lanes were separated by red and white plastic floats threaded on polyester rope and strung the length of the pool. There were eight lanes, each about two-and-a-half meters wide. This meant some students had to share lanes. During our first exercise we held onto foam flutter boards and using only our bare feet kicked our way down and back the length of the pool five times. I could not seem to generate any speed. Snails on the edge of the pool outpaced me. We never wore fins during swim workouts. The instructors wanted us to learn how to propel our bodies through the water with our bare feet. Down the length of the pool and back, fifty meters, counted as one lap, and we did five laps. Almost immediately after the first set, we had to do another five laps of flutter boards. I was already getting tired. Next we swam five laps using only one arm; the other arm we kept extended in front of us. Then it was another five laps of one arms, and I struggled to keep pace. Then it was two more iterations of five-lap flutter-board drills. By this time I was totally exhausted. I busted many time limits and earned numerous penalty drops.

Drops are pushups or flutter kicks. Each time a trainee busts a time limit, screws up, or annoys an instructor he earns a drop. We accomplished some drops on the spot. When an instructor yells, "Drop!" trainees immediately begin doing the appropriate number of pushups according to which week they are in. After loudly counting out sixty pushups, they do one more pushup for pararescue and then remain in the front-leaning rest position. When the instructor is satisfied, he will say, "Recover." and the trainee will scramble to his feet and stand at attention until the instructor gives the command, "Carry on!" Sometimes instructors will drop the entire class. For time-limit and exercise violations the instructors keep a written record of drops that students accrue during the day. At the end of the training day, and after dinner, students gather in the dungeon to pay their penalty drops, sometimes ten to fifteen iterations of pushups and flutter kicks.

Everyone knows how to do pushups, but flutter kicks are less familiar. To do flutter kicks a trainee lies on his back with his feet held six inches off the ground. To accomplish the exercise, the trainee keeps his legs straight and alternately raises his right and left legs up and down in short scissor kicks. Four kicks count as one repetition, a four count exercise. Flutter kicks work the abdominal and hip flexor muscles and help prepare you to swim with fins through ocean waves.

The swim workout continued. I wasn't a trained swimmer and had only recently learned how to swim with my face in the water using three-stroke breathing. My hangover was not making matters any easier, beer foam floated around me in the water. At this, the moment of my greatest misery, a guy in the lane next to me casually remarked, "Well, warm ups are almost over." I had just been thinking to myself what an agonizing workout this had been and was hoping we were nearing the end. I was extremely annoyed that this kid would try and mess with my head, especially on my first day. Refusing to fall for this obvious ploy, I played along. "Yeah, warm ups. What's next?" "Underwaters," he said. I was mortified when the instructors announced they were preparing the pool for under-waters. We had to swim twenty-five meters underwater to the other end

of the pool, turn and kick off the wall while still submerged, finally sur-
facing for a brief lung full of air before sprinting freestyle back to our start
point. Since we were in week one, we only had to do six underwaters. As
the weeks went by, we would eventually work up to twelve underwaters.
After the underwaters, warm-ups would be over and we would begin the
actual swim workout. It finally dawned on me that my classmate in the
next swim lane had not been messing with me at all; he was just making a
casual, helpful comment for the benefit of the new guy. My mind was
nearly destroyed. I was already exhausted, had a satanic hangover and we
had only just completed swim warm-ups! I mentally screamed at the
instructors, "Are you kidding me! Have you lost your freakin' minds? This
is ridiculous!"

The main workout consisted of *only* a two thousand meter swim. This
was the longest swim I ever completed in my life: forty times down and
back. I was tired and sputtering after the first lap. Except for a surprising
aptitude for swallowing pool water, my swim technique sucked. I felt as
comfortable in the water as a camel, and my slow lap times reflected my
lack of skill. During the swim I was penalized a million drops. Afterwards,
I thought I was the most tired and demoralized person in the class, until
two guys self-eliminated—sissies.

The final part of the swim workout was "water harassment." *These days*,
the official, politically correct name for this training is "water confidence,"
but harassment is a more accurate description. Water harassment is designed to train PJs to remain calm and effectively deal with underwater
emergencies. This training also prepares students for the rigorous military
scuba school later in the pipeline. As a result, PJs are exceptionally skilled
and comfortable in the water. Water harassment, a technique invented by
PJs, involves pairs of trainee buddies wearing masks and treading water in
the deep end of the pool. The students have to keep their faces under water
and share breaths through a single snorkel which simulates a scuba regulator. One swimmer takes two breaths through a snorkel and then passes it
to his buddy. While the second swimmer takes his two breaths, his buddy
holds his breath, keeping his face underwater and awaiting his next turn
to breathe through the snorkel. This is known as buddy breathing and is a
technique used in scuba diving in case one partner runs out of air or experiences an equipment malfunction while at depth. In that case, the two

divers share the one functioning scuba regulator, two breaths each, until they can safely ascend to the surface. Divers need to keep cool heads to resolve underwater emergencies and equipment malfunctions. Panic is the enemy and the harassment is designed to force the trainee to perform despite unpleasant mental and physical sensations, such as air hunger, panic, and the threat of imminent drowning.

The first buddy pair enters the deep end of the pool and begins buddy breathing. The games begin when, like a hungry shark, an instructor menacingly stalks the two trainees. Suddenly, the instructor darts forward, grabs the snorkel, and tosses it about ten feet away where it slowly sinks to the bottom. It is the duty of the last person to have taken a breath, to retrieve the snorkel. As the swimmer dives ten feet deep to recover the snorkel, his buddy floats motionless, his face underwater, holding his breath, patiently conserving oxygen. The swimmer returns with the snorkel and hands it to his buddy, but before his teammate can grab it and breathe, the instructor sadistically snatches the snorkel and again tosses it away. The swimmer, still holding his breath, dives to get the snorkel, but the instructor grabs his facemask and floods it with pool water. The swimmer has a choice. He can clear his mask of water, by blowing valuable air into it through his nose, or he can continue to swim with his mask full of water blurring his vision. The swimmer makes the right decision and retrieves the snorkel. All this time both trainees are holding their breath, battling the urge to surface and suck in a lung full of sweet fresh air.

With lungs burning and vision dimming, the swimmer hands the snorkel to his buddy. After taking only two breaths, his buddy returns the snorkel and, finally the instructor allows the swimmer to breathe *his* two breaths. While the trainees try to breathe, instructors splash water into foam around them while screaming insults. Despite the distractions, the snorkel travels back and forth between the trainees until once again, an instructor snatches it, tosses it across the pool, and floods both students' masks. This harassment continues until the instructor is satisfied with the trainees' performance. Without exception, every trainee had to endure water harassment. Although this training can be somewhat subjective, the instructors operated under strict guidelines to ensure consistency. Nonetheless, this training proved to be the undoing of many prospective trainees. Some trainees trembled uncontrollably at the mere mention of water harassment. Some students quit, while others refused to give up and would choose to pass out rather than surface prematurely. Officially known as a shallow-water blackout, we called these near-drowning experiences "seeing the wizard."

After the swim workout the instructors surprised us with a special treat: a grueling game of water polo. I was not happy with this development. I had already had my fill of swimming for the next hundred years. There is a lot to know about playing water polo: how to tread water, game strategy, and how to avoid being drowned by opposing players. Of course I knew none of these game subtleties and nearly drowned numerous times. I spent so much time underwater, that afterwards I could feel small gills starting to sprout on the sides of my neck. After pool torture it was lunch time. Yeah! Only half a day of agony left. We showered and dressed in the locker room and then ran in formation to the chow hall. PJ students have to run everywhere they go. While we ran, we sang motivational cadence songs called "Jodies." I was starved. At the dining hall I ate a pile of food as big as my head . . . and then ate five desserts!

After lunch we jogged to the running track for our timed, two-mile runs. I hate running more than anything. I'm not a natural runner. Long, fast runs are very painful to me. Run workouts were always my nemesis; I would rather have my eyeballs rubbed with sandpaper. We ran two miles in the first week and each subsequent week the distance increased by an additional mile. We ran five days a week which included competition day. Each mile had to be completed in under seven minutes. For each mile run slower than seven minutes we had to run a hundred-yard penalty sprint at the end of the workout. My conditioning could never keep pace with the weekly distance increases. The daily runs never got easier. I ran a lot of penalty sprints; sometimes it was if my lungs came out and fell on the ground. I painfully made it through the first Saturday competition. I knew that as time went on the training would get successively harder, but now I knew what to expect: daily agony for the next two months.

The exercise standards and run and swim distances increased each week, but the instructors varied the types of workouts. Each day always consisted of a calisthenics workout, a run routine, and a grueling swim session, but the kinds of run and swim workouts varied. There were straight distance workouts, sprint routines, and instructor's-choice workouts. Each week had minimum standards for running, swimming, and calisthenics that trainees had to attain in order to progress to the next week. Competition day established class ranking according to how each person performed and improved. The run distance for week one was two miles and the swim distance was two thousand meters; week two required three mile runs and three thousand meter swims; week three featured four mile runs and four thousand meter swims; and so on. This progression continued until week six, max-week. Calisthenics repetitions also increased accordingly as the weeks advanced. During max-week, we ran a minimum of six miles and sometimes as much as twelve miles during Fartleks. We swam six thousand meters a day and did insane numbers of pushups and calisthenics. Max-week standards remained the same from week six onward.

Over the following weeks I settled into the routine of organized training and torture. I also became tight with my teammates along the way. Shared pain and misery builds strong friendships and esprit de corps. As strange as it may seem, we had a great time while we were having an agonizing time. Our team shared and buffered all the highs and lows. When we were not groaning in agony, we were laughing. Our instructors were not evil, they were just very picky about who they allowed into the brotherhood and wanted to get rid of any sissies in our ranks. Ultimately, so did our team, so does every PJ. Indoc is extended torture, but the day after graduation everyone will say, "That was awesome!" It *was* awesome, but it was also unbelievably hard.

During Indoc I dreaded the start of each day. Each person comes to terms with his inner demons in his own way. I prayed to God for strength, promising good works. I visualized myself in the future, wearing my maroon beret and conducting business as usual in the air force. I imagined myself having already overcome all training challenges and living life as a PJ. But the runs were such agony! During every run I wanted to quit, but I forced myself to hold on for just that *one* run. When the run ended I moved on to the next training event, immediately forgetting the intense suffering I had just experienced.

Looking back on my time at Indoc, I think that *forgetfulness* must be one of the human mind's primary self-defense mechanisms. Women experience unbearable pain during childbirth and I'm told that afterwards they tend to forget the true depth of their suffering. If women had complete memories of their birthing ordeals, they might never be willing to become pregnant again and our species would become extinct. Without consciously trying I somehow forgot the true magnitude of my daily pain and suffering. A few miles into my next run my amnesia dissipates and the horror of past runs comes flooding back into my mind. It is just too painful to go on. I make a decision. I will quit after this *one last* run. Seconds after crossing the finish line I am already forgetting, "That wasn't so bad." Maybe the trainees who quit, the ones who nearly went insane, the ones who broke down in tears, maybe those guys couldn't forget.

Every other weekend the entire team packed a truck and bus with climbing and camping gear—tents, ropes, sleeping bags and military rations—and traveled northwest of San Antonio to Enchanted Rock, Texas. Enchanted Rock is an enormous, pink granite dome that juts 425 feet above the ground and covers 640 acres. The instructors designed these field trips to familiarize us with the basic techniques of rock climbing, knot tying, land navigation, and mountain rescue. This training also prepared us for the more advanced mountain training to come later at the Pararescue School. The training was intense; I was convinced all the instructors were insane. We were out on the rock at first light and only returned to camp when it got dark. We learned to rappel and rock climb with only the most rudimentary gear. It was fun but extremely scary and tiring. Of course, the instructors worked us ridiculously hard all day long. At dusk we carried a litter loaded with a patient down steep rocky slopes back to camp. One of the instructors played the role of an injured climber and lay in the metal basket litter. Six trainees carried the litter, periodically switching-out with other teammates. One evening I was trailblazing at the front of the litter. Occasionally, a prickly pear cactus blocked my path. I maneuvered around the larger, invincible plants, but stomped down the weaker, two-foot-high cacti that were in my way

As we struggled to carry the two hundred pound litter, twilight deepened and it became harder and harder to see. I aggressively stomped what I thought was a small cactus that was in my way. In the growing shadows I didn't realize that I was only seeing the top two feet of a giant cactus that jutted above the lip of an arroyo. The rest of the massive cactus was hidden below the edge of the gully. My stomp carried me forward over the edge of the drop-off. I instinctively let go of the litter, extended my arms to break my fall and tumbled into the welcoming embrace of the "mother of all" cacti. My spontaneous girlish, high pitched scream startled everyone into immobility, stopping their forward travel. My bemused teammates cautiously peered over the ledge and saw me crucified on a giant prickly pear cactus. I felt like I was nailed to the plant, unable to move a muscle. Apparently, my rampant stomping of baby cacti had earned me bad cactus karma and the enmity of Mother Nature. As my teammates carefully pried me off the bloody cactus patch, I swear I could hear the other nearby cacti chuckling softly. Back in camp, PJ instructor Dave Young later came to my tent with pliers and de-spined me; it only took a couple of hours.

We broke camp Sunday night and returned to our barracks, filthy, bedraggled, and exhausted from the non-stop training. I ached from abused muscles and five hundred puncture wounds. When we arrived back at the base after midnight, I didn't care that I was covered in grime; I was so tired I immediately collapsed onto my bed and fell into a coma. In a few short hours, I would have to face max-week and our hardest workouts.

As usual, the next day began with loud noise, cursing, grumbling and a team run to breakfast. In max-week we made our longest runs, longest swims, and the most repetitions of calisthenics. I was not in top form, and as the day wore on my penalty drops mounted. After dinner we gathered in the dungeon and did our drops. Each drop was sixty pushups or eighty flutter kicks. After the drop session, Sergeant Bruce made a special announcement. While we had been training, the instructors had graciously carried out a "white glove" inspection of our rooms. They obviously knew we had returned late and exhausted from Enchanted Rock. We had been camping and living in filth for two days and had not had time to clean. Bastards! My roommate John Dwyer and I earned twenty-nine demerits. Most of the other rooms received a similar number of discrepancies. Instead of heading to our racks to sleep, it was back to the dungeon for another instructor supervised drop session. The cadre expected me to do twenty nine iterations, alternating sixty pushups and eighty flutter kicks—this after a full day of our hardest workout to date.

I looked around at my stunned teammates to see if they were up for rushing the instructors and killing them. No. The drops began. I seethed inside from the injustice of it all. I didn't see how it was even possible for a human to do this. It was ridiculous. My rage was soon replaced with an all-out struggle to survive this drop session. The instructors were relentless. Despite the unreasonable circumstances, the instructors often made us start an exercise over because someone showed poor form or was not in sync with their teammates. Imagine being on pushup forty-five of a sixty pushup set and hearing, "Start over, Bill Sine is cheating." They did this often, sometimes unfairly, just so the team would start to get mad at the person that was causing them extra exercise sets. Is your mind strong enough to deal with undeserved peer pressure and scorn? The instructors will find out. The room stank of human steam, anger and despair. Sweat droplets by the thousands cascaded from our bodies. Men moaned and grunted, gritting their teeth in exertion. As the minutes crawled by, our team slowly gained strength. Our anger fueled our resolve, and despair transformed into determination and pride. They would not break us, no one would quit; we were invincible. When the exercises finally ended, we were shaking and quivering, barely able to stagger up the stairs to our rooms. It was ten at night. Subtracting meal times, our team had survived a brutal fifteen-hour workout!

I successfully completed the rest of Indoc, but no day was ever easy. During the final test it was freezing outside. The water in our pool was sixty-seven degrees: *very* cold. When I finished the four-thousand meter swim and hit the showers, I stood under streaming hot water for five minutes before I was warmed enough to start shivering. I was so cold my shiver reflex had shut down. From a trainee's point of view, Indoc seemed designed to tear a person down, not build them up. The weekly increases in distance and exercise repetitions seemed too extreme to allow a human body to adapt; there were not enough opportunities to rest and recuperate. The routines that seemed designed to tear a man down and make him quit were, in reality, selecting for physical durability and mental toughness. Two weeks after graduating Indoc, my fitness and strength dramatically increased, because my muscles finally had a chance to rest and build. This is the same rebound effect dedicated athletes experience as they adjust their workouts to peak before a major athletic event. The instructor's had prepared us to overcome any physical or mental barrier the pipeline would throw in our way.

Years later, I learned that the training routines in Indoc were far from arbitrary. The instructor's used the latest athletic and medical science of the period combined with a host of 'PJs' personal experiences to establish formal standards for Indoc. They consulted with prominent physical therapists and swim coaches. Their efforts formed the foundation, training regimens and philosophy that exists in Indoc to this day.

On November 12, 1975, our instructors administered the final test to my class. The ordeal took most of the day. My performance was not spectacular, and I ranked midway in my class. I was in a severely weakened state. We had forty-eight minutes to run a minimum of six miles, or a maximum of eight miles. We received extra points for distances above minimums. We had to exercise until time ran out; we couldn't stop once we reached the six-mile minimum. I ran a little more than six and a half miles in forty eight minutes, not exactly a record setting pace. We had to swim a minimum four thousand meters in one hundred minutes up to a maximum of six thousand meters, all without swim fins. I swam 4,545 meters in one hundred minutes. I was obviously never in consideration for a place on the U.S. Olympic Swim Team. In forty-five seconds I did eighteen chin-ups followed a short time later by fifteen pull-ups, also with a forty-five-second limit. I managed a hundred and sixty sit-ups and then a hundred and sixty four-count hello darlings—lay on your back with feet held six inches off the ground and spread and close your legs—and a hundred and thirty flutter kicks. In a minute and a half I did sixty-three push-ups and in fifty-five seconds I did twenty-six Chinese push-ups. (For Chinese push-ups you place your hands and feet about two feet apart creating an upward vee-shape with your body. You place the thumbs and forefingers of both hands together making a triangle on the ground. Keeping your legs straight, touch your nose to the middle of the hand-triangle and return. This is one Chinese push-up.) I passed donning and clearing mask and snorkel, and I passed water harassment. Most importantly, I passed the overall test and would move on to the next stage of PJ pipeline.

There have been many changes in PJ training over the years. Changes take place because of shifting policies or safety concerns. Changes often reflect prevailing societal or scientific world-views, or sometime it just depends on the personalities of the instructors in charge. These days at Indoc they have swim coaches, exercise physiologists, and psychologists on staff to assist the PJ instructors. The running gag over the years has been, "Training was harder when I went through." You hear this mantra throughout the special operations community. But the ultimate test of training effectiveness is operational performance. In every historical era PJs have always demonstrated heroism, valor, and unmatched professionalism. Times and training methods change but pararescuemen remain the same: the best of the best.

A fascinating article in the January 1985 *Armed Forces Journal International* titled "Yasotay and the Mangoday of Genghis Khan" by Ethan Heral focused on the Mangoday, the elite special operations force led by the Mongol warlord named Yasotay. In the thirteenth century Genghis Khan united the Mongol tribes and conquered and ruled the largest empire in the history of the world. A military genius, he pioneered the use of special operations commandos. According to the article, Mangoday warriors were a step above the Khan's regular force of hard-core Mongols. Genghis used them to infiltrate enemy strongholds and as suicide shock troops. The Mangoday were so single minded in their attacks that one caught on fire from an enemy's flaming-oil weapons, he would continue to fight until he fell dead to the ground. The average Mongol's life was one long selection process for warrior skills and endurance, but the Mangoday possessed a unique mental perspective based in Zen Buddhism. They did not fear death and during battle fought without helmets to be more exposed to death. Mangoday philosophy was based on the observation of starving wolves. Yasotay, the founder of the Mangoday and its greatest warrior, noticed that as wolves became progressively more hungry their bravery and ferocity increased even against strong opponents, such as armed men. Eventually, prolonged hunger induced tranquility in the beasts but without diminishing their courage. The Mangoday were so effective that the Great Khan ordered Yasotay to recruit more warriors but admonished him not to sacrifice quality for quantity.

Yasotay used a rigorous process to select soldiers for his unit. Mangoday warriors took the candidates on a forced march that lasted seven days. During the entire march, they were not allowed to eat any food, only to drink water. On the first day, the Mongols marched for eighteen hours and were allowed to rest for six hours. On the second day, the Mongols marched over the vast steppe for nineteen hours and rested for five hours, still consuming nothing but water. On the third day, they marched for twenty straight hours and slept for only four hours. This pattern continued, with the Mongols marching longer each day and sleeping less, all without eating. On the sixth day the Mongols only rested one hour, and then performed attacking maneuvers and intense military drills the entire seventh day. After this ordeal, those Mongols still wishing to become Mangoday took an oath. They pledged to obey their supreme commander and to be true to their comrades, orders, and leaders. They swore to be prepared to lay down their life and to consecrate themselves to God. They foreswore personal ambition without considering the consequences. After reciting the oath, the new Mangoday were accepted into the unit. If a Mangoday soldier could look down from Mongol heaven upon modern day commandos, I'm sure he would say, "Being a warrior was a lot harder in my day."

Half of our team passed the final test. Half failed water harassment the first time, but most passed on the retest a week later. We graduated Indoc without fanfare. The next day we left Texas to attend our next pipeline school. That first PJ course forged human steel. Mentally, physically, and spiritually we would bend but not break. I was a physical fitness badass. After Indoc, none of the other military schools in the pipeline were physically challenging. I was unstoppable and on my way to becoming 175 pounds of lean, mean, green, spring steel, sex appeal, airborne pararescueman!

CHAPTER 3

_____

ENGLAND

_____

I want to be a rescue ranger
Live a life of sex and danger
—*PJ Running Song (Jodie chant)*

MY PJ CLASS GRADUATED 2 JULY 1976, AND RESCUE HEADQUARTERS assigned me to the 67th Aerospace Rescue and Recovery Squadron (ARRS), Royal Air Force (RAF) station Woodbridge, United Kingdom. I was a brand new nineteen-year-old PJ fresh from the pararescue school, what more experienced PJs called "a pup." Prior to my air force enlistment, I had never traveled outside the Midwest. I chose England as my first assignment, because I wanted the opportunity to travel around Europe, visiting countries like Germany, Spain, France, Scotland and Wales.

RAF Woodbridge is located in Suffolk, East Anglia, a short distance from the North Sea. The largest nearby city is Ipswich, with a population of a hundred thousand. The 67th ARRS had both helicopters and fixed-wing aircraft. PJs flew on Sikorsky HH-53 helicopters nicknamed Super Jolly Green Giants. We also flew on the HC-130 Hercules, the long-range search-and-rescue/combat-search-and-rescue version of the venerable C-130 cargo transport. The HC-130 is a large, four-engine, turboprop plane with radar and communications upgrades. With thirty-five PJs on its roster, the 67th ARRS boasted one of the largest PJ teams in the world.

At the 67th we trained non-stop. One of our frequent training missions was practicing aerial gunnery. Our HH-53 helicopters were equipped with miniguns. During combat rescue pick-ups the flight engineer and PJs use the miniguns to protect the helicopter from enemy soldiers. For targets, we tossed smoke flares into the North Sea and tried to shoot them to pieces. We also practiced free-fall swimmer deployments, which we called "low and slows." This involved jumping from the helicopter door into the sea while flying ten feet above the waves and traveling at ten knots forward airspeed. I learned that it takes a lot of skill to work in the powerful waves beneath a hovering helicopter. The enormous HH-53 helicopter's rotor wash creates extremely powerful and violent gale-force winds. is. The giant rotors whip salt spray with such force that the impact of the water droplets stings exposed flesh. Water work beneath a Super Jolly is strenuous and confusing, even while wearing a wetsuit and face mask for protection. It's like working blind in crashing ocean surf during a hurricane. Blind, because looking through the face mask is like looking through a car's windshield during a thunderstorm without windshield wipers. In the midst of this watery chaos, we practiced recovering mock patients from the sea using the helicopter's rescue hoist. Rising and falling on dark ocean swells, a PJ acts the part of an unconscious victim. Other PJs low-and-slow close to the limp victim and muscle him into a steel, coffin-shaped litter equipped with foam flotation. Once the patient is strapped into the litter, the helicopter hovers overhead while the flight engineer lowers a slim steel cable and hook, part of the rescue hoist. With the huge chopper hovering only forty-feet above, wind-whipped waves and salt spray batter the PJs complicating their task. One mistake working with the quarter-inch-thick hoist cable, a stray loop caught around an arm or neck, can result in death or a lost limb when the cable tightens. These operations require endurance, skill, and focus. They are incredibly difficult and dangerous, which is why we trained constantly.

We also practiced parachuting into the cold North Sea. Water parachute jumps, especially at night, are a grueling physical ordeal. Because of the freezing water, we wore unisuits. Also known as dry suits, unisuits are one-piece rubber suits with water-tight rubber seals at the wrists and neck. The suit keeps water out so the PJ inside stays dry. The more familiar wet suits are not water-tight. They work by trapping a layer of water between the porous neoprene of the suit and the diver's skin. The diver's body heats the thin layer of water, keeping him warm. Dry suits are vastly superior to wetsuits in very cold water, because a diver can wear warm, dry insulation inside his suit. Compared to modern-day dry suits, the Poseidon unisuit I wore in the 1970s was extremely bulky and restrictive. The suit was so unwieldy and exhausting to put on that PJ regulations required two people be present when a unisuit was used and mandated periodic rest breaks. If a person put on a suit incorrectly they could suffocate.

The first time I put on a unisuit, my teammates guided me, step-by-step through *improper* donning procedures. At one point, I was in a squatting position with my hands inside the arms of the suit and my head positioned below the opening to the hood. My buddies told me the correct procedure was to stand up, straightening my legs and forcing my head through the neck seal and into the hood. I dutifully followed their instructions and suddenly found the tight rubber neck seal clamped over my mouth and nose making it impossible to breathe. My hands were trapped inside the thick rubber arms of the suit, so I could not could not free myself. I flopped about helplessly on the floor, minutes away from death by silly suffocation. Shortly before I expired my mischievous teammates freed me from the suit, and allowing me to survive. (They probably didn't want to be bothered with the paperwork that follows a training accident.) Everyone laughed at my antics . . . good times.

One of our most demanding training missions was practicing night scuba jumps. We put on our open-ocean parachute gear in the dark confines of the HC-130 as it flew at a thousand feet above the waves. Gusty winds buffeted the plane, and the stuffy constrictive unisuits combined with the jerky movements of the airplane caused many PJs to get airsick. The loadmaster passed out barf bags to those who needed them. If one person vomited it often caused a chain reaction of uncontrolled retching. We sometimes used this phenomenon to prank newcomers. A PJ would fill his mouth full of soup with chunky vegetables and sit next to a new PJ. At the proper time, and in full view of the butt-of-the-joke, the PJ would vomit the soup into a clear plastic bag and lick the dribble off his lips. If well-acted and timed, this spectacle would often trigger vomiting in the victim.

Suiting up for the jump was an ordeal. After dressing in the unisuit, I strapped on a pair of heavy steel scuba tanks, and on top of the tanks I positioned my parachute and harness. Next I snapped on a forty-pound medical kit to the webbing positioned on my belly, below my reserve parachute. Finally, I connected a square, canvas-covered container behind me, below my butt. It held an emergency one-man life raft we called a "butt boat." We also wore large swim fins, strapped a knife and flare to our lower leg, and put on a mask, snorkel, and scuba-breathing regulator. Weighed down with so much cumbersome gear, I literally had to waddle to the open paratroop door to leave the aircraft. My exit was an undignified tumble into the 130 mph slipstream.

As soon as I jumped from the plane, the slipstream shook me violently as I slowly counted to four—it was a staticline jump—waiting for the welcome jerk of the parachute as it opened and caught the air. (After four seconds, if my main parachute failed to open I would need to pull the ripcord of my reserve parachute.) I always experienced momentary disorientation as the parachute opened and jerked me around. And then, suddenly, I was floating in the night sky, enveloped by silence and cold. I looked up and confirmed I had a healthy parachute canopy. I looked below and located my target, a life raft lit with strobe lights. Using my parachute toggles to steer towards the raft, I prepared for water entry. As I descended I performed my water-entry procedures, disconnecting straps and buckles so I could quickly escape my gear after I hit the waves. The winds were a brisk 20 mph, so after landing I expected my inflated canopy to drag me across the sea, pulling me underwater. Moments later I splashed down, but when my parachute deep-sixed me beneath the waves I didn't panic. Despite being towed under the frigid black water, I calmly breathed off my scuba tanks while I released one side of my parachute from my harness. This spilled the air from my canopy and collapsed the parachute, abruptly ending my subsurface ride beneath the waves. When I bobbed to the surface, I quickly freed myself from the parachute harness and finned towards my target. PJs in our Boston Whaler picked up the jumpers and recovered our parachutes, stuffing them into large canvas bags. Once all the gear and jumpers were safely onboard, the boat master navigated back to the river inlet and cruised up the River Ore to dock near the picturesque and historic village of Orford.

Orford is a small coastal village that dates back to the twelfth century. The ninety foot tall stone keep of Orford Castle overlooks the village. King Henry the Second built the castle in 1165. This is the first real castle I ever saw close up, and it is quite imposing. Orford is also home to a couple of historic pubs, the Jolly Sailor and the King's Head Inn. These were originally thirteenth century smuggler's inns. After a cold, wet day training in the North Sea we would always stop at the Jolly Sailor for a couple of pints of ale. We drank beer and warmed ourselves before a roaring fire, even playing a few games of push penny. I was amazed at how ancient and historic everything was. The Jolly Sailor was older than America, even the push penny game board was more than a hundred years old. After a few pints of ale, we would drive the narrow twisting roads back to Woodbridge and the PJ section.

There is a common thread that runs through every PJ team: unique personalities. Pararescue is peopled with unusual characters who generate nonstop drama and adventures; there is never a dull moment on a PJ team. Everyone is interesting and I spent a large part of each day laughing. The Vietnam War had just ended, and many of my teammates had seen action. One PJ, "Swerve" Petty, had taken a .50-caliber bullet in the arm and sported a very impressive scar, a serious badge of honor. Others had participated in various combat rescues and were highly decorated. One PJ had even been temporarily kicked out of Vietnam for being too violent and eccentric. Two of my friends, Kevin and Rick, were infamous for their over-the-top adventures. They lived on a sailboat, but knew very little about seafaring. That didn't stop them from sailing to various countries hundreds of miles away. On their first attempt as intrepid seamen, they missed the entire country they were aiming for. Dead tired, they anchored in an unknown harbor and crawled into their bunks and passed out. In the middle of the night the tide receded and their sailboat rolled over on its side, sinking into the mud and spilling Kevin and Rick out of their bunks. Luckily, their boat refloated when the tide returned.

When they finally made it back to England, they didn't realize they had violated a whole slew of British customs regulations. Kevin and Rick came to work as usual, blissfully unaware of any wrong doing, until customs officials dragged them away and swarmed over their boat searching every nook and cranny for contraband. On another occasion, during a surprise dorm inspection, their rooms were discovered devoid of all beds and other furniture but stacked floor-to ceiling with sheep and horse pelts they had bought in Iceland. They planned to sell the hides for a profit, but the inspection short circuited their scheme. There is always something interesting going on at a PJ team!

There were endless opportunities for excellent military training in Great Britain. We were fortunate that we were only a few hours' drive from Snowdonia, North Wales. Snowdonia is a region famous for its granite cliffs, rock climbing, and spectacular mountain scenery. Wales boasts some of the best hiking and climbing in Europe. Many of the techniques and equipment used in modern sport climbing were developed on the granite crags in North Wales. Climbing in Wales is challenging, because Welsh weather is notoriously changeable. Even in summer, the weather is often rainy, windy, cold, and miserable: perfect weather for rescue training. In winter, snow and freezing sleet often add to the misery. Wretched weather complicates and hinders mountain rescue operations. With cold wet hands it's hard to tie knots and manipulate ropes and equipment. The rock is slippery and treacherous. The damp cold penetrates to the bone and slows your thought processes. Whistling winds flap garments and garble verbal communication, while fog and blowing snow obscure visibility, making it hard to coordinate team efforts. Training in Wales taught us how to conduct rescue operations under worst-case conditions. A hard day spent in the Welsh elements also taught me to appreciate a crackling fire and a tumbler of single-malt scotch whisky.

Our PJ team regularly traveled to Capel Curig, North Wales, to rock climb and polish our climbing and rescue skills. Over the years PJs had established a close relationship with the mountain-rescue community in North Wales. Especially helpful were members of the local Ogwen Valley Mountain Rescue Team. Tony Jones, a marine geologist and rescue expert, was especially helpful. Tony allowed us to stay in Helyg (pronounced hay-lig) Hut, an stone cottage built in the nineteenth century and purchased by the exclusive Climber's Club in 1925. George Mallory, the famous Everest climber was president of the club. Tony was custodian of the hut. It is located near Tryfan, one of the highest mountains in Wales and one of the country's most recognizable landmarks. The hut is conveniently located in the heart of Welsh rock-climbing country and is nestled a short distance from numerous rescue training areas. It was a great privilege, and a great convenience, to be invited into the hut and we loved it.

When we trained in Wales, we usually brought ten PJs and drove pickup trucks from Woodbridge to Wales. Our unit had a contract with the RAF-base commissary and we packed large coolers with enough food to last us through a week of hard training. Working long and hard in mind-numbing cold, we ate like kings after we returned to the warm hut, taking turns cooking our culinary specialties, such as stews, chili, and pasta.

One time we had loaded our pickup trucks with food and equipment and were backing out of the PJ compound to begin the drive to Wales. Suddenly the truck I was on lurched and there was a loud scraping and crunching noise from underneath. Our driver immediately slammed on the brakes, and we all jumped out to see what had happened. During pack-out, someone had forgotten to load one of the large plastic milk crates, leaving ten, one-gallon jugs of milk, packaged in a hard plastic compartmentalized container on the ground behind the vehicle. The crate was crushed under the truck's frame and gallons of milk gushed down the street in a white frothy torrent. Our top sergeant was furious. Red faced and apoplectic, he began cussing and yelling at everyone until PJ Brian Berg calmly said, " Sergeant Wagner, no sense crying over spilt milk!" Everyone cracked up and all semblance of discipline vanished as everyone laughed uncontrollably. Wagner eventually threw up his arms, acknowledging the hopelessness of trying to be serious in the face of a perfect retort and slunk sheepishly back into the truck.

I occasionally wrote home, detailing my exotic adventures. Eventually, I convinced my younger brother Bobby to visit me in England. I planned the highlight of his vacation around a hardcore rock-climbing adventure in Wales. When Bobby arrived in England I showed him around the unit and gave him a tour of the local pubs and castles. A few days later we drove to Snowdonia with my PJ buddy Tim Williams. When we arrived in Wales we pitched tents in the meadow behind Helyg Hut. Over the next couple of days Tim and I proceeded to give Bobby a crash course in rock climbing and rope work. We punctuated our daytime climbing lessons with night-time drink fests at Cobdens, our favorite watering hole. Soon Bobby knew the basics of pub etiquette and rock climbing and wanted to go on a serious climb, something scary. I had the perfect adrenaline junky adventure in mind, a very sketchy climb at the limit of my ability. We could actually die on this outing—perfect scary fun.

The next day we drove to Tremadog, one of the best climbing areas in

Wales. The rock is volcanic dolerite and the cliffs soar to 250 feet. Serious rock climbing is a life and death proposition. If a climber is inexperienced or careless, he can get into some very terrifying and sometimes fatal predicaments. Lead climbing is the most difficult and hair-raising type of rock climbing. Rock climbing involves a team of two climbers tied in at each end of a sixty-meter climbing rope. The lead climber is the first person to climb, and the belayer, who controls the brake, climbs after the lead has blazed a route upwards. The lead climber connects one end of the rope to a special sit harness that he wears around his waist and thighs. A modern climbing rope is a miracle of engineering and can withstand seven thousand pounds of force without breaking. Climbing ropes are also specially designed to stretch and absorb the energy of a climber's fall. If a climber used a nonstretching steel cable, the instant stop at the end of a fall would snap the climber's spine and rip him in half. The belayer also wears a sit harness and controls the movement of the rope through a mechanical friction device. The lead climber can ascend a rock face, pulling rope smoothly through the belayer's friction device, but the belayer can apply the brake and stop all movement of the rope in an instant.

The belayer anchors at the bottom of the climb, while the lead climber makes his way up the cliff pausing every five feet or so to wedge a metal device, called a chock, into a crack in the rock. Chocks are solid wedge-shaped chunks of aluminum attached to a foot-long steel cable with a loop at the end. The climber carries different size chocks on his harness to fit different sized cracks. The chock is the piece of gear that will save the lead climber if he falls. After wedging a chock into a crack in the rock, the climber clips his rope into the chock's cable loop with an oval-shaped aluminum snap link called a carabiner. When a lead climber is about to fall he will loudly shout, "Falling!" This prompts his belay man to immediately apply the brake, preventing any further rope from being let out. If a climber is five feet above his last chock, he will fall five feet down to the chock and continue to fall a further five feet past the chock until rope slack disappears and jerks him to a stop. The forces generated in a fall are enormous, and even a short fall can have devastating consequences. Imagine falling five feet and banging an elbow on a granite ledge. That's an instant recipe for squirting blood and a broken arm with jagged bones sticking out. If a climber falls ten feet above his last chock, he will fall twenty feet. To keep falls as short as possible, it's important for lead climbers to place chock protection every five feet. Unless a climb is absolutely vertical, a falling climber will probably bang into protruding rocks on the way down and suffer broken bones.

For adrenaline junkies, rock climbing provides plenty of, "I am surely going to die!" moments. If a falling climber's sloppy chock protection fails, gravity could make him pay for his carelessness with his life. Falling is not the only way to die. Avalanches or falling rocks from above can smash your bones or crack your helmet like an egg, caving in your skull and immediately ending your climb. The most exquisite form of climbing terror is when a lead climber gets "ass-holed." This happens when a climber moves too far above his last piece of chock protection and gets stranded. A climber knows that if he falls when he is twenty five feet above his last chock, he will fall twenty-five feet down to the chock and an additional twenty-five feet past the chock before his rope will stop his fall. That's a fifty-foot fall. Even if his equipment works perfectly, there is no guarantee he will come out of that situation unscathed, and he could even be killed.

Imagine being ass-holed under these circumstances: You are twenty-five feet above your last chock, clinging desperately to a sheer granite wall. You know that if you fall, you will plummet at least fifty feet, possibly snapping your spine and crushing internal organs. You can't climb back down; climbing down is harder than climbing up, because you can't see where to place your hands and feet. You are stunned when you figure out your next climbing move. The maneuver is ridiculously hard, almost certainly beyond your abilities. Your heart sinks when you realize the magnitude of your situation. You either overestimated your skill or blundered off your planned route. Every course of action is a gamble, and you are playing for your life.

The move requires you to launch from your slick, precarious foothold, leaping to grab a tiny ledge with one hand. You mentally calculate that you only have a 40 percent chance of successfully making the move. If you miss, you'll fall fifty feet. You vividly visualize the life and death consequences of your success or failure, so you naturally hesitate to make the move. But you are perched precariously on a vertical rock face getting more tired with each second that passes. You know the longer you wait to move, the weaker you will be, and the less likely you will be able to make the move.

As you fight this internal mental battle your chances of making the move, steadily drop. And you are painfully aware of this. Your legs start to shake and vibrate uncontrollably. "Sewing machine leg" is caused by fatigue and fear and is beyond conscious control. Your shaking limbs further saps your strength and your will. You are ASS-HOLED! As a lead climber you have to have uncommon courage. You cannot hesitate to go for those sketchy moves. This will give you the best chance to succeed, although you accept that there will be times when you will fall. If all this seems like a bit too much, don't take up rock climbing.

It was finally time to take Bobby on a serious climb. After a scenic drive through picturesque mountains and emerald green valleys, we arrived at Tremadog. I decided I would take Bobby on a climb that was rated "hard very severe." This is a pretty difficult climb, and I wasn't sure I was good enough to lead such a hard climb. The climb was three pitches, meaning we would use three lengths of our sixty meter climbing rope to get to the top. I would lead the climb, stopping at about one hundred feet up to set up a new belay system to protect Bobby as he climbed to my location. As Bobby climbed, I would belay from above him, taking in slack. If he fell I would put on the brake, instantly stopping his fall in only a couple of feet. On the way up, he would remove the chocks I had set in cracks for my protection. When Bobby reached my position, I would set up a new system and lead the next pitch while my brother once again belayed from below.

The first pitch was moderately difficult, but I was able to climb it and set up a belay to bring Bobby up. Bobby started to climb, occasionally removing chocks and clipping them to his sit harness. Since I pulled in his slack as he climbed, he would only fall a foot or two if he fell, assuming I applied the brake when he yelled, "Falling!" Bobby was climbing good, but he still fell twice screaming out, "Falling!" in undisguised fear. Falls of any length are no joking matter when you are a hundred feet above the ground.

The next pitch included a twenty-foot traverse. A traverse is a movement horizontally across a rock face. This involves facing the cliff and edging sideways, balancing the toe tips of your climbing shoes on tiny ledges and small bumps on the rock called nubbins. The ledge we traversed was almost an inch wide, which sounds small, but in the climbing community an inch is as wide as a highway. Interspersed along the traverse were sections

where a climber had to support their entire weight on miniscule rock nubbins. Nonclimbers would consider these foot holds microscopic and would
be mystified as to how anyone could possibly stand on anything so insubstantial. Specially designed rock climbing boots with hard rubber soles is
part if the explanation, and the climber's skill and strength make up the
rest of the equation.

I negotiated the difficult traverse and established a belay on a convenient ledge. Bobby began to climb as I pulled in his slack. As he climbed,
he removed the chocks that I had placed, and soon Bobby was at the beginning of the traverse. He began to creep across the narrow ledge, balancing
on his toes a hundred feet above the ground. To add excitement and en-
hance his climbing experience, I called out, "Hey Bobby! Look down.
You're pretty high above the ground. I'm amazed you're balancing on those
tiny footholds like that. Looks like you could fall at any second." Bobby
laughed nervously but could not resist looking down. I laughed, "This is
what you wanted. Keep it up; you're climbing like a gecko." At one point,
Bobby experienced sewing machine legs, but made it to my ledge without
falling. I clapped him on the back, "Good job Bobby." I setup for the last
and hardest pitch; we were over two hundred feet above the ground. In
the corner of the ledge was a stout tree with a thick branch about shoulder
height. I used nylon webbing to connect the back of Bobby's harness to
the branch as an anchor and safety. Soon we were ready to go. "Remember
if I yell, 'Falling!' you set the brake, stop my fall, and save my life . . . simple.
Once I get on top, I'll belay you up."

I began to climb the hard, gray granite cliff. This pitch seemed impossible. The stone wall was splashed with green and yellow blotches of lichen
and was totally vertical. I had no problems placing chock protection during
the first half of the eighty-foot high pitch. At about forty feet above Bobby,
I placed a bomber piece of protection. Climbers use the word bomber or
bomb proof to describe the perfect chock placement, one that you think
will definitely save you if you fall. I continued to climb, but the route
became ridiculously hard. Handholds and footholds were very thin. Suddenly, I found myself ten feet above my last piece of protection. My grip
on the cliff was so tenuous, that even if I wanted to place protection, I
could not remove a hand from the rock to fish around for a chock clipped
to my harness. I needed both hands and feet just to stop from falling off

the rock face. I had no choice but to continue to climb, hoping to reach a less extreme section so I could place chock protection. I edged upwards, now twenty feet above my last chock. A slip here would result in a forty-foot fall. I was at the limits of my skill and endurance; knowledge of the possible outcome of a long fall gave me the strength to continue on. I was splayed across the rock like a spider and wished I had a spider's climbing skill. I slowly struggled upwards, totally giving up on placing further protection. I was now thirty feet above my last chock: a sixty foot fall. I fully realized I was in a serious climbing pickle. I had either overestimated my skill, or had strayed off the route onto a harder section of rock. I had only myself to blame.

I could not afford to fall now. I knew these types of situations killed climbers. Far below me Bobby was blissfully unaware of my predicament. I prayed he remembered how to brake a fall and would not panic. Ten feet from the top I desperately scrabbled and clawed the rock. My muscles quivered with exhaustion, but I refused to give up. Finally, I hung by my fingertips, grasping the top ledge. My forearms were unfeeling blocks of wood, numb with fatigue. I willed my trembling arms to function and did a slow pull up and slowly dragged myself up the rock face. I was almost there. My eyes cleared the edge and I could see grass and meadows and the promise of rest and safety. With a relieved smile on my face, I reached for a hand hold to pull myself up the final few inches. When I reached for that last hand hold, my other hand inexplicably slipped. I instinctively screamed, "Falling!"

I peeled off the rock and plummeted eighty feet down the vertical cliff; course granite rock was a deadly gray and brown blur only inches in front of my face. In only two seconds I accelerated to over 40 mph. When I reached the end of the slack, my rope tightened and stretched to near breaking, struggling to absorb the titanic energies involved in stopping a 180-pound man falling eighty feet. Caught in the inescapable grip of gravity I was completely powerless as I was tossed about like a ragdoll. I finally came to rest dangling upright a few feet above the ledge where I had started my climb. My torqued joints and vertebrae ached and tingled from the beating they had taken. Bobby was suspended in air next to me, wide-eyed and white as a sheet. All he could sputter was, "What the hell Bill!" I told him, "Just stay calm. Keep the brake on." When I fell, it had caught Bobby completely by surprise, but he had instantly applied the brake saving my life. When I reached the end of my fall, the rope stretched and yanked Bobby upwards and smeared him into the rock face. As the stretching rope slowed my fall, my boot soles had actually thumped his helmet making him see stars. I told Bobby to slowly let out slack and we both lowered the few feet down onto the ledge. Feeling shaken and vulnerable, we teetered on the narrow space two hundred feet above the ground. Bobby was still freaked out. He was trembling and still unbelieving of what had just actually happened. He had also picked up some scrapes and bruises when the forces of the fall lifted him off the ledge and ground him into the rough granite wall. Though my fall had caught him completely by surprise, Bobby had reacted like a seasoned climber and maintained his break hand throughout my fall. I also felt weak and shaky after my close call. The magnitude of what had just occurred was sinking in. I glimpsed a flutter of wings out of the corner of my eye, but when I looked there was nothing there. It was probably just my Guardian Angel departing the scene, another job well done.

We were definitely done climbing for the day, but we were not out of the woods yet. I needed Bobby to rappel down and locate Tim. I told him to explain the situation and have Tim walk the path to the top. Once there he could find a spot directly above and set up a rappel. I needed Tim to rappel down the way I had climbed up, removing the chocks I had placed in the cracks. I had borrowed all our climbing gear from the PJ section, and I needed to return as much as I could. From our precarious perch on the thin ledge, I set up a rappel to the ground. My rope had a damaged section caused by the fall, and would not see any further use as a climbing rope. But we had enough good rope left to reach the bottom if I tied two ropes together. I didn't want to leave Bobby by himself on the high ledge, so I sent him down on the rappel. It was fortunate that we had trained him hard in the preceding days, because he had to do a complicated knot bypass procedure in order to negotiate around the knot that joined the two climbing ropes. Despite his shaken condition, Bobby successfully bypassed the knot, but not without some drama that is burned into his mind to this day. A failure at this point would have stranded him, hanging in midair a hundred feet above jagged boulders. After he passed the knot he continued his rappel and his feet soon touched solid ground.

Bobby soon found Tim and filled him in on our close call. Tim grabbed gear and took off up the steep trail to the top. After all the adrenaline and excitement, Bobby was played out. He soon fell behind but pressed on and was once again in great pain as his legs and lungs burned from the climb. Tim practically sprinted up the hill. A short time later I could see him above. Bobby returned down the path while Tim rigged a retrievable rappel and collected my chocks. We both rappelled to the ground and soon met up with Bobby in the parking lot. We headed directly for the nearest place that offered comfort and medical treatment: the local pub.

At the pub we celebrated a time honored climbing tradition reserved for those special occasions when we almost die. We proceeded to drink a couple of creamy pints of Guinness. Looking back on those events, I shouldn't have picked an unfamiliar climb, especially a climb so difficult; 20/20 hindsight strikes again. I did learn from my mistake, however, and the next time I experience a similar situation I'll react very differently. And afterwards I'll drink more than just a couple pints of Guinness.

CHAPTER 4

OKINAWA

PARARESCUE HAIKU
Very hard training
Sissies cry in the bleak night
They do not succeed
—*William F. Sine*

33RD AEROSPACE RESCUE AND RECOVERY SQUADRON (ARRS), KADENA AIR BASE, JAPAN 1980

OKINAWA IS LOCATED HALFWAY BETWEEN KYUSHU AND TAIWAN, THE largest island in the Ryukyu chain of islands that stretches for seven hundred miles, and has a population of about a million people. The rock and coral island is sixty-seven miles long and varies in width from two to fourteen miles wide. U.S. Marine and Air Force bases take up 12 percent of the island. Okinawa has beautiful beaches and is renowned for its scuba diving. The climate is hot and humid, and occasionally tropical cyclones called typhoons pummel the island.

During World War II Operation Iceberg, the invasion of Okinawa, was the largest amphibious assault during the war in the Pacific and one of the hardest fought campaigns of the entire war. Only 340 miles from the Japanese home islands, Okinawa was slated to act as a springboard for American bombers to attack Japan. Sixty thousand allied troops stormed the beaches and fought for eighty-two days, from April through June 1945. The Japanese lost one hundred thousand soldiers and twelve thousand

Americans were killed in action, while one hundred and fifty thousand Okinawan civilians perished during the battle. In preparation for the assault, the allies amassed an armada of thirteen hundred ships and softened up the beach heads with intense naval bombardment. The landing commenced on Easter, 1 April 1945, and instead of being called D day, it was designated Love Day. Okinawa is dotted with thousands of concrete burial crypts. Local lore has it that the naval bombardment was especially intense, because reconnaissance aircraft mistook the thousands of cement crypts for reinforced concrete bunkers.

Kadena Air Base is the center of American air-power in the Pacific. More than eighteen thousand Americans and four thousand Japanese live or work on Kadena AB. Marine and air force bases take up 19 percent of the island. Air force and marine personnel and their families make up a significant percentage of the island's population. Located near the Kadena AB flight line, the 33rd Rescue Squadron had both HC-130 transports and HH-53 helicopters. There were good opportunities for rescue missions during an assignment to Okinawa. There were also a lot of chances to travel and see the Orient. Our duties often required trips to the Philippines, Korea, Guam, Wake Island, and sometimes Thailand or Australia. Our squadron had around twenty PJs assigned. Our PJ section team room became our home away from home. We built a western style bar complete with swinging saloon doors and decorated the walls with western artifacts and paintings of John Wayne. An obvious departure from our wild west theme was a large saltwater aquarium and an oil painting of PJ Bill Eby. During a visit to Korea Bill commissioned an oil painting portrait of himself. However, he insisted the artist follow special instructions. The painting depicted Bill with his lower lip bulging with a large wad of tobacco. He also insisted the artist paint his head with the top of his skull missing, so that his brain was exposed like a bucket of earthworms. When he gave the painting to his wife for their wedding anniversary, she burst into tears and the painting ended up in our bar.

We had friendly relations with our Japanese PJ counterparts and occasionally invited them to our bar. After we entertained them during a Halloween party, they hosted our PJ team at their home base in the city of Naha. The evening began with an impressive Kendo sword-fighting demonstration. Afterwards we gathered in a small banquet room. Our hosts had arranged the tables in a large hollow square so that we all faced each other. They provided two bamboo casks of sake to slake our thirst. Japanese chefs piled our plates high with shrimp tempura and other delicacies. The leader of the Japanese PJs spoke English and insisted we go around the room with each person standing and telling a little about themselves. We alternated between Japanese and American introductions. Staff Sergeant Bill Eby was the highest ranking American at the party and the last to speak. When it was his turn, he stood and launched into an animated speech in fake Japanese, complete with bizarre gestures and facial expressions. Normally impervious to embarrassment, I was mortified. Our Japanese hosts appeared more confused than offended. Luckily, the large amount of sake everyone consumed masked the slight breech of protocol, and everyone laughed. To this day I wonder what Eby's speech sounded like to the Japanese PJs.

PJ training dominated our daily routine. One day I flew an aerial-gunnery training mission over the crystal blue waters surrounding the island. I always loved to fire the powerful 7.62mm minigun off the aft ramp of the Super Jolly. I stood behind the weapon and gripped the yoke of the gun and aimed the cluster of six barrels out the back of the helicopter. Wind swirled around me, keeping me cool in the stifling heat. We flew over the water at one hundred feet, the huge helicopter banking left and right at high speed. During hard turns, G forces threatened to crush me to the floor as I watched for the target smoke flare to appear on the waves. When we pulled out of a turn, I saw the wooden flare spewing smoke and aimed the gun. When I depressed the left trigger, electric current flowed into the machine gun and the six barrels spun so fast they blurred. Two thousand rounds per minute exploded from the muzzles with fire and thunder. The torque and recoil forces of the weapon are beyond the ability of any man to control, so the gun is bolted to a steel plate attached to the aircraft floor. I walked the red tracers over to the target until my rounds, each one a lethal high powered bullet, chewed into the wood casing of the flare. Once I locked on target, I squeezed the second trigger and the gun accelerated from two thousand to four thousand rounds per minute. I cackled maniacally as I obliterated the target, disintegrating the wooden smoke flare into the foaming sea—awesome!

Target destroyed, I released the triggers and began to prepare the weapon for the next firing pass when the pilot paged me over the intercom. He postponed the remainder of our gunnery flight, because base operations radioed to divert us to the Northern Training Area (NTA) to save a marine. The NTA is a morass of tangled jungle and treacherous ravines. The ground is perfect for military field training. The rough terrain is home to poisonous snakes, giant centipedes, banana spiders, and ravenous mosquitoes. Marines operate a hard-core combat skills course in the NTA that we nicknamed the "Marine Mud School." It's a good school that I had previously attended with some PJ teammates. En route to the NTA, information on the mission began to trickle in to our pilot.

A bee had stung a marine and the man was experiencing symptoms of a life threatening allergic reaction known as anaphylactic shock. This condition can stop your breathing and kills quickly if not immediately treated. I readied my medical equipment while our helicopter flew at top speed to the NTA. I prepared the litter, securing it to stanchions and positioned my oxygen unit near the head of the litter. Most importantly, I prepared my epinephrine syringe and reviewed administration procedures. Epinephrine is synthetic adrenaline and counteracts the effects of an allergic reaction. If all goes well, the patient immediately shows a positive reaction after an injection, and his condition will dramatically improve.

The pilot landed our helicopter on a landing pad crudely chopped out of the jungle and the flight engineer and I jumped to the ground and rushed over to a crowd of marines. The stricken man lay on a canvas pole litter in obvious physical distress, struggling to breathe. I verified the circumstances, quickly measured his racing pulse and respirations, and injected the recommended dose of epinephrine. His condition instantly improved and we moved him into the helicopter for transport to the hospital. With the patient safely secured on a litter, I set up oxygen and monitored his vitals on the way to the hospital. After the epinephrine injection the marine's condition dramatically improved. It was akin to raising a drowning man's head out of water, suddenly allowing him to breathe. We landed at the hospital pad and carried our patient inside. I briefed the receiving physician and reboarded my helicopter. This was my first solo rescue mission as a PJ—a definite save.

We lifted off and flew towards the gunnery range to resume training. We planned to finish our gun runs and begin water operations and hoist work. On the way to the range our pilot received another mission tasking. We immediately diverted towards a nearby island off the coast to evacuate a civilian in medical distress. I reconfigured the helicopter to receive a patient as the pilot received more information. I could hear the radio transmissions in my headset and occasionally requested additional information. This patient was in bad shape, suffering from a bleeding ulcer and shock. A bleeding ulcer is magnitudes more serious than a common ulcer or stomach ache. Gastric acid eats through a person's stomach lining, perforating blood vessels and causing continuous bleeding. A bleeding ulcer can kill, especially if the patient has other underlying conditions or is fragile. I obtained as much medical history and background information as I could while we sped towards our destination.

We landed on flat ground near a residence and I left the aircraft to examine the patient. I like to obtain a solid set of vitals (pulse, respirations, and blood pressure) before loading a patient. Once onboard, the helicopter's turbo shaft engines scream at over one hundred decibels and earplugs and helmet make it impossible to use a stethoscope. We loaded the patient and lifted off into the salt air. Once we were airborne, I started an IV and administered fluids. The ability to start an IV in a shaky, vibrating helicopter is a core PJ skill. The patient appeared very ill and had a racing pulse and systolic pressure under one hundred, definite signs of severe shock. I talked to my pilot and requested he contact a flight surgeon. A short time later, I conferred with the doctor via radio. I wanted to apply MAST (military anti-shock trousers), and after discussing the patient's signs and symptoms, he agreed.

In 1980, MAST was cutting edge medical technology. MAST is an inflatable pair of pants made of heavy duty nylon fabric secured with velcro. Like a fighter pilot's G suit, the trousers squeeze blood in the legs and pelvis and force it into the patient's core to support circulation to the brain and other vital organs. Used in conjunction with aggressive IV therapy, MAST increases a patient's blood pressure and keeps him alive until his arrival at an emergency room. MAST is controversial, some medical studies show they are helpful, but other studies conclude they are harmful. I was trained to only use MAST as a last resort to treat severe shock. I applied the trousers, a difficult task in a confined space during a bumpy helicopter ride, and successfully increased the patient's blood pressure. I started two

IV s and pumped as much fluid into the patient as I could. The patient stabilized, but I continued to closely monitor his condition.

After we landed at the hospital, I accompanied the patient into the facility and briefed the receiving physician on the treatment I had administered and, most importantly, how to remove the trousers. If someone improperly removes MAST it can result in an immediate and catastrophic drop in blood pressure. After I handed off my patient to a doctor, I boarded my helicopter and we returned to base. We were low on fuel and cancelled further training for the day. I did not mind at all; operational lifesaving missions trump all other considerations, and I had just had two successful rescue missions on the same day.

Not all my adventures involved rescue missions. My PJ buddy Dan Inch and I were flying a long range training mission over the Pacific Ocean when our HC-130 started having engine problems. One of our engines failed and the pilot had to shut it down. An HC-130 has four engines and can fly on three in an emergency, but the plane has to land as soon as possible. We headed for the nearest airfield, a runway on Midway Atoll. Midway consists of a remote cluster of small islands in the middle of the Pacific Ocean, about halfway between America and Asia. The fifteen hundred acre Midway Atoll is a territory of the United States and a designated wildlife refuge. The atoll has an airfield and small air force contingent, but aircraft maintenance support is very limited. After landing, our mechanics diagnosed the problem and announced the bad news: we needed to replace the engine. A transport aircraft from Hawaii would have to fly a new engine to our location and our mechanics would have to install it. This whole process would take about a week. In the meantime we were stranded on Midway Island.

During World War II, Midway was the scene of a huge naval battle between Japanese and American aircraft carrier fleets. Coral encrusted hulks of sunken warships litter the ocean floor around the island. Dan and I made friends with some of the Filipinos who worked the barges and small ships that operate from Midway's lagoon. The sailors claimed to know the location of some nearby shipwrecks in relatively shallow water. For a few dollars, they agreed to take us to a wreck where we could scuba dive. Dan and I grabbed scuba tanks from our gear and loaded everything onto a barge. We were glad to change our routine of lifting weights and drinking beer.

There is no tourist industry on Midway so scuba diving is not an everyday occurrence. The crystal clear water is a diver's dream and the coral reef is pristine. Sea creatures don't recognize divers as a threat and are unafraid.

We rode a rusty barge on the turquoise sea and chatted amiably with the Filipino sailors while we prepared our gear. The water was so warm we wore only swim suits and dive tanks. The barge positioned over a wreck and we jumped into the bright blue water. Once submerged, we saw the superstructure of a ship jutting up from the sea floor and finned towards it to explore. With Dan in the lead, we cruised through an underwater gallery of brightly colored fish and brilliantly hued forests of coral. Suddenly, Dan began to gesture frantically. I continued towards him while trying to figure out what he was trying to communicate. The mystery was solved when I came face-to-face with a giant moray eel. This eel was bright neon green and had probably been living in this cave, continuously growing since prehistoric times. I guessed the eel was a "she" because her mouth was always open and males rarely look so mean. She was as big around as I was at the waist, but she was much longer and stared at me with her mouth gaping open. The eel had no choice—she couldn't close her mouth because it was packed to overflowing with jagged fangs. I frantically windmilled my arms, backpedaling through the water with all my strength. The eel decided to let me live, and I escaped and made a wide detour around her lair. Protected by their giant "Mother of all Eels," her youngsters brazenly poked their snickering heads from the cave and laughed at me, calling me a dull-toothed, sissy air breather and hurling other embarrassing eel insults at me.

I shrugged off their scorn and swam towards Dan who was cringing wide-eyed against the rusty, barnacle encrusted side of the wreck. "What's wrong now?" I wondered. A large menacing shadow passed over me. I looked up to see the pale belly of a giant shark. It slowly passed over me like the Imperial Star Destroyer in the opening scene of *Star Wars*. Dan and I cowered out of sight in the rusting derelict, temporarily safe from the monster shark. From the look of its saucer-sized black eyes and triangular-shaped razor teeth, I guessed the shark was a rare species of *sharpimus toothimus gigantus*. We were trapped, reduced to nervously monitoring our dwindling air supply while we waited for the fearsome shark to leave. Finally, the sea monster left and we warily swam to the surface and scrambled onto the deck of our barge. We ordered an immediate to return to port and hoped the shark didn't sink our vessel on the way back. Once we were safe on dry land, we celebrated our survival by drinking twenty-five cent Lone Star beers and rehashing our adventure. Our entire dive had been spent eluding sea monsters; it was a good day.

Eventually our plane engine arrived and our mechanics restored our aircraft to flying condition. We took off from the airfield and headed towards our next destination. A few hours into our flight, we lost another engine. This time, we made an emergency landing on Wake Island. Wake Island is a remote coral atoll surrounded by beautiful aquamarine waters of the Pacific Ocean. Like Midway, it is a territory of the United States and has a small air force runway and installation. Once again, we would have to wait for an engine to be flown from Hawaii with the estimated time of arrival being a week. Our crew checked into rooms and settled in. The accommodations were relatively comfortable with units of two rooms connected by a shared bathroom. A short walk from our room took us to a placid lagoon, a perfect place to fish and relax. Palm trees swayed to gentle shore breezes while small herds of hermit crabs patrolled the beach.

The warm water was crystal clear, perfect for snorkeling. Two huge moray eels lived in some coral caves and a myriad of colorful, exotic sea creatures swam in the lagoon. I spied a strange animal and had a great idea for a practical joke. I scooped up the creature and took it to shore. I found a bucket, filled it with sea water and slid the sea cucumber into its temporary home. My practical joke victim would be my pilot, a lieutenant colonel who also happened to be our squadron executive officer, second in command. Given his rank and responsible position in the squadron, he was a serious person not inclined to frivolity. The copilot was also a humorless officer. They were perfect targets for a Dan Inch and Bill Sine practical joke. The two officers were in rooms that shared a bathroom. When we learned the copilot would be away from his room for an hour or so, the game was on.

I snuck into the vacant copilot's room next to our victim, carrying a bucket with the sea cucumber. I crept through the room, being careful not to make any noise. I removed the sea cucumber and slid it into our victim's toilet, being careful not to splash any water. The sea cucumber looked like a world record, giant turd. It was jet black, about fourteen inches long and thick around as a coke can. Neither of our pilots was a scuba diver and I guessed they would never suspect the giant turd was really a sea creature. The humongous turd impersonator lay motionless in the bottom of the toilet bowl, leaking a faint reddish dye.

When they discovered the state of the toilet the pilots began a heated argument, blaming each other for not flushing the disgusting mound of excrement. This was a serious breach of etiquette for an officer and gentleman. The hapless pilots finally tried flushing and the toilet backed up and flooded the bathroom. They had to summon a plumber who immediately recognized the turd for what it was, a sea cucumber, and said it must have somehow crawled up through the pipes. Neither pilot ever guessed they were the victims of a practical joke. The prank was flawless and I still have the picture of the cucumber in their toilet.

From Okinawa, we occasionally traveled to Korea for training. Every year between 1976 and 1993, usually in late March, American military forces in Korea and the South Korean military held a joint exercise called Team Spirit. This exercise was a huge event with thousands of players from all around the world. Rescue forces played a prominent role in the exercise and rescue units deployed to South Korea from all over the globe. Rescue squadrons brought their aircraft, flying HH-3 and HH-53 helicopters across the ocean from Okinawa and the Philippines. PJs and rescue crews from Alaska and other stateside units flew to Korea for the exercise. The rescue squadron and PJs stationed at Osan Air Base in South Korea hosted the other rescue units.

Exercise players stayed in a tent city erected on an expansive field. A tent city is more than just rows of tents set in a grid pattern; it is a community with shopping tents, latrine and shower tents, beer tents, barbershops, massage tents, and all the amenities normally found in a town. The individual canvas tents are eighteen feet wide and fifty-two feet long and can easily hold twelve cots each. There is a large space heater in the center of each tent and you have to be careful not to accidentally brush up against it or you will lose some skin. The heaters are absolutely necessary because Korea is ridiculously cold in March.

During the exercise PJs participated in two kinds of missions: helicopter rescues of stranded crewmembers and overland patrols to recover isolated pilots. Overland missions were multiday affairs, coping with strength-draining mountains and freezing temperatures. At night, PJ teams infiltrated with ninja-like stealth using night-vision goggles while security police, playing the role of enemy forces, tried to ambush them. PJ teams had to elude pursuing dogs and hunter-killer teams in order to overcome all obstacles and accomplish their missions.

Helicopter rescue missions involved flying one hundred foot, low level routes to avoid simulated enemy air defenses, often escorted by fighters, to pick up friendly pilots stranded behind enemy lines. Sometimes a helicopter would land to pick up a pilot, and an exercise evaluator would emerge from hiding and declare the helicopter had been "shot down." All the crewmembers would have to leave the helicopter and another crew would take their place and fly the aircraft back to base. The "shot down" crew became evaders and had to spend the night in the forest moving to a pickup site. Everyone knew this scenario was a possibility and flew with a rucksack packed with field gear including food, water, and a sleeping bag. If a crewman forgot his gear, his teammates would have to share theirs to keep the unprepared flyer alive in the cold.

Early one morning, our helicopter lifted off into the frigid morning air to recover a pilot who had been "shot down." My teammate was my good PJ friend John Willis. We had a mixed flight crew from our Okinawan and Philippine rescue units. In the early, early morning it was so cold that when I breathed I exhaled icy fog into the air. We cruised into the rural interior of the country, contouring mountains and dipping into remote valleys. Suddenly, our aircraft shuddered in the sky—something was wrong. An ominous thumping sound accompanied the shimmy. The pilots calmly dealt with the situation, which appeared to involve our rotors. They suspected a blown rotor pocket. HH-3 helicopter rotors are compartmented and pressurized with nitrogen. Loss of pressure indicates a problem with the integrity of the rotor blade and activates an indicator. The pilot banked the chopper and we cleared the aircraft for an emergency landing in a dirt field. Once on the ground, the pilots shut down the aircraft and the screaming turbine engines slowed to silence. We exited the chopper and confirmed that a rotor pocket was blown, the metal peeled back. This helicopter would not fly again until we replaced the entire rotor blade. The pilots radioed our position back to base and explained the situation. We were stranded until a replacement rotor blade could be flown to our location.

Our immense helicopter sat motionless and out of place in a frozen field in a remote Korean valley. Shy farmers and their families cautiously began to show themselves, like wary Munchkins after Dorothy's house crushed the Wicked Witch of the East. Their curiosity finally overcame their reluctance and the entire village slowly gathered around our helicopter. The crowd consisted of smiling old men dressed in colorful silks and women with babies bundled on their backs. Everyone was friendly and enjoying this unusual event. An old man wearing a green silk jacket approached the helicopter, and our pilot met him just outside the crew door. None of the Koreans spoke English, so we used gestures to communicate. The village headman offered food and hospitality, and our pilot accepted. The old man shouted some commands and several people scurried off to do his bidding. Soon, members of the crowd became bolder, peeking into the aircraft, some trying to gain entrance. We diplomatically kept the crowd from overrunning our helicopter.

Villagers with containers of food soon arrived and passed out bowls of kimchi, a staple Korean food made from pickled cabbage. It's a spicy hot dish and very heavy on the garlic, not what most Americans would choose to eat for breakfast. However, we accepted their hospitality as we did not want to offend them. We dug into the kimchi using wooden chopsticks they provided. Next they handed out bowls and filled them from a ceramic teapot. The teapot faked me out, faked everyone out. I was expecting a hot beverage and was surprised when a cold white fluid filled my bowl. It looked like milk with pieces of rice floating in it. The pilot gingerly tasted his drink and his eyes grew wide. "Everyone stop!" he ordered. "This drink is alcoholic—we can't drink it!" Air Force flyers are prohibited from drinking alcohol twelve hours before flying and absolutely cannot drink during actual flying operations. The whitish drink was makolli, the oldest alcoholic beverage in Korea, its origin dating back two thousand years. It is a nutritious drink made from fermented rice and is as potent as very strong beer. Someone pointed out—maybe it was me—that we would certainly offend our hosts if we refused the drinks; our bowls were already filled. Our Korean fan club was gathered round gazing at us expectantly, waiting for our reaction to their generous hospitality. I whispered a suggestion to our pilot, and he motioned the crew into the aircraft for a secret pow-wow.

"I have an idea." he said. "The crew will do an aircraft walk around. We'll point at parts of the aircraft and act official. Meanwhile, the PJs will stay out of sight inside the helicopter and drink all the makolli. After all, they're not actually flying the aircraft." John and I looked at each other and grinned. "Yes sir!" We replied in unison. While the rest of the crew acted out their parts of the deception, John and I dutifully did our part for God and country and gulped down two large teapots of makolli. We drank the alcoholic equivalent of a half gallon of extra strong beer apiece. We drank it in mere moments, and we drank it on empty stomachs. We thought of asking for a re-fill but decided that might be pushing it. The crew returned to the helicopter, and John and I returned the empty teapots to our hosts. We were all smiles as we gestured our thanks and appreciation for their hospitality. The Korean villagers were also pleased and became even more friendly and outgoing. Suddenly, John and I were laughing and interacting with the crowd. We were jolly ambassadors of good will, holding babies and taking photos. That makolli is good stuff. So that's what Korean farmers do in these remote valleys. They walk around in silk pajamas and drink booze for breakfast . . . not bad.

Later that afternoon a helicopter arrived with our new rotor blade and landed nearby. Our mechanics immediately began to work on replacing the rotor and accomplished the blade swap in record time. We had spent the entire day in the valley with our Korean friends, but it was finally time to take our leave. We boarded our helicopter and fired up the engines. The Koreans scattered as our helicopter powered up and our rotors spun faster and faster. Soon our blades formed a disk shaped blur, and we lifted off in a cloud of dust.

We were trying to fly back to base, but it was getting dark and we were lost. Then it started snowing, softly at first, then harder and harder. It was difficult to see, flying through thick snowflakes in the dim light. We were also running out of fuel. Our situation was getting serious. Our pilot decided to climb to altitude to acquire the TACAN (tactical air navigation). TACAN is a radio signal that provides direction and distance to an airfield. The plan worked and we got a heading to our airfield. As we descended and flew towards the base I looked out the left window, scanning for obstacles and other aircraft. The weather worsened; we were flying in a blizzard. The pilot began to make a left turn and I screamed, "Stop left! Break right!" The pilot yanked the aircraft to the right and saved our lives. Because of poor visibility in the snow storm we had almost flown into the side of a rocky bluff. The whole crew was shaken. It was too dangerous to continue flying. The pilot told us to quickly scan for a suitable landing site.

Suddenly the low level fuel light came on. This meant we were flying on fumes and had only minutes to land. The pilot banked the helicopter hard left and made an approach to a snow covered road. For the second time that day we landed in a remote Korean valley. We were out of fuel and unsure of our exact location, but at least we were safe on the ground. Before we landed, the pilot had made radio contact with the base. Base operations knew we were safe, but not exactly where we were. Snow fell thick around us in the dark, deadening sound and piling up on our helicopter. As night deepened the temperature began to drop—we would have to spend the night in our aircraft. I could see our pilot was feeling very down. I plugged a hot cup into the bulkhead of our helicopter and made some hot chocolate. After the pilot drank it he was a new man, decisive and back in command.

Korean officials began to arrive at our aircraft. We were playing war games and our chopper was equipped with M60 machine guns mounted in the left and right windows. The local police decided to post an armed guard overnight. This was preferable to us rotating guard duty as none of us spoke Korean. It would have been poor form for an American to shoot a curious villager because we misread a situation. We arranged canvas pole litters on stanchions mounted inside the helicopter. Litters would substitute as beds, and we laid out our insulating pads and sleeping bags. I convinced the pilot to send PJ John Willis on a mission. John was a very resourceful PJ. His mission was to go to the nearest village, find out where we were, make his way to Osan Air Base, and return with the cavalry the next morning. John walked down the road and faded into the swirling snowflakes.

We closed the door and prepared to spend the night in the drafty, unheated helicopter. The temperature would drop into the low teens during the night. The uninsulated aluminum helicopter was like a giant freezer, but we were prepared. We used aircraft battery power and the hot cup to prepare steaming soups and drinks. We snuggled into fluffy down sleeping bags, warm down to minus twenty degrees. Our closed-cell foam pads insulated us from the ice-cold surface of the litters. We slept warm and toasty and exhaled cloudy plumes of water vapor that condensed and coated the inside of the helicopter with frost.

I woke up to the sound of tentative knocking on the helicopter door. I looked at the luminous dials on my watch. It was five o'clock in the morning. I reluctantly abandoned the warm comfort of my sleeping bag and opened the sliding aluminum hatch in the side of the aircraft cabin. A Korean guard stood shivering outside. He only wore a light jacket. Eyes watering from the cold, he said in hesitant English, "Please. Can I come in? I am very cold." I invited him in, found him a seat and tossed him a blanket. I set about waking the crew and soon we had battery power, and I fired up the hot cup. Color returned to our guard's pale face and he began smiling. Only lightly dressed, he had guarded our chopper all night in the freezing cold.

Dawn broke and the sky was crystal clear. Our helicopter sat in the middle of a silent white wilderness. At least that's what I thought until the school children arrived. A village was nearby and kids of all ages walked past us on their way to school. Our huge green, snow covered helicopter in the middle of the road was an unexpected sight. The curious children crowded round with smiles on their faces. We dug into our rations and started handing out candy and dehydrated strawberries. Eventually the novelty of our presence wore off, our goodies ran out, and the kids trundled off to school. A short time later John Willis returned with the posse: a maintenance crew and barrels of fuel. As it turned out, we were only ten miles away from Osan Air Base. We hand-pumped fuel into our helicopter and flew back to base. That night at the beer tent, we had lots of interesting stories to tell.

I lived in Okinawa for eighteen adventure-filled months. I enjoyed experiencing the culture shock. The Orient was a fascinating place to explore. I was due to receive an assignment to another base soon, but I liked the Far East and did not want to return to a rescue base in the United States. I resolved to stay in the Pacific Theater for a few more years and put in a request to be stationed in the Philippines or Korea. When I received my orders, they read 31st ARRS, Clark Air Base. For my next assignment, I was going to the Philippines!

CHAPTER 5

_____

PHILIPPINES

_____

If everyone is thinking alike, someone isn't thinking.
—*George S. Patton Jr.*

IN 1982 I LEFT OKINAWA AND TRAVELED TO MY NEXT ASSIGNMENT, the 31st Air Rescue Squadron at Clark Air Base, Republic of the Philippines. Americans who live in the Philippines affectionately refer to the country as "The PI." The Philippines is a group of more than seven thousand islands in the western Pacific Ocean, north of Indonesia and across the South China Sea from Vietnam and southern China. The United States has a long history of involvement with the Philippines starting in 1898 with the Spanish-American War. The Filipino people are friendly to Americans because we liberated their country from the Japanese during World War II. The Filipinos suffered greatly under Japanese imperial occupation until Gen. Douglas McArthur returned as promised and defeated the invaders. The Americans lost more than sixty thousand men, but the Philippines lost a million people.

Filipinos admire Americans and their affluent life-style because most of them are very poor. Filipinos treat Americans like celebrities and view America as an almost mythical land of plenty. It is not unusual for a Filipino family to prominently display American consumer products, such as canned goods, in their home as status symbols. The Philippine people have obvious Chinese and Malaysian ethnic traits, but they also have strong historical ties to Spain and Latin America and until recently Spanish was their official language. The Philippines has evolved a unique culture that blends Asian, American, and European influences.

In the 1980s the area around Clark Air base in Angeles City is a hub of commerce. The streets teem with industrious Filipinos hustling to make a living. Rusty cars and trucks clog narrow streets and honk their horns with abandon. Jeepneys ferry passengers around town for only a few pesos and serve as public transportation. The jeepney is the official vehicle of the Philippines. Jeepneys are long, open-sided jeeps and have bench seats for passengers. The best jeepneys are very ornate, their hoods festooned with a multitude of fancy chrome horses and ornaments, multihued streamers, and hand-operated rubber-bulb horns. Safety standards are third-world-relaxed in the PI, and jeepney drivers casually smoke cigarettes while they sit with plastic containers of gasoline nestled between their feet. The clear plastic jugs have a tube that connects to the engine and serves as the jeepney's improvised gas tank, making it easier for the driver to monitor and conserve fuel. Jeepneys are not the only transportation available. Small, sidecar-equipped motorcycles called tricycles, also serve as cheap taxis, crowding the streets near popular establishments. The alleys are lined with side-by-side food stalls, and street vendors occupy every corner. Small street-side hibachi grills serve barbecued chicken and spicy chunks of marinated pork grilled on wooden skewers.

The entrances to the air force base act as bustling market places. Street urchins gather near the gates and beg coins from people entering or leaving the base. Newly arrived Americans are conspicuous *marks*. Their inexperience is writ clearly on their naïve faces. They invariably feel sorry for the scruffy looking kids and pitch them some coins. In seconds, swarms of unruly children surround the flustered do-gooder, jostling and pleading for their share of pesos. Sadly but necessarily, newcomers quickly learn to harden their hearts and not give money to beggars.

One evening a few of us PJs took a new arrival named Dan downtown to introduce him to the culture. Immediately after leaving the gate we encountered a bunch of raggedly dressed street kids. They blinked sad brown eyes and held out their hands begging for money, but we ignored them. Dan flashed us an accusing look, as if we were heartless bastards. He fished some coins out of his pocket, and tossed them to the children. A frantic mob of kids immediately overwhelmed Dan, hopping up and down, clamoring for money. Dan finally broke free from the grasping children, and we set off down the street. Suddenly, Dan stopped dead in his tracks, belatedly realizing his expensive scuba diving watch was missing. While we laughed and said, "I told you so!" Dan rubbed his naked wrist and stomped around the street in disbelief, bemoaning the loss of his watch. Then an innocent looking little boy timidly approached Dan. Obviously feeling sorry for the kind-hearted American, the cute little ragamuffin timidly spoke, "Mister, I know who stole your watch. Give me a hundred pesos and I'll get it back for you." Dan breathed a sigh of relief, thanked the little angel profusely, and gave him a hundred pesos worth eight American dollars. The little boy quickly scuttled into the crowd never to be seen again. We laughed so hard we were choking. Dan had just set a new *chump* record, losing an expensive watch *and* a hundred pesos all within minutes of leaving the base. We dragged him into the nearest bar to console him with cold San Miguel beer.

The PI has a special place in my heart because in 1984 my son was born there. I was taking my pregnant wife to the hospital because she was complaining of bad stomach cramps and had awakened with blood on her panties. Medical genius that I am, I eventually noticed that her stomach pains were regularly coming and going; she was having contractions. When the nurse examined her at the hospital she said, "You're going to have a baby today." According to my Lamaze class, I was supposed to have packed a lunch and readied for the momentous occasion. I had brought nothing; I was totally unprepared.

My wife's labor dragged on all day and into the evening, and I was starving. My friend and fellow PJ Pat Sinon delivered a large pizza and saved the day. By now my wife's contractions were only a minute apart. The nurses were amazed to see me consume a sixteen-inch pizza between her contractions, one minute per slice. Finally, they rolled Leslie into the delivery room and I followed with my bulging pizza belly. My son refused to come out. The doctor declared that after one more unsuccessful attempt he would bring out the forceps. The forceps looked like giant plastic tweezers—scary. Following a nurse's instructions, I pushed the top of my wife's stomach towards her feet as she strained, and suddenly William Daniel

Sine was born. I stood transfixed, frozen in horror as they cleaned my crying son with a damp cloth. I was dumbstruck because he had a prominent, pointy, cone-shaped head. The cone was so pronounced that when they put a stocking cap on his head they didn't even need to roll up the bottom of the hat. I warily approached the doctor and asked about my son's pointy head. He laughed and said Billy's head would eventually regain a normal round shape. My wife was a tiny thing, only five feet tall and one hundred pounds. Billy's journey through his mother's tight birth canal had temporarily squished his soft head.

While I enjoyed the cultural and domestic adventures of living in the Philippines with my family, now increased with the addition of Billy, I was having even more fun at work. The PI was a hot spot for rescue missions and I was always prepared to spring into action. It was a beautiful day when I went to work in August of 1985; the weather was bright sunshine, warm breezes, and clear blue skies: just another day in paradise. I was on rescue alert along with the rest of my helicopter crew: pilot, copilot, flight engineer, and another PJ. If anyone needed rescuing, we could launch and be airborne within thirty minutes. I drove a pickup truck stacked high with rescue gear to the flight line where my helicopter was parked. In the heat and humidity my flight suit clung to my sweaty skin as I wrestled my medical kits, scuba gear and rescue equipment onto the Jolly.

The rest of the crew soon joined me and we quickly prepared the helicopter for flight. We would remain on airborne alert as we performed our routine training flight. The pilot ran through the flight checklist, flipping cockpit switches and checking gauges until the twin turbine engines whined and the rotor blades formed a blurred disc overhead. Flight checks completed and the rotors up to speed, our helicopter lifted smoothly into the air and soon we were cruising above a green and brown checkerboard of rice paddies and plowed earth.

An hour into the flight our squadron duty officer radioed that we had a rescue mission. An A-4 Skyhawk pilot was on a training sortie when his jet experienced mechanical failure. After the jet's engine flamed out he was forced to eject from his aircraft over remote mountains carpeted with dense jungle. The pilot's wingman watched the bailout and tracked pilot's descent until his parachute snagged on the top of a tree in the middle of a rain forest. The wingman noted the coordinates and passed them back to the base command post. Our mission was to find and rescue the stranded pilot. We immediately changed course and flew towards his last reported position.

Captain Francis Tan of the Singapore Air Force hung from the top branches of a towering tree that leaned out over a steep mountain precipice. His bailout parachute had barely snagged on branches, and he dangled helplessly a hundred feet above the ground. Captain Tan was almost frantic, because his parachute was slowly but surely slipping off the tree. When he used his handheld survival radio to talk to our pilot I could hear desperation and fear in his voice.

As our helicopter neared his location Captain Tan was in pain, suffering from the agonizing effects of harness induced pathology (HIP). He hung in an upright, seated position with gravity exerting an inexorable downward force and the leg straps of his parachute harness digging painfully into his groin, crushing nerves and collapsing veins. Blood pooled in his legs and blood flow back to the heart was restricted. Toxins accumulated in his blood and there was a risk of sudden cardiac arrest and even upper airway obstruction. Some victims have lost consciousness in fewer than ten minutes. After thirty minutes anybody would experience serious difficulties. Fatigue, dehydration, and other injuries will hasten and amplify the effects of HIP. Decreased circulation can also cause kidney failure. The bottom line: HIP damages many different organ systems and can kill relatively quickly. Captain Tan had already been hanging in his parachute harness for two hours, and his legs were already paralyzed and wracked with pain; he was in serious trouble.

Yelling into his radio, the desperate pilot pleaded with us to hurry. He was terrified, because he believed that it was only a matter of minutes before his parachute would tear free and spill him onto the rocky slope a hundred feet below. As our Jolly sped towards Captain Tan, I mentally explored various ways to save him. Once on scene it would be my job to perform the actual rescue and provide medical treatment during the flight to the hospital. I had a large inventory of state-of-the-art rescue equipment, but the most versatile and useful device at my disposal was the rescue hoist.

The rescue hoist has two hundred feet of quarter-inch thick steel cable, wound on a reel, and mounted on the right side of the aircraft fuselage. The flight engineer operates the hoist from inside the helicopter. He pushes a lever forward and backwards to lower and raise the cable. I planned to ride the hoist to the ground, touching down as close to my patient's tree as possible. I would use tree gaffs, ankle-mounted lumberjack spikes, to climb the 150 foot tree. I needed to climb to a position above the pilot, secure one end of a rope to the tree trunk and the other end to Captain Tan. Once he was tied to the rope, I could disconnect him from his parachute. He would then be suspended from the tree by my rope, not his parachute. I could then ease him to the ground, controlling his descent with a special mechanical lowering device.

During the flight to Captain Tan's location I formed a vivid mental picture of the incident site. When we reached our destination I would be able to see the actual situation and fine-tune my plan. When we did arrive on scene I spotted the downed pilot hanging suspended in space. I was stunned! His body dangled high over a mountain slope, surrounded on all sides by miles of impenetrable jungle. The mental picture I had formed was overwhelmed by the actual reality. The Skyhawk pilot seemed hopelessly out of reach. For a moment, I was at a complete loss. None of the plans I had brainstormed during our flight were feasible. I could not hoist to the ground near him because the mountain slope was too steep. To make matters worse, the Jolly pilot informed me that Tan was twenty-five hundred feet up the side of the mountain and with our helicopter's heavy load of fuel and equipment we didn't have enough power to hover at that altitude. The nearest place to land was in a dry riverbed five miles from the mountain. There was no way I could carry a hundred pounds of gear and travel five miles up a mountain slogging through dense tropical rain forest, especially with only a couple of hours of daylight remaining. We flew over the mountains and surrounding jungle fruitlessly searching for a closer landing site. We flew in circles high above where Captain Tan hung like a puppet. His hopelessness of his predicament was breathtaking, and my mind raced to come up with a solution. We were his only hope for survival, and he continued to plead with us to hurry. It was late afternoon. The jungle night loomed ahead, and the dark of night would make rescue impossible. If we could not save Captain Tan before nightfall he would probably die.

Suddenly, we spied a navy helicopter off in the distance. We radioed the other aircraft and discovered it was on a routine training mission from the nearby naval base at Subic Bay. Our pilot explained our dilemma, and the other crew agreed to help. This naval version of the H-3 helicopter had a light fuel load leaving it with more power available than our aircraft. The pilot of the navy helicopter informed us he could easily hover at twenty-five hundred feet and also had a hoist onboard. To this day, I'm amazed that the navy aircraft miraculously appeared out of the blue with the exact capabilities we needed to rescue Captain Tan. This pilot from Singapore had some attentive guardian angels looking out for him. Both our helicopters landed in the dry riverbed and I transferred to the navy chopper with my rescue gear.

Although both helicopters were the same basic model, the interior of the navy aircraft was configured differently than our air force version. My helmet intercom was incompatible with the navy system and a crewman had to lend me his helmet so I could talk to the pilot. I put on the navy helmet and plugged its cord into a communications box. Once I was up intercom the pilot asked me what I wanted to do. I laid out my plan, which I worried sounded a bit crazy, but the pilot calmly agreed to give it a try. The pilot would establish 150 foot hover over the downed pilot. I reasoned that we needed to hover as high as possible above him to minimize the effects of the helicopter's rotor wash. I worried that in a low hover the intense down draft from our helicopter's spinning rotors would blow the parachute off the treetop. I wanted the hoist operator to lower me on a forest penetrator. A forest penetrator is like a chair that attaches to the end of the cable. The penetrator has three paddle-shaped seats, which fold down and lock into place, and seat belts to keep the rescuer and victim from falling off. I planned to secure myself onto one paddle and fold down a second seat to accommodate Captain Tan. Once the entire length of the cable was played out and I hung suspended 150 feet below the helicopter, I would attempt to pendulum over to Tan and grab him. Then, in midair I would maneuver him onto the penetrator paddle and attach his seat belt. With the pilot securely seated I'd disconnect him from his parachute, we would swing free of the tree, and the hoist operator could raise us back into the helicopter.

Now I had a plan; all I had to do was execute. I strapped myself onto the penetrator, and gave a thumbs up signaling I was ready to be lowered. The hoist operator let out cable, and I slowly descended towards Captain Tan. Moments later I hung 150 feet below the chopper from the thin steel hoist cable, but was still 100 feet above him and the steep mountain slope.

The helicopter pilot slowly maneuvered his chopper until I hung level with my patient. Directly across from me, the pilot dangled just out of my reach. Wide eyed and anxious, he swung in his parachute harness and clutched at anything within reach, even insubstantial leaves and twigs. Following my hand signals the hoist operator began to push the cable to swing me over to the captain. I swung back and forth, slowly at first, but then gradually gaining momentum in wider and wider arcs. Just when it appeared I would be able to reach my target, branches in the tree canopy above blocked the cable, stopping me short and ruining my attempt to grab him. I could read disappointment and fear on Tan's face and gestured to reassure him I was not giving up. Time after time I swung closer and closer to him only to be foiled at the last second. Suddenly, my cable slid through a small gap in the branches, and I swung into the tangle of parachute suspension lines above him. I grabbed hold; loose parachute cord draped my body. I hugged the bundle of parachute lines and considered my next move. Tree-top foliage screened me from view, making me invisible to the men in the helicopter hovering above. The crew could only see the hoist cable arching down from their helicopter and then angling up and vanishing under the green tree tops. The navy H-3 pilot expertly used ground reference points to establish the helicopter in a steady hover to give me a stable platform to work from.

I laboriously lowered myself hand-under-hand down the parachute lines until I reached Captain Tan and dragged him onto a penetrator paddle so he was seated across from me. I worried about the loose parachute lines wrapped around my body—bad news if the helicopter moved and the cords tightened around me. But my first priority was to fasten his seatbelt and disconnect his harness from his parachute canopy. At that point, he would be attached to the rescue cable and not the tree. I told him to hold on tight and began to pass the seatbelt behind his back. Suddenly, part of the parachute tore loose from the tree. Everything was a confused blur as we fell, and then a second later a violent jerk stretched my spine as we came to the end of the cable. We had only fallen a few feet, but now I hung head-down, suspended by parachute cord wrapped around my left leg. Hanging like this, upside down in midair, I felt like a snared rabbit.

Captain Tan's arms encircled me in a death grip. I talked to him, trying to calm him down. He would have been even more frightened, had he known the full extent of our danger. If the canopy ripped completely free from the tree, the helicopter's rotor wash would inflate the parachute and suck us up into its whirling rotor blades where we would be chopped to pieces. If mechanical problems developed on the chopper the pilot could be forced to abandon his hover and move away. That would tear my leg off, since my thigh was literally tied to the tree by multiple strands of 550-pound-test parachute shroud lines. The H-3 pilot could also decide that being tethered to a tree by a steel cable posed an immediate danger to the helicopter and crew and order the hoist operator to use the hoist's guillotine system to sever the cable. If that happened my patient and I would be stranded, hanging upside down a hundred feet in the air with absolutely no hope of rescue. We would be dead men.

I urged Captain Tan to hold on as tightly as he could. I had been in the process of connecting his seat belt when we fell. The belt's fastener was snagged by parachute cord and pulled taut out of my reach. In order to be winched into the helicopter, I needed to free us by cutting through the seat belt and the parachute suspension lines trapping my leg. Fortunately, I kept a folding knife in a leg-pocket of my flight suit. Rivulets of sweat stung my eyes as I struggled to free my knife while hanging upside down. I finally removed the knife from my pocket, but it slipped from my sweaty hand and fell. Luckily the knife was tied to me with a long lanyard and I was able to retrieve it. Thank God! Both of our lives depended on that knife.

I slowly began to saw through the tough nylon webbing of the seatbelt. I realized that without the belt I would not be able to secure my patient to the penetrator. He would just have to hang on tight. I finally slashed through the last few threads and severed the seatbelt. Next I needed to cut through the parachute lines that snared my leg. Each nylon cord could suspend 550 pounds. My arm ached from the effort, and it seemed I would never be able to cut through all the cords. Sweat poured into my eyes and blurred my vision. The humidity and ninety degree tropical heat were taking their toll on my strength. Each time I sawed through a cord I had to do an upside down sit up. My stomach muscles were on fire. Finally, only a few lines remained.

I warned Captain Tan that in moments I would cut the last cords. I disconnected his harness from his parachute canopy. "Hold on tight!" I yelled. He tightened his grip as I slashed the last lines that entrapped me. I felt the sickening sensation of falling in the pit of my stomach and experienced a moment of vertigo. There was a brutal jolt as our fall reached the end of the steel cable, and then a dizzying moment when we were swinging out over empty space. We swung back and forth above the floor of the valley, suspended in emptiness. Our pendulum motion gradually subsided, and the hoist operator winched us up to the helicopter. As we neared the door of the chopper, I looked back to where we had hung inverted only moments before. Completely oblivious and indifferent to the intense drama of the past few minutes, the tree was decorated with colored streamers of nylon parachute fluttering from its branches.

The hoist operator dragged us into the aircraft and we flew to the riverbed a few miles away. I transferred my now secure patient onto our air force helicopter, which was better configured for medical evacuations. Once onboard, I secured him into a litter suspended from the aircraft ceiling by canvas straps and metal brackets and administered a bag of IV fluids. I performed a thorough medical assessment and concluded his leg paralysis was due to poor blood circulation and pinched nerves, a temporary condition caused by hours of hanging in his parachute harness. I cared for my patient during the flight back to base, keeping him as comfortable as possible and monitoring his vital signs. Our pilot radioed ahead informing the emergency room medics about the status of our patient. When we arrived at the helicopter landing pad near the hospital, medical staff met us with a stretcher. I followed them into the hospital and briefed the doctors on the pilot's injuries and the treatment I had performed.

A couple of days later I visited Captain Tan in the clinic. He was in excellent spirits and had regained the use of his legs. He eventually made a full recovery. And, when he checked out of the hospital, his flying squadron hosted a huge pig roast for our rescue unit. We swapped stories, shared food, drink, and camaraderie, and toasted the PJ motto, "That Others May Live."

The pilot and crew of the navy helicopter showed great courage and superb airmanship. While I worked to free Captain Tan and struggled to overcome various complications, the H-3 pilot maintained a stable hover despite having no radio communications or visual contact with me. From my adrenaline altered perspective the entire rescue took a few minutes, but

I found out later that the navy pilot hovered rock-steady for over twenty minutes. The navy hoist operator was also supremely skilled and performed spectacularly. My own air force crew also did a fantastic job. Every aspect of this mission showcased our crew's adaptability and skill. Our pilot devised the brilliant scheme to use the navy helicopter to complete the mission, and his clever thinking ultimately led to Captain Tan's rescue.

PAMPANGA PROVINCE, PHILIPPINES, 1985

Rescue missions were not my only source of adventures in the Philippines. The mountains were covered with mysterious jungle that begged to be explored. The jungle reminded me of Tarzan movies I watched as a kid growing up in Ohio. I was mesmerized by the giant trees draped with thick vines and the colorful birds and exotic creatures. As a PJ stationed in the Philippines I had plenty of opportunities to explore the rain forest. I twice attended the jungle environmental survival school at Naval Air Station Cubi Point at Subic Bay. This school was run by the navy, but the chief instructors were Negrito natives.

Negritos may be the original inhabitants of the Philippines. They arrived in the islands as long as thirty thousand years ago. The name Negrito evolved from a Spanish word meaning "small and black." They have dark complexions and are small enough to qualify as pygmies. Negritos are masters of the rain forest. They can trap or snare any jungle creature. They catch chickens, lizards, parrots, wild pigs, bats, and river shrimp. They even know how to trap the nocturnal, big-eyed civet cats that live and feed in the tops of the towering trees.

Negritos know the uses of every plant. They know which ones are nutritious and which are medicinal. They know which vines to cut to get fresh water. They can use bamboo to make a pressure cooker for rice, or to make a fire from scratch. They can build a shelter in minutes and show you how to do it, but it will still take you hours to build one. They make machetes called bolo knives from the leaf springs of junkyard cars. They make the bolo handles from water buffalo horn, scrapings of which will coagulate blood and stop cuts from bleeding. They make bows and arrows and are expert marksmen. They are jungle wizards.

Once when I was walking with a Negrito he pointed out a hole in a bamboo stalk. He grabbed a banana leaf and quickly slapped the leaf over the hole. He used his bolo knife to cut loose the bamboo segment. He tied the leaf in place, and we took the piece of bamboo back to camp. I could hear something moving inside the hollow segment. He tossed the bamboo on the edge of the campfire and waited until the heat killed whatever was inside. With a flourish he removed the leaf and proudly emptied eight tiny bats onto the ground. We placed the little bats on hot coals near the edge of our campfire. The fire burned off their fur and cooked them. My PJ buddy Dan Inch and I brushed off the scorched fur and ate the bats with soy sauce and rice. I didn't like the taste, but I ate them anyway. Bat didn't agree with me, and I woke up in the middle of the night retching uncontrollably.

Negritos are expert trackers. They can follow the faintest footprints on the jungle floor. If they are tracking you, walking in streams won't fool them. You can't hide from them, because they can also smell you like a bloodhound. They will know that you walked through their jungle as easily as we would know if someone came into our home and moved a piece of our living room furniture across the room. They can also build man traps to kill you. The Negrito version of the "Malayan Gate" sends a bamboo beam mounted with razor sharp spikes whipping into an enemy's chest.

In World War II, Japanese soldiers killed the aborigines on sight. But the Negritos got their revenge and terrorized any Japanese soldier who entered their rain forest. One of their tactics was to setup a fake camp in the path of a Japanese patrol. When the soldiers discovered the abandoned village, it seemed as if the Negritos had been surprised in the middle of a meal and fled. The Negritos left large bowls of delicious smelling boiled potatoes behind. The starving Japanese soldiers would glut themselves on the mouth-watering food. Then they would die. The food was really poisonous tubers that only looked and tasted like potatoes.

When you treat Negritos with respect they are very friendly and love to laugh. White men amuse them with their clumsiness in the jungle. If you want to explore the rain forest, hire a Negrito as your guide; they are the ultimate forest experts. We were friends with a Filipino we called Boy who worked at our squadron. Boy knew Negritos and would set up weekend camping trips in the jungle. Sometimes we would look for World War II artifacts in hidden caves. Our air force flight surgeon sometimes came along. He would collect rare orchids from tree tops. When he spotted an orchid growing on a lofty branch, a Negrito boy would scramble up the tree, saw off the limb, and lower the flower to the ground with a long cord. Everyone was fascinated with the jungle for different reasons. I was interested in jungle survival. I wanted to know which plants were good to eat and how to hunt and snare animals. I bought a pellet rifle thinking that on my next jungle trip I would bag some game and eat like a king.

A few of us PJs hired Boy to arrange a weekend camping trip. We planned to hike half a day into the jungle-covered mountains and set up camp. Boy also arranged for a Negrito guide. We drove to a remote village, parked our cars, and traveled on foot into the forest. Like typical white men we had large backpacks stuffed with food and supplies. At a rendezvous point, Boy introduced us to a Negrito named Nara. Nara was barefoot and wore only a loin cloth. He had a bolo knife and a bow with arrows. That was all he needed. At night he built a sleeping platform from bamboo and used his loin cloth as a blanket. He couldn't speak English, so Boy translated. We hiked for a long time, crossing rivers and fighting our way through thick vegetation and up slippery, vine choked ravines. Our eventual camp site was a long way from civilization. In every direction as far as the eye could see there was only rain forest.

We set up camp near a stream and I grabbed my pellet rifle and went off into the jungle to shoot some tasty forest creatures. I was excited about my hunt and hoped to shoot some delicious chickens. Wild jungle chickens look different than their American relatives. They are black with bright red and yellow markings on their wings, but they taste just like the domestic chickens we are used to eating. Only a few hours of daylight remained, so I immediately got started. I hunted and hunted and never saw a single animal. I never saw a chicken or snake, not even an insect. When I walked into the jungle, the forest became quiet and lifeless. It started to get dark, so I headed back to camp empty handed and extremely disappointed.

When I arrived at camp, Boy asked me about my hunting safari. I explained that I hadn't seen any game. There is just nothing out there. Boy smiled and asked if I would let Nara borrow my rifle. I reluctantly said, "Sure!" It was approaching twilight and I was convinced there were no animals around. I'd combed the forest for more than two hours and never saw a thing. I handed the gun to Nara. Without moving so much as a step, he raised the barrel and pulled the trigger. "Phhht" went the pellet gun, and a dead bird fell at our feet. I couldn't believe it! While I stood with my mouth gaping open in astonishment, Nara trotted into the forest with my rifle. About thirty minutes later he returned, smiling innocently. He had two jungle chickens, a couple of brightly plumed parrots, and a bat. "You've got to be kidding me!" I thought. I swallowed my pride and asked Boy if Nara would give me a hunting lesson the next day. Boy translated, and Nara agreed.

That evening my friends and I sat around the campfire, drinking cheap ESQ rum and toasting hotdogs over a campfire. I listened mesmerized to the complex jungle music. Insects, birds, and other unknown denizens of the forest formed a mysterious and compelling orchestra. The many different sounds blended and complemented each other so perfectly they seemed almost choreographed. I snapped out of my reverie when Nara came over and asked to borrow my rifle again. This time he taped a flashlight to the barrel and walked over to an enormous jungle tree. The tree was about a hundred and twenty feet tall, and there were no branches until fifty feet up the trunk. Nara positioned his ankles about two feet apart and tied them together with a piece of rope. He slung the rifle over his shoulder and, somehow, used the rope tied between his ankles to quickly shinny up the smooth trunk. In seconds he disappeared into the lofty treetop, invisible in the night.

"I think I'll pass on the whole night tree climbing and hunting thing." I explained and headed back to the campfire. When Nara returned later that night, he had lots of game. Some of the animals were probably unknown species. Nara had killed some bizarre looking creatures, including a bird with a face that looked like a frog. Tomorrow, I resolved to learn to hunt like Nara!

The next day I followed Boy and Nara into the jungle for my hunting lesson. They took me to a tree that had berry bushes cascading down one side of the trunk. Nara said, "This is where we hunt. Birds and animals like to eat these berries." He built a blind within sight of the berries. It took him about five minutes to build the blind out of bamboo, leafy tree limbs and vines. Later, when I built a blind by myself, it took me two hours. Afterwards, I felt like one of the three little pigs, the one who built the stupid straw house that fell down.

Boy spoke, "Nara asks if you know what to do if a cobra comes into the blind with you?" "Chase it away with loud screaming?" I guessed. Boy translated and they laughed. "One thing you can do is squirt insect repellant in the snake's eyes." Boy told me. "That's why I always carry this bottle." he explained. There are a lot of deadly snakes in the jungle. Besides cobras, there are bamboo vipers. These snakes are bright green and are camouflaged so well they are almost invisible in the foliage and bamboo. Probably only Negritos can see them.

I gave up trying to duplicate Nara's hunting skills. He could make animal calls from leaves. He put a leaf in his mouth and mimicked the sound of a chicken. A short time later, chickens walked over to him and he killed them. I could never attain that level of expertise. Animal impersonation skills must be genetic, because I could never make the proper sounds. When I tried an animal call it seemed that some creatures made sounds in reply. Nara said it was just the animals laughing at me. On my last day in the jungle I made a blind near some berries. It only took me an hour. I sat motionless for more hours waiting for game, only moving occasionally to brandish my bottle of insect repellant at an imaginary cobra. Minutes before it was time to break camp and head back to civilization, I finally bagged a sparrow. "Yes! I am the great white hunter!"

ANGELES CITY, PHILIPPINES, 1986

Excitement was not limited to rescue missions and jungle treks; I also had urban adventures. When I first arrived at Clark Air Base, I attended a newcomers briefing on the customs and culture of the Philippines. The spokesperson taught us some of the do's-and-don'ts of life in the Philippines. The briefer specifically warned of pickpockets and described some preventative measures, such as carrying wallets in a front pocket instead of a back pocket. He also warned us never to play cards for money with a Filipino. He said con men routinely tricked Americans into card games and cheated them out of their money. Violence often ensued after these encounters, with the American always outnumbered and at a great disadvantage. These tips were common knowledge for anyone living in the PI. I always remembered the precautions and took them to heart.

I lived off base and became very familiar with the customs and habits of the locals. After a couple of years I thought I was street smart and felt safe from pick pockets and con artists, but I always wondered how the Filipinos worked the card scam. I was curious how anyone could be tricked into playing cards for money. What kind of card games did they play, and how did they cheat? One day I was walking downtown and a Filipino waved his arms and got my attention. He said, "Hey friend, do you remember me?" He looked familiar, but I couldn't quite place him. I guessed, "Are you the tailor who made my suits?" "Yes! My name's Johnny, remember? How are you doing?" he asked. I had a couple of custom suits made about a year earlier, and this Filipino looked like the tailor. It was not surprising he remembered me, because Filipinos are famous for their sharp memories. It is not uncommon for an American to visit the PI and return years later, only to be startled and amazed when Filipinos remember him by name. I kind of felt embarrassed by my deficient, American memory. I started talking with Johnny. He was very animated and told me he had started business selling furniture and souvenirs. He wanted to show me his store, hoping I would be impressed. He offered to pay for a tricycle ride to his shop. I would earn a good discount if I wanted to buy furniture, and if I liked his store I agreed I would give his business cards to my friends.

I didn't have any plans, so I hopped into a tricycle with Johnny. We sat in the sidecar and talked as the driver dodged potholes and swerved around traffic. After awhile, I realized we were traveling pretty deep into the city. I commented to Johnny that his shop seemed a long way from the base. He assured me we were almost there. We continued into the depths of the city, until finally, the tricycle stopped outside a bar on a traffic-choked street in the heart of Angeles City. Johnny said he had some quick business to attend to inside. He offered to buy me a beer while I waited. We entered the bar and sat down at a small table. Johnny ordered me a beer and introduced me to his friend Elvis. "Elvis will keep you company for a few minutes. I'll be right back." Johnny excused himself and disappeared into a back room.

I was beginning to sense that something was not quite right. I closely examined my surroundings. The bar was small and shabby, a local hangout for regular guys. A few tattered tables and chairs were pushed against the far wall. The ceiling fan's large blades circled slowly, not making much of a breeze. A few guys sat at the counter, smoking cigarettes and talking. The front door was propped open. I didn't feel I was in any immediate danger. Besides, I was a good wrestler and an experienced black belt in karate and had successfully competed in kick boxing matches.

We engaged in small talk for a while and at some point Elvis brought out a deck of cards. "Let's play some cards while you wait." he suggested. "Let's play for the phone number of a good looking woman." he joked. I agreed to play, because I was curious. By this time I had realized that Elvis and Johnny were setting me up for the card scam, and I wanted to see how they did it. I just had to be careful that curiosity didn't kill the cat, me being the cat. I was having too much fun! "Can I get another beer?" I asked. "Sure friend, it's on me." Elvis said. We played draw poker for a few minutes, and then Elvis suggested we play for a few pesos. "You can deal." he said. I readily agreed, because I didn't think it was possible for Elvis to cheat as long as I was the dealer. The exchange rate at the time was eight pesos to a dollar, so playing for a few pesos was not exactly high rolling. I still felt I was in control of the situation. I won a few hands before finally losing. "I won the last hand; it's my turn to deal." Elvis exclaimed. "Dealer chooses the game. Let's play seven card stud."

We placed a five peso ante to start, and Elvis dealt each of us two cards face down and one card face-up. "Highest card bets." he reminded me. Elvis proceeded to deal our next cards face up, and we bet after each card. I peeked at my face-down cards and realized I had a full house, an almost unbeatable hand in poker. I knew I was being duped, so I cautiously bet only ten pesos. Elvis would have to have four-of-a kind or a straight flush to beat me, and the two fives he had showing told me the tale. Elvis readily matched my bet and dramatically upped the stakes, raising me five hundred pesos.

My curiosity was satisfied. Now I knew exactly how the crooked card game operated. I had a full house, which under normal circumstances would be a winning hand. Although Elvis only had a pair of fives showing, I knew with certainty that he also had the two remaining fives face down. Somehow he was manipulating the cards, but I couldn't see how he was doing it. Elvis was pretty slick. Nonetheless, I knew that he was cheating. His four-of-a-kind would beat my full house. I had two choices. I could fold my hand and lose all the money I'd contributed to the pot, or I could match Elvis's bet and continue to play. If a gambler thought he was in an honest game, he would probably match the bet thinking his full house was a sure winner. The con artist would bet large amounts of money on the remaining cards, knowing he had a winning hand.

I narrowed my eyes and pursed my lips, as if struggling to decide whether to wager five hundred pesos or fold my hand and call it quits. I knew there were five men between me and the door and watched them from the corner of my eye. Even if I folded and accepted my losses, I knew they would not let me leave without taking all my cash. They had strength in numbers and would strong arm me if they could. The men stared, intently watching my next move. I set down my beer and took five one hundred peso notes from my wallet. The men at the bar relaxed. My adrenaline surged, pumping through my brain, sharpening my focus as I prepared for action. I moved as if to place my bet on the table, but instead my hand bumped my beer bottle, spilling it onto Elvis' lap. Elvis reacted instinctively to the cold beer, pushing back from the table and rising to his feet. I jumped up from my chair making a loud show of apologizing, and in the ensuing pandemonium I snatched all the money off the table and bolted for the door! My tactics took everyone by complete surprise. I had a small head start, but the Filipinos recovered quickly and scrambled to cut off my escape. I dashed to the door and barely made it to the exit ahead of the Filipinos. The thugs were nearly upon me when I suddenly wheeled round and kicked the nearest man square in the chest. My kick cracked ribs and launched the shocked Filipino through the air into the other men, tumbling them to the ground. For the moment, my assailants were a jumble of tangled bodies on the floor. I darted out the door and raced down the busy sidewalk, dodging pedestrians.

I looked back and saw the furious Filipinos swarming out of the bar. Running full tilt, I grabbed onto the rail of a passing Jeepney and swung myself into the vehicle. The wide-eyed passengers shrunk back, trying to keep their distance from the crazy American. I yelled to the driver, "Step on the gas!" and thrust a hundred peso note into his hand. I looked back and saw all six of Johnny's henchmen piling onto one tricycle. The jeepney driver realized we were being pursued and stomped the gas pedal to the floor. The jeepney surged into traffic and accelerated away from the tricycle. The tricycle was only designed for one driver and two passengers. With six bodies hanging on, the overloaded motorcycle was slow and unstable. The motorcycle driver held the throttle wide open and the tricycle rocked side to side, almost tipping over, as the frustrated riders yelled curses and flailed their arms futilely. My jeepney continued to speed through the city, pulling away from our pursuers. Finally, I could no longer see the tricycle behind us.

When I was sure I had escaped, I thanked the driver and got off at the next stop. I hired a tricycle of my own and carefully made my way back to my neighborhood, keeping careful watch for Johnny and his friends. I knew that Johnny was in a frustrated rage. Not only had I foiled his plans, I had also made off with a thousand pesos of his cash. Even though I had great fun and came out of my escapade in good shape, my escape was risky and could've had a very different outcome. I feel a disclaimer is appropriate for those people who think it is fun to con street hustlers, "Kids. Don't try this at home."

CHAPTER 6

ETHIOPIA

There is a Reaper, whose name is Death,
And, with his sickle keen,
He reaps the bearded grain at a breath,
And the flowers that grow between.
—Henry Wadsworth Longfellow, "The Reaper and the Flowers"

IN 1986 I LEFT THE PHILIPPINES AND MOVED TO THE 1730TH PARA-rescue Squadron at Eglin Air Force Base, Florida. On the domestic front, my hands were full being a single parent to my five-year-old son Billy. As you can imagine, this responsibility kept me quite busy. Sometimes, my child rearing techniques clashed with traditional methods. I focused his training on reading, wrestling, karate, sports, and having fun. I also wanted my son to be well rounded and involved in outdoor activities. One day Billy's kindergarten teacher phoned me at work. In a grave tone of voice she informed me Billy had been involved in a serious incident at school. She refused to elaborate but insisted I come to the school for a disciplinary meeting. My mind raced as I drove to the school. I wondered what type of behavior could possibly land a five-year-old in such hot water.

When I arrived at the school, the teacher ushered me into a private office. Billy sat next to me—he looked scared. We both faced the grim faced teacher. She reminded me of the woman in the famous painting, "American Gothic." She sat rigidly behind her desk, her eyes unblinking. The atmosphere was reminiscent of a criminal court proceeding. "Maybe

Billy had accidentally killed someone." I thought. There was a moment of uncomfortable silence. The teacher's face was stiff and emotionless. Finally, her lips moved and she intoned, "Billy, tell your father what you did."

Under the disapproving gaze of his teacher, Billy began his confession. "Well, I was eating lunch next to Suzy. We had green Jell-O. It was jiggling around. Suzy bent down to look at her Jell-O real close, and I . . . pushed her face into it." I barely choked off a belly laugh and quickly looked away, struggling for control. Somehow I sensed that Billy's straitlaced teacher would frown upon me laughing uncontrollably about this issue. With Zen-like concentration, I mastered my emotions and turned to face my son. My expression was serious, my tone was stern, my acting was impeccable, "Billy, how do you think that made Suzy feel?" "Bad." said Billy. "That's right." I said. "I don't want you to ever do such a thing again. Do you understand?" "Yes." Billy meekly replied. I looked at the teacher. She seemed disappointed I hadn't tortured my son with hot irons. Reluctantly, the she allowed us to leave. This incident was representative of many child-rearing situations I dealt with over the years.

When I wasn't dealing with single parent emergencies, I continued to perfect my PJ skills. In 1986, I attended Army High Altitude Low Opening (HALO) parachute school and became Military Free Fall (MFF) qualified. I was no longer restricted to static line parachuting; I was an MFF parachutist, in layman's terms a sky diver. During this assignment, I had numerous adventures including participating in high altitude high opening (HAHO) parachute jumps. HAHO operations involve a PJ team jumping from as high as thirty-five thousand feet and activating their parachutes shortly after leaving the plane. Jumpers pull their ripcords at staggered intervals to create altitude separation between team members. The jumpers breathe through facemasks connected to a portable oxygen tank and communicate with voice activated interteam radios. The purpose of these jumps is to infiltrate enemy territory undetected by being invisible to enemy radar. The plane flies a high altitude route that offsets many miles from the actual objective. At the determined exit point, jumpers dive from the plane and deploy their parachutes almost immediately. Still twenty five thousand feet above the ground, they fly their high-performance canopies as far as thirty miles to the landing zone, all the while presenting a practically invisible radar image. If all goes well they will land behind enemy lines, silently in the dead of night, completely unexpected and unseen.

Jumpers must overcome severe challenges during HAHO jumps. They must prebreathe pure oxygen for an hour before jumping. This purges nitrogen from their bloodstreams and prevents them from getting the bends. They must also endure temperatures as cold as sixty degrees below zero. With hands held above shoulder height, as is the case when gripping the toggles and steering the parachute, their hands will freeze in a matter of seconds. This happens because with hands held above heart level circulation is restricted and hands will freeze regardless of how well insulated the gloves are. I've seen jumpers land with their hands so cold it took them thirty minutes just to shed their parachute harness. On one of my HAHO training jumps a jumper lost his helmet on exit and his head was so cold he needed medical attention after he landed—talk about brain freeze!

There are a lot of things that can go wrong and ruin a HAHO operation. It is very difficult for a team to group into a formation and maintain it mile after mile at night while following a magnetic azimuth. In order to land together on the drop zone jumpers use a compass or GPS to follow a directional heading while following the lead jumper. Helmet visors tend to fog up, blinding jumpers and complicating matters. A parachute malfunction can cause severe altitude separation between jumpers and ruin their formation. Interteam radio failure and other equipment malfunctions can also play havoc on a formation. A failure in a jumper's oxygen system can result in unconsciousness. There is a lot that can go wrong.

HAHO jumps are serious business. On my first HAHO, we prebreathed pure oxygen for an hour from large green steel tanks while we sat dressed in full combat gear. In addition to weapon, rucksack, and load-bearing gear, each of us wore a portable oxygen tank, oxygen mask, and compass board. When it was time to jump we stood and switched over to our personal oxygen cylinders. The pilot lowered the aft ramp, and the back of the plane opened onto an ink black night. The interior of the plane instantly plunged into subzero temperatures and fogged my visor. Although we were not quite in the jet stream, the wind outside was 100 mph. The plane's navigation computers had calculated winds along our route and determined where our team should exit the plane in order to land on the drop zone.

When the red jump light turned to green, we dove from the plane into the freezing night sky. I counted ten seconds in my head and pulled my ripcord. I knew my fingers would soon freeze making it impossible to grip the steering loops with my hands, so once under canopy, I immediately pushed my hands through the toggle loops and steered with my wrists. I maneuvered into my place in the formation and, when prompted, chimed in on my radio, which demonstrated that my interteam radio was working properly. We had a lot of miles to cover before we landed and I was busy constantly adjusting my altitude and direction to maintain my place in the formation. I followed the jumper in front of and below me. Many minutes later I prepared for a landing in a desert clearing. The landing zone, small open area, was overrun by mesquite trees, their thick limbs twisted into menacing barriers. I must have been slightly off the wind line, because when I flared my canopy I didn't slow down and was moving at more than 20 mph straight towards a burly tree. A thigh-thick branch filled my vision. In my heightened mental state I could see individual leaves and every detail of the coarse bark. If I hit that branch at top speed my body would break in pieces. I raised my knees to my chest, hoping to impact the horizontal branch on the thick soles of my jump boots. I had a fleeting thought, "If this doesn't work I am toast." My feet hit the branch with such force that the stout limb snapped off clean, sounding like a gunshot. All the other jumpers saw me careen into the tree, heard a loud crack, and watched me disappear into a tangle of underbrush. Everyone thought I was surely dead, but I was completely unscathed. I leaped to my feet covered in bark and leaves but otherwise without a scratch. My guardian angel is a badass! Since I jumped HAHO in the 1980s, there have been many advances, such as steering toggle extenders to allow maneuvering while keeping your hands below your heart and special gear that warms jumpers. Despite the dangers and complexities, I loved HAHO jumps precisely because they were so difficult and challenging.

At the unit my day to day activities revolved around training, instructing, and evaluating our PJs. Although PJ training is fun and exciting, what every PJ really wants is a good rescue mission. PJs never know when they may be called upon to use their skills. Sometimes the timing is unpredictable and sometimes the type of mission is unexpected. On 7 August 1989 Congressman Mickey Leland and his entourage of fourteen died on a remote mountainside in Gambela, Ethiopia. Congressman Leland was chairman of the House Select Committee on Hunger and on his way back to the states from a visit to the Fugnida Refugee Camp in Ethiopia. The camp was overflowing with desperate people who had escaped fierce fighting in neighboring Sudan. The congressman's delegation consisted of staffers, U.S. Agency for International Development officials, Ethiopian bureaucrats, and a U.S. embassy representative. En route to Ethiopia, their De Havilland Twin Otter aircraft encountered a violent thunderstorm. Investigators later speculated that the pilot crashed his plane into a rocky bluff while trying to find a landing site. After the plane full of dignitaries failed to show, the Ethiopian government searched unsuccessfully to locate the missing aircraft.

On 8 August headquarters ordered helicopters and PJs to Ethiopia to search for Congressman Leland. We immediately prepared to deploy to Africa. Our commander selected me as the PJ team leader for this operation. I did a quick country study, learning that Ethiopia is located in the Horn of Africa, the easternmost projection of the continent. The country is about twice the size of Texas and, as can be expected of such a large country, the geography is diverse. Armed with my newfound knowledge of our destination I supervised gear preparation, ensuring we could respond to any situation. The 55th Special Operations Squadron loaded four HH-60 helicopters onto a C-5 Galaxy aircraft. The Galaxy is our military's largest cargo transport, larger than a 747 jumbo jet, and six Pave Hawks can fit inside. The HH-60's rotors are designed to fold back so the helicopter takes up less room and can be more easily transported on a large aircraft. Along with the helicopters our eight PJs boarded a C-5 with our gear, including assault rifles and pistols.

After a long flight, we arrived at Bole International Airport in Addis Ababa, the capital of Ethiopia. The C-5s taxied to the parking area and shutdown their engines. The back of our plane opened onto a media frenzy. It was pandemonium on the tarmac with crowds of people rushing pell-mell towards us. News personalities and bulky TV cameras were everywhere. Embassy officials met our group and immediately freaked out when they saw the PJs openly carrying rifles. (We had brought the weapons for protection against wild animals in case we were sent into the jungle.) The diplomats ordered us to immediately box the weapons so they could be returned to the United States. They let us store our pistols out of sight inside the aircraft.

Now that we had arrived in Africa, there was a lot of work to do. Our maintenance crews had to unload the helicopters and get them ready for flight. Our PJ team had to unload gear, setup operations at the airfield, and get settled in at our hotel. Our illustrious intelligence shop had erroneously predicted tropical weather and balmy temperatures. The winter weather was cold and wet, not what any of us expected. I immediately contacted our unit and requested winter gear be sent on the next aircraft flying to Ethiopia.

One thing was obvious—this was a huge operation. An HC-130 and PJs from England were already on scene. We also had four more PJs and extra equipment scheduled to arrive in a few days. Master Sergeant Emilio Jaso from RAF Woodbridge was the ranking PJ team leader. I would act as assistant team leader with oversight of our helicopter assets. We seamlessly integrated PJs, helicopters, and HC-130s for the search effort. Major General James F. Record, who at the time was operations director at CENT-COM, was in overall command of the task force. In order to perform their search mission, the planes had to be flight worthy. To make the planes fly, we brought a lot of mechanics and established a strong supply chain.

The embassy arranged hotel accommodations in the capital. Addis Ababa is the largest city in Ethiopia with a population of about three million. The city is located at the base of Mount Entoto at an altitude of eight thousand feet, higher than Mexico City. Our hotel was the finest in the capital and boasted high-class restaurants and nightclubs. The nightclubs featured various shows and performing artists including traditional Ethiopian dancers. The dance show was amazing. The performers jerked like marionettes, their joints and limbs popped to strange rhythmic music. Their performance was mesmerizing; I had never seen anything like it.

Ethiopia is an ancient land. Paleontologists have unearthed mankind's earliest known evolutionary predecessors in Ethiopia's rift valley, including three-and-a-half-million-year-old Lucy. Ethiopia is also the birthplace of coffee. Arabica coffee is native to Ethiopia and connoisseurs have been drinking it for a thousand years. Legend has it that a goat herder from

Kaffa discovered coffee beans and gave them to monks who placed them in water to preserve them, accidentally preparing the first coffee beverage. Since that time, coffee has spread around the world. Coffee is an important part of Ethiopian culture, and they drink it during an elaborate ceremony performed three times a day. Another little known fact is that Judaism and Christianity have deep roots in the African country. Ethiopia's famous Queen of Sheba visited King Solomon nearly a thousand years before Christ and embraced the novel concept of a one all-powerful God. Almost from its beginning, Ethiopia had strong Christian influences and beliefs. Despite the spread of Islam across Africa, Ethiopia's official religion remains Christianity.

In the heart of Addis Ababa is the Mercato, the largest open-air market in all of Africa. I visited the market with some PJs and a guide. The Mercato covers several square miles and contains thousands of vendors selling mostly agricultural products, although you can find almost anything. To a Westerner, the market appears raw and haphazard, the polar opposite of the polished tile, tidy shelves, and fluorescent lighting in American supermarkets and department stores. The Mercato is a confusing warren of narrow alleys. Crowds of people search the maze for bargains. Occasionally one has to step around a diseased person lying naked and prostrate in the street—it is a shocking, alien environment.

The highlight of our excursion was a visit to an illegal ivory shop. A taxi driver arranged our visit to the secret store. Hard faced men with Russian AK-47 assault rifles guarded the ivory and patrolled nearby alleys. In 1989 the international community banned the sale of ivory to protect endangered elephants. However, destitute poachers could care less about endangered species and conservation. Our escorts did not know it, but we came to look, not buy. The shop was crammed full of every sort of ivory product. Elaborate carvings of all shapes and sizes crowded the showroom. There were even stacks of raw elephant tusks, each one dense and heavy. There were plenty of active buyers pacing the floors, mostly Europeans. The shop buzzed with the rapid fire chatter of patrons and vendors haggling prices. I wondered how the buyers planned to smuggle their purchases past customs.

The Soviet Union maintained a strong presence in Ethiopia. Russia provided Ethiopia with economic aid and military equipment. Before we left the United States our intelligence shop briefed us that there was a very real possibility we would be approached by Russian spies. *I imagined a gorgeous Russian agent with long, shapely legs and exotic accent striking up a conversation with me at the bar. I would play hard to get, inadvertently letting slip that I was privy to vital military secrets. After a few drinks I would appear vulnerable and she would overwhelm me with her feminine charms, coaxing me to her room and seducing me. In her bedroom suite overlooking lush gardens she would exhaust her repertoire of erotic stratagems only to discover I was immune to all her attempts to pump me for information. Too late she would realize she had fallen in love with the handsome American and offer to become a double agent.* Dream on brother—unfortunately that never happened.

The Soviet Union was also cozy with Ethiopia's dictator Mengistu. Mengistu Haile Mariam came to power in 1977. It is rumored that he used a pillow to smother his predecessor, the King of Kings, Emperor Haile Selassi. Mengistu was a brutal dictator responsible for the death of tens of thousands of Ethiopians during what came to be known as "The Red Death." Mengistu readily embraced communism and visited the Soviet Union numerous times. In the mid-eighties Mengistu orchestrated the adoption of a soviet-style constitution. With Mengistu at its head the Worker's Party of Ethiopia became the ruling faction, complete with politburo. As we drove the streets of the capital en route to our hotel we passed giant banners and billboards prominently displaying the image of Mengistu. Lean men in uniforms prowled the streets carrying assault rifles. The country had a totalitarian feel. I wondered what leverage our government used to persuade Mengistu to allow our intrusion.

After we settled into our hotel we planned the next day's search operation. The two HC-130s had already conducted an unsuccessful reconnaissance of likely crash sites. Helicopters can fly lower and slower giving searchers a better chance to spot wreckage. The next day we launched helicopters and HC-130s with PJs onboard. We carried medical gear and equipment to allow us to operate on the ground. HC-130s refueled our helicopters during flight, so we were able to search non-stop for many hours. A few congressmen and their sergeants at arms showed up at our hotel and insisted on flying aboard our helicopters. They were identified as friends and colleagues of Mickey Leland. We outfitted them with flight suits and helmets. These congressional hangers-on served no useful purpose on our aircraft and were actually a hindrance, but we were forced to babysit them—orders from on high. At first I thought it was all publicity and political theater. But something didn't fit: instead of emotional pleas to find their missing colleagues the congressmen seemed more interested in recovering a mysterious briefcase.

We flew our search aircraft over lush green fields and jungle-covered mountains. Our helicopters flew low, about a hundred feet above the ground. Mushroom shaped Tukul huts made from thatch dotted the countryside. Occasionally we saw prides of lions and troops of baboons. We flew ten hours straight and found nothing. The next day we continued the search. Around midday a PJ onboard a helicopter glimpsed wreckage partially hidden by dense forest. He spotted the scorched, crumpled remains of a plane on a steep jungle covered mountainside. With great difficulty the HH-60 hovered above the site and used its rescue hoist to lower the PJ onto a level area two hundred and fifty feet above the crash site. The operation was very dangerous because of tall trees, boulders, and an extremely steep, seventy-degree slope. Another helicopter arrived and lowered a second PJ. A horrendous scene confronted the PJs as they climbed down to the crash site. The air was thick with buzzing insects and the stench of decaying bodies. All the people in the wreckage were dead, their bodies twisted, burnt, and badly decomposed. The PJs located twelve bodies and Congressman Mickey Leland's passport, positively identifying the missing delegation. A congressional sergeant at arms was onboard the circling helicopter and ordered the PJs to look for a specific briefcase. Fire had nearly destroyed the briefcase, but the tightly stacked sheaf of papers inside resisted the flames and only the edges were charred. The PJs scooped up the damaged documents and hoisted back onto the helicopter.

A short time later two other helicopters arrived on scene and the aircraft with the secret papers immediately began the two hour return flight to Addis Ababa. One of the newly arrived HH-60s lowered a PJ and doctor to the wreckage. The second helicopter attempted to lower additional PJs, but experienced mechanical problems. After briefly surveying the crash site the helicopters retrieved all personnel back onboard. The pilots debated the pros and cons of leaving PJs at the site overnight, but decided to return to Addis Ababa with all crewmembers. During the evening exodus back to Bole Airport, extreme weather forced one of the helicopters to land near a village seventy miles away from Addis Ababa. Their crew spent the night in thatched Tukul huts and enjoyed the hospitality of the Ethiopian villagers.

Once back in Addis Ababa, I attended a strategy meeting with Major General Record and all the key players in the task force. Darkness and thick fog prevented any immediate return to the crash site. General Record decided the recovery operation would begin in earnest early the next day. The general laid out the objectives and priorities of the operation. It was important to secure the crash site. Specially trained Air Force Fly Away Security Teams (FAST) normally guarded sensitive wreckage. Three-man FAST teams were available, but in this instance were not trained or prepared to operate under these conditions. The wreckage was on a remote jungle covered mountainside with near vertical slopes and wild leopards and baboons. PJs were the only group with mountaineering equipment and the proper training to operate safely at the crash site. PJs were also the only ones with the required combination of weapons, survival training, and bivouac equipment to camp in the jungle.

The general also wanted reliable communications from the crash site back to headquarters and the embassy. The radio technicians did not have man-portable gear they could set up on-site, and were not prepared to operate in austere environments. The solution: PJs would position a team on a mountain peak near the crash site. We had portable satellite radios capable of reaching Addis Ababa and other radios to talk to helicopters and aircraft. Each PJ also had a handheld UHF survival radio.

It was difficult just to access the site. Among the hundreds of deployed personnel only PJs were trained to use the hoist and rappel ropes needed to reach the wreckage. General Record decided PJs would establish fixed-rope systems and escort a very limited number of critical personnel, such as a mortician to the site. We ended the meeting and built a flying schedule for the following day. Master Sergeant Emilio Jaso and I organized the PJ plan of operations and briefed the teams. Strangely, every single congressman and staffer had already left the country. I wondered why they didn't want to stay while we recovered the bodies. Maybe they were more interested in that briefcase and now that they had it there was no reason to linger in a third world country.

At first light on 14 August two HC-130s flew to Gambela airfield with men, supplies, and equipment to set up a forward operating base. Gambela was forty miles from the crash site, about a twenty minute helicopter flight. Two helicopters, each carrying five PJs took off but were turned back by bad weather. Another helicopter was still grounded at the native village. Eventually the weather cleared enough for the helicopters to reach the wreckage site, which was located five thousand feet up the side of a mountain. My helicopter did not have a rescue hoist, so my team of PJs (Sergeants Scott Copper, Jerry Sowles, and Maurice Sweet) and I rappelled to a flat area about two hundred and fifty feet above the wreckage. Sergeants Emilio Jaso, Rick Weaver, and Mike Fleming soon joined us. We used axes to chop down trees and established the high meadow as the primary base camp for the rest of the mission. We were terrible lumberjacks and our axes mostly bounced harmlessly off the tree trunks. The wood was so hard we nicknamed the timber "iron trees." Another helicopter deposited Sergeants Dan Daily and Norman Simpson on top of the peak to set up the satellite-radio base station. For the next two days they were isolated from our main group and relayed information from our team at the crash site back to headquarters.

Our next order of business was to set up fixed ropes down to the wreckage. We used three, sixty-meter mountain climbing ropes to construct the system. We rigged the lines so that we could attach lanyards onto the ropes and work safely. We descended to the wreckage, thoroughly searched the area and made pencil sketches of the site. Two hours before sunset helicopters lowered two doctors and a photographer. We took them on a short tour of the wreckage then back to camp where they were hoisted up to a waiting helicopter. Sergeant Jaso also hoisted up while Sergeants Graham and Bollinger remained with our main party to spend the night. All the aircraft returned to Addis Ababa as night descended over the jungle.

We set up tents, built a fire, and prepared our camp. We had reliable radio contact with our two teammates on top of the mountain, five hundred feet above. Our intelligence shop had researched the dangers we could face in the jungle, such as, leopards and baboons. There were also numerous species of deadly vipers, such as mountain adders, and cobras. It would have been nice to have a few high-powered rifles and hand grenades, but we had to make do with our 9mm pistols and a roaring fire. We turned in knowing we had a hard day ahead. The night noises were loud and creepy, unnerving to those of us with no jungle experience. In the middle of the night Jerry Sowles roused the entire camp. He claimed he saw a giant baboon on the far side of our clearing. He was agitated, waving his pistol around. He pointed, "There it is! Can't you see it?" We strained our eyes, but none of us could make it out. Finally, I walked over to where Jerry was pointing. His fierce baboon was a harmless tree stump. Shadows can play tricks on a restless mind. We all had a good laugh and went back to our sleeping pads. I poked fun at Jerry, "Don't shoot your teammates in the middle of the night. A lot of them look like baboons." "Ha ha, very funny; go back to sleep." The rest of the night passed uneventfully.

Shortly after first light two helicopters arrived and began lowering people to our camp. In addition to four additional PJs our group now included a civilian mortician, two doctors, a photographer, and a videographer. The mortician was in charge of all matters pertaining to the body recovery. He wore a black baseball cap with *MORT* emblazoned in bold white letters, and was an expert in body-recovery operations. Being masters of originality we called him Mort. We provided safety harnesses for non-PJs and briefed them on procedures. We tethered them to the fail-safe rope system. Their lanyards would slide freely up and down the safety rope, but if they slipped and fell the tether would automatically grip the rope and stop the person from falling farther down the slope. A PJ escorted each visitor at all times.

Recovering deceased personnel is one aspect of a PJ's job that is extremely unpleasant. This is especially true if the corpses are broken, burnt, and rotting. The crash victims had experienced all three. Their bodies had lain decomposing in the jungle for eight days before we arrived. During this time they were at the mercy of bacteria, blowflies, and other jungle scavengers. Most of the victims had worn seat belts that tore their bodies in half upon impact. Seat belts cannot protect people from the extreme deceleration forces sometimes encountered in a plane crash. PJs carefully escorted the specialists down to the crash site. The putrid smell was indescribable. A by-product of human decomposition is the formation of noxious gases, such as ammonia and hydrogen sulfide. The stink was so oppressive the air felt thick. Flies swarmed around us with bits of rotting human remains stuck to their feet. Initially, I tried to wear a surgeon's mask to keep bugs off my lips and mouth. Because of our intense physical exertions, masks made it too hard to breathe. We put dabs of Vicks Vapor Rub in our nostrils to help disguise the overpowering odors.

Mort directed our efforts at the crash site. PJs Daily and Simpson sat atop their mountain perch and kept General Record apprised of our progress and needs. We kept one PJ at base camp at all times and all of us communicated with handheld radios. Our mission at the crash site was to place each corpse into a vinyl body bag. Mort micromanaged this delicate operation taking great care to ensure that body parts and pieces belonged to the same person before placing them in their bag. The remains were writhing with maggots of all shapes and sizes. Repellant though they may be, maggots are important to accident investigations, especially plane crashes. Maggots can help determine exact times of death, and most importantly, whether explosives were involved in the crash.

It took an unburdened person twenty minutes to climb from the crash site up to the base camp. Instead of trying to drag heavy bags of remains two hundred and fifty feet up a steep slope we moved the body bags one hundred feet off to the side of the wreckage where we could hoist them off the mountain. Around midday a Pave Hawk flew to our location and hovered above the recovery site we had prepared. They tossed down a tagline and we attached it to the foot end of a rigid metal litter. We muscled a body bag into the litter, attached the helicopter's hoist cable, and gave the "thumbs up" signal to the flight engineer. He stood in the open helicopter door one hundred feet above, gazing down at us. We were buffeted by the downwash from the choppers whirring rotors and struggled to keep our footing on the steep slope. The engineer raised the litter, and we used the tagline to prevent the rotor wash from twirling it like a top. The litter reached the helicopter door and the engineer dragged it into the chopper. Noxious fluids leaked from the body bag, blown into sticky mist by the rotors. Sickened by the powerful smell, the flight engineer leaned out the door and vomited a stream into the downwash. The helicopter crew unloaded the litter and lowered it back down to us; only four more bags to go. We placed the next body bag into the litter, now slimed with rotting human juices, and signaled for a raise. After six bodies were lifted into the helicopter, it banked away from the slope and flew to Gambela airfield. At Gambela, they removed the bodies from the helicopter and loaded them onto a refrigerated cargo plane bound for a morgue in Addis Ababa. Refrigeration dramatically slows maggot activity and decomposition.

During this whole operation we could see Ethiopian helicopters circling miles away. I'm sure they had binoculars trained on our location. I thought it very mysterious that the Ethiopian military agreed to keep their distance. This was their country after all. Ethiopia was friendly with the Soviets, and the dictator Mengistu was no great friend to the United States. We did not allow Ethiopian accident investigators to visit the crash site and there were no Ethiopian observers on the ground with us—unbelievable. I was mystified as to how our government was able to lock out the Ethiopians.

We continued with the necessary work of bagging bodies. We had one bag designated for body parts we could not match with a specific person. I dreaded that bag. I hated it because we had to keep opening it to add pieces. The bag contained so many maggots it moved and undulated, making faint rustling noises. The dead bodies were soft and came apart when we tried to pick them up. Our clothes were covered in putrid slime. We would have to discard our clothes after the operation. The helicopter returned and one by one we hoisted bags off the treacherous slope. When we finished, the aircraft departed to Gambela with its load of corpses. Now there were only a few bodies left at the crash site.

We continued to bag bodies until finally there was only one corpse left. A large man, weighing well over two hundred pounds, lay tightly wedged between two boulders deeply imbedded in the earth. His shirtless torso had a sickly greenish sheen. The only way to dislodge the man was to wrap arms around him in a bear hug and pull him from the rocks—not a pleasant prospect. We huddled in a silent group and looked at the dead man, building our resolve. Finally, SSgt. Ken Bollinger spoke, "I'll do it." The rest of us sighed in relief. Ken had a body builder's muscular physique. He would need his great strength to free the wedged corpse. Sergeant Bolliger positioned a vinyl body bag next to the man-in-the-rocks. Then he lay on top of the corpse and worked his arms under and around the dead man's chest. He intertwined his fingers, locked his grip and squirmed to his knees, struggling for leverage. As Ken heaved upwards we watched in awe as his muscles bunched and his face reddened with herculean exertion. And suddenly, the man-in-the-rocks came apart in the middle, his entrails spilling onto the ground. Some of us groaned and turned away, but Sergeant Bollinger was unfazed. He methodically filled the body bag with the largest parts of the corpse, then scooped the remaining organs and pieces into the bag. When he was finished not a speck of the person remained on the ground. We gave him kudos as he slowly stood. His uniform was slick with gore and stank of death, but he appeared totally unfazed. We all praised him, "That was hardcore Ken." he looked at us quizzically, genuinely taken aback. "No big deal." he said.

Finally the crash site was completely clear. We had removed all the bodies in two and a half days. Now our commanders gave permission for a small Ethiopian delegation to visit the site. Helicopters lowered them and we escorted them. They stayed long enough to make a cursory examination of the wreckage and pose for group photos. They were all smiles— it was strange. Helicopters ferried our party to Gambelo airfield, including our radio operators on the peak. We could not salvage our clothes; we threw them away and changed into fresh uniforms. We even abandoned our boots. Maggots had worked their way into nooks and crannies of our shoes and occasionally fell onto the floor.

Now that the mission was accomplished, we would pack up and be on our way home in a matter of days. One thing had been nagging at the back of my mind: the briefcase. I was curious and asked the first PJs on scene about the contents of the mystery briefcase. The case was partially destroyed, and the sheaf of documents inside was exposed. "What was so important about those papers?" I asked. He said he had only glanced at the documents, but they involved intelligence on various political factions and support for antigovernment rebels. At the time the information was interesting but not earth shaking. I forgot all about the incident. Many months later, in May of 1991, I was at my new assignment in Iceland watching network news on TV. The report showed rebels advancing on Addis Ababa with tanks. Eventually, the rebel fighters surrounded the capital and forced the dictator Mengistu to flee to Zimbabwe where President Robert Mugabe gave him asylum. Ethiopian courts eventually convicted Mengistu of genocide and sentenced him to death in absentia. I flashed back to the Ethiopian mountainside and the enigmatic briefcase. Suddenly everything made sense. Maybe the rebel overthrow of the mass murderer Mengistu was a successful U.S. covert operation. The removal of Mengistu barely registered a blip on the world's radar. It made me wonder about what goes on in the shadows just below the well lit surface of world events. I've discovered one thing while participating in military operations around the world and examining the print and television coverage. What you think you know when you watch the evening news is only the tip of the iceberg.

CHAPTER 7

ICELAND

Our most important baggage on our journeys is wisdom.
—*Viking proverb*

AFTER A THREE YEAR TOUR OF DUTY IN THE PHILIPPINES MY FAMILY moved to Eglin Air Force Base, Florida, near the small city of Fort Walton Beach. Fort Walton Beach is a popular spring break destination on the Emerald Coast. Nestled on the gulf side of the Florida panhandle, its beach sand is as white as snow and the crystal clear water is eye-popping, a neon swirl of turquoise and green. The summers are hot and the winters are mild. Fort Walton Beach is a great place to live and raise a child. As a single parent I worried about how I would cope while performing military duties around the world. Surprisingly, I found that being a single parent in the military, while hectic, was manageable. Friends and family looked after Billy when I was out of town. My friends and coworkers were incredibly understanding and supportive. Wayne Jones, a fellow PJ, and his wife Jean became Billy's second family. Wayne and Jean, along with their children Jessica, Mali, Aaron, and Charles adopted Billy while I was away, sometimes for many weeks. The air force also provided many programs to help single parents, such as day care and family services.

In January 1990 the Air Combat Command PJ functional manager offered me a job as the detachment chief for the PJ team at Keflavik Naval Air Station, Iceland. I was a master sergeant and this was my first opportunity to live every PJ's dream: lead my own PJ team. Moving up through the military ranks a person lives many experiences, positive and negative. Although, for the most part my PJ bosses were awesome, many times I thought to myself, "*One day when I'm the boss,* I'll *do things a little differently, smarter and more logically.*" Gradually, I worked my way up the ladder to higher rank and gained experience as I polished my leadership skills. Finally, I was poised to take the helm of my own team, and I couldn't wait to begin. I wanted to forge the ultimate PJ team and have a lot of fun doing it.

When I received orders to Iceland, I felt anxious about abandoning the child care arrangements it had taken me years to develop. In Iceland, I would have to start from scratch, building a fresh support system at a new base where I didn't know anyone. Keflavik was a naval base, and navy organization and traditions were alien to me. I soon learned, however, that the navy is very similar to the air force, except their focus is understandably on ships instead of airplanes. Navy customs and jargon are very different from air force talk. Navy terminology relates to ships. There are no floors in buildings, only decks. You do not go to the bathroom; you use the head. Navy personnel are called seamen and refer to their base commander as "The Skipper." Every time I heard someone say "The Skipper" I couldn't help but think of the sitcom, Gilligan's Island.

Keflavik Air Base is an ideal place for a single parent to raise a child. The small base is located on the coast near the town of Keflavik. It is a very safe, interesting place for kids. Only a few hundred thousand people live in Iceland and violent crime is almost nonexistent. There is an American school on base and plenty of sports activities, such as, floor hockey, soccer, and baseball. Kites are very popular, because Iceland is ridiculously windy. *Average* daily winds are 20 mph, but are often much stronger. During fierce wind storms I saw steel dumpsters tumble across fields. Residents have to install special straps on their car doors to prevent wind from ripping them off the hinges. To take advantage of the strong wind Billy and I soon owned some high performance kites.

No surprise, I also continued to have occasional clashes with the traditional child-rearing authorities. Soon after I arrived on the island I had a run-in with my son's first grade teacher due to my irreverent PJ sense of humor. When Billy lost a baby tooth I arranged the traditional parent-child Tooth Fairy ritual. Only six years old, Billy already suspected I was really the Tooth Fairy and schemed to catch me in the act. With each lost tooth, he was getting harder and harder to trick. To defeat my precocious youngster I decided on a bold plan of action. When I tucked him in I made an exaggerated show of placing the tooth under his pillow. I conspicuously displayed his tooth between my thumb and forefinger and slid my hand slowly beneath his pillow. Unbeknownst to him, I hid a crumpled dollar bill in the palm of my hand. With a flourish I pretended to place the tooth under Billy's pillow, but with expert parental sleight of hand, I kept the tooth and deposited the dollar bill instead. I issued a stern warning not to try and stay awake to see the fairy and left Billy's room grinning slyly. I assured him I would guard against the tricky fairy creature.

I knew Billy would not be able to resist checking under his pillow. Sure enough, only a few minutes later he burst from his room wide-eyed with excitement. He clutched a dollar bill tightly in his fist and bounced around the room, "Dad! Dad! The fairy took my tooth and left a dollar!" I said, "I know son. I used my ninja skills and caught that thieving fairy leaving your room. I trapped her in a plastic bag and put her in the freezer." Billy was even more excited and begged to see the captured fairy. I opened the freezer and gave him a quick glimpse of a large shrimp I had wrapped in plastic. Viewed through multiple layers of wrap, the shrimp kind of looked like a frozen fairy. I stressed the magnitude of the occasion, "Tooth fairies are magical, elusive little things with their wings and all. I think we are the first family ever to capture one!" Billy was hopping all over the house and it took me quite awhile to finally calm him down and get him to sleep.

The next day I got an unexpected phone call at work. My son's teacher wanted to talk to me about Billy, "Now what?" I thought. When I arrived at the school, Billy's teacher met me at the door. Once we settled into her office, she explained she was worried about him. Earlier that day, Billy told his first grade class his father had killed the tooth fairy and had her in a plastic bag in the freezer. He was very convincing. Some little kids started to cry. I explained the previous night's fairy drama to the teacher. I was chuckling—she was not. She looked at me as if I had a giant booger hanging out of a nostril. Despite the look, I could tell she was attracted to me so I told her no thanks, I already had a girlfriend. Her sputtering red face made me uncomfortable and I quickly left. Later I swore Billy to secrecy about our fairy hunting activities. For dinner that evening, we breaded and fried up a couple dozen fairies and ate them with cocktail sauce and fava beans.

Despite the occasional child-rearing controversy, Keflavik was a great PJ assignment. Iceland is a volcanic island of glaciers and icy rivers about the size of Kentucky. Originally a forested land settled by Norwegian Vikings in the ninth and tenth centuries, the island seems mostly barren. Iceland boasts the largest glacier in Europe, Vatnajokull, which is roughly the size of Rhode Island. Iceland is also one of the world's most volcanic places, straddling the Mid-Atlantic Ridge where the North American and Eurasian tectonic plates separate. This is the source of Iceland's intense volcanic activity and widespread availability of geothermal energy. Almost every town has its own swimming pool heated with volcanic energy produced deep beneath the earth's crust. Locker rooms are in buildings equipped with showers and other amenities, but the swimming pools are open to the elements. Outdoor pools are usually enclosed within high cinder block walls to blunt the ever present wind gusts. Pools are surrounded with hotpots built into the concrete and tile deck surrounding the main pool and resemble hot tubs or Jacuzzis. Each hotpot has a different temperature, some icy cold and others hot enough to cook lobster. It's a unique experience to soak in bubbly hot water while snowflakes swirl around your head.

Iceland has a proud whaling tradition and is one of the few nations that continue to commercially hunt whales. When I flew local helicopter training missions off the coast, I would often see pods of speckled dolphin or orca numbering in the dozens. During these flights, we would fly a few hundred feet above the whales, shadowing their pods. The huge killer whales sliced effortlessly through the waves their black and white skin glistening as smooth and perfect as new plastic. Once we saw a dead sperm whale washed up on the rocky shore. Sperm whales are the largest toothed predators in the world. The infamous Moby Dick was a sperm whale. The dead whale was about forty feet long and probably weighed thirty tons. Each of the fifty ivory teeth in its ten ton head weighed more than two pounds. I tried to talk the pilot into landing the helicopter on the shore, and letting me off next to the dead whale so I could pry out a giant ivory tooth with my scuba knife. I couldn't convince him, however, even after offering him the whale's blow hole.

Iceland is a peaceful country with no military of its own. During the cold war, the American naval base at Keflavik acted as a deterrent to Russian aggression and as an early warning outpost. Navy P-3 Orion aircraft patrolled the surrounding seas searching for Russian submarines and air force jets intercepted Russian Bear bombers encroaching on Icelandic airspace. This was classic cold war NATO stuff.

The Icelanders favorite U.S. military unit was the 56th Aerospace Rescue and Recovery Squadron. The 56th had HH-3 Jolly Green Giant and later HH-60 Pave Hawk rescue helicopters and saved hundreds of people over the years. Over many decades the 56th rescued sailors of all nationalities as well as hikers in the remote glacial interior. When I was stationed in England in the late 1970s we used to fly our HC-130s to Keflavik and pull rescue alert for two week rotations. Our large HC-130 cargo planes provided air refueling for the helicopters assigned to the 56th. This extended the helicopter's range so they could hoist injured sailors off ships far out at sea.

And now, here I was, almost twenty years later, stationed in Iceland, assigned to a rescue helicopter squadron with my own PJ team. We had a small unit, never more than twelve PJs, so everyone had to pull their weight. Once a newly arrived PJ was checked-out on aircraft and procedures, he was immediately included in the alert rotation. A helicopter crew and two PJs were on rescue alert twenty-four/seven. Alert periods lasted two days. When we were on alert we carried beepers or radios and could not drink alcohol. If there was a potential rescue mission, the squadron would beep the alert crew. No matter the time of day or night the crew would scramble to the flight line and get the helicopter airborne in less than an hour. Every PJ on the roster took his turn pulling rescue alert, hoping for the big mission.

After I settled into my new squadron I soon became qualified on unit procedures and entered the alert rotation. During my very first alert I was scrambled. Scrambled is how we referred to being called up and activated for a rescue mission, because once notified everybody is "scrambling" to get the alert aircraft airborne. I was thrilled to get a mission so soon after my arrival at my new unit. I had not been in the squadron long enough to have flown with all the crews and I was a complete mystery to most unit members. Most of the squadron flyers only knew me as the new PJ boss.

I loaded a cart with my alert gear and pushed it from the hangar onto the icy tarmac where the helicopter waited. Our hard working mechanics were already at the bird, getting her prepped for flight. The rest of the crew loaded their belongings and manned their stations. The helicopter came to life as the power cart fired up, providing electricity to the aircraft. Maintenance troops removed plugs from engine intakes and freed the rotors from the tethers that prevented the gusty winds from turning the rotors while the helicopter was parked and dormant. We took our places, ran the checklists, and taxied for takeoff. Lifting off into stiff headwinds we flew towards Iceland's interior to recover the victim of a farming accident. During the flight I prepared the cabin to accept a patient, setting up litters and organizing the space. After an uneventful flight we found the location and landed the helicopter in a nearby fallow field. There was already an Icelandic doctor on scene with the patient. This unfortunate farmer was working in his fields and somehow caught his right arm in some type of farm machine and the whirling blades had neatly severed it. Our mission was to transport the victim, his arm, and the attending physician to the main hospital in the capital city of Reykjavik.

The doctor packed the severed arm in ice and carefully placed it in an insulated container. The hope was that surgeons could reattach the arm at the hospital. My job was to configure the helicopter for the medical transport and assist the doctor, who would be unfamiliar with the aircraft systems. Once I secured the patient in a litter and familiarized the doctor with our oxygen system, we faced a routine flight to the hospital.

The flight to Reykjavik was proceeding uneventfully and the patient was stable and doing well, so I thought this was a good opportunity to have a little fun with the flight crew.

I called the pilot on intercom.

"Go ahead PJ." the pilot responded.

"I've been talking to this doctor back here and he seems to think it's not looking good for this arm." I explained.

"What do you mean?" asked the pilot.

"Well," I said, "he says the arm was unattached for a long time, probably too long to sew it back on."

"That's too bad." The pilot sounded understandably disappointed.

I waited a few minutes before giving the pilot further fictitious updates. "The doctor says he's a hundred percent certain they won't be able to sew on the arm now. It's been detached too long. The patient also realizes they can't sew his arm back on and has accepted the bad news. He's a pretty tough character. Anyway, I talked to the doctor and patient about this whole situation. Since they can't sew the arm back on, they said I could have it."

There was shocked silence on the intercom.

"What?" asked the pilot.

"They won't be able to sew the arm back on because it's been separated from his body for too long. The muscles and nerves have been without blood and oxygen for so long that cell death is irreversible. The hospital will just throw the arm away, so I asked them if I could have it, and they said yes."

Once again, there was an uncomfortable silence on the intercom. I could almost hear the gears whirring inside the pilots head.

"Wha . . . what will you do with it?" stammered the pilot.

I answered, "I'm not really sure. At first I'll just keep it in my freezer. I just think it would be a waste to just throw a good arm away."

"Are you serious?" asked the pilot.

"No." I said, "I'm just messing with you."

But, the doctor told me that, ironically, right before the accident the man was heard to say, "I'd give my right arm to be ambidextrous."

Another crewmember chimed in, "That guys pretty tough. I think we should give him a hand!" I heard laughter over the intercom.

"You guys are sick!" said the pilot.

Later on we dropped off our patient at the hospital and took off for our home base. About halfway back to Keflavik I came up on the intercom. "Oh shit!"

"What's the matter PJ?" the pilot asked.

"When we dropped them off at the hospital they forgot to take the arm!"

The pilot asked nervously, "Are you serious?"

"No," I replied.

When my PJs were not flying alert missions they were training. Because we were in Iceland our PJ team practiced a lot of winter rescue scenarios to prepare for glacier rescues. We practiced downhill and cross-country skiing along with crevasse rescue and ice climbing. Occasionally we loaded our specially built four-wheel-drive trucks with camping and rescue training gear and drove to the base of a small glacier called Eyjafjallajokull. This glacier sits atop an active volcano and blankets thirty-nine square miles in thick ice. This is the same volcano that erupted in 2010, filling the sky with dense ash and disrupting European air traffic for weeks. The exploding volcano spewed forth a 150 million cubic yards of silica particles and dark gray ash, and the immense plume rose more than 33,000 feet into the sky.

Near the glacier we turned off the paved road and drove across the volcanic landscape, fording several shallow, swift-flowing and streams to reach our training area. At times the rushing water came halfway up the door and threatened to topple our truck. By the time we pitched our tents our nerves were frazzled from the drive. The centerpiece of the wilderness panorama was a magnificent waterfall that filled the air with mist and colorful rainbows. We trained on the icefall, the part of the glacier that flowed down a steep slope and gradually petered out on the plain. A myriad of deep crevasses rent the jumbled surface of the icefall. They looked like deep jagged cuts in the surface of the ice. Some crevasses appeared bottomless and led to a swiftly flowing subterranean river of melted ice, hundreds of feet below the glacier. Other crevasses were only a hundred or so feet deep. After a short search we found an ideal crevasse for training and a couple of PJs rappelled seventy feet to the bottom. The vertical ice walls of the crevasse were perfect to practice ice climbing. The ice walls were deep crystal blue and hard as stone. We climbed with ice axes and crampons until our arms were numb and our legs trembled with fatigue. We also practiced pulling each other out of the crevasse with rescue ropes and pulleys, rigging mechanical advantage haul systems that multiplied a man's strength.

The countryside was devoid of trees, and relentless winds whistled across the gravelly plain, chilling us to the bone and bending and flapping our tents. Our gear was designed to withstand the special environmental demands of Iceland, so we lived in relative comfort. After five days of training we were ready to test our skill and resolve with a climactic trek across the glacier. The adventure began with a drive to the far side of the glacier and a day's walk to an A frame cottage that perched near the edge of the ice. We planned to spend the night and begin our trek across the ice at first light. That night the aurora borealis, also called northern lights, put on quite a light show. Mesmerizing sheets of pale pink and green fire rippled across the night sky. It was an evening to remember.

The next morning we roped up and began our hike. Our goal was to navigate across the glacier back to our base camp. The glacier was about twelve miles across and was slashed with crevasses. Some of the crevasses were covered with snow, mantraps for the unwary. As a necessary safety precaution we all connected to a climbing rope with forty feet of slack between each man. When a PJ plunged through the thin snow and fell into a hidden crevasse, the rest of the team could stop his fall and pull him out. It was a good thing we roped in; the PJ in front of me suddenly disappeared. My heart nearly stopped as I went down on the ice and arrested with my ice axe. We pulled him out unhurt and continued on. It was nerve wracking. At any moment someone could fall into a hidden crevasse. We were able to walk around many of the crevasses, and some were narrow enough to jump across. Sometimes a crevasse went on seemingly forever, and we would follow it until we found a snow bridge that spanned the gash in the ice. Poised to stop his fall, we would send each man across the fragile snow bridge one at a time, splayed out on his stomach to distribute his weight across the surface of the fragile snow bridge. We crossed numerous snow bridges squirming on our belly's like snakes.

These were the days before GPS and we used a map and compass to navigate. Our map was mostly useless, just a sheet of white indicating the featureless wilderness of ice with the occasional contour line indicating elevation. We used an altimeter to help locate our position on the map. We trudged across the ice mile after mile, striding across the crystal surface in our many-spiked crampons. We were human pack mules loaded with gear and lugging massive backpacks. We finally came to the ice fall with only a couple of hours of daylight left. Our bright yellow tents far below were a welcome sight. It took another two hours to pick our way through a jumble of house-sized blocks of ice, down the ice fall and over to our camp. It was an awesome experience.

In addition to rescuing people from glaciers and crevasses, one of our more common missions was rescuing sailors at sea. In American waters the coast guard is normally responsible for rescue operations, but recovering distressed sailors hundreds of miles from shore is beyond their capability. Only a few military rescue units have the technology, aircraft, training, and ability to successfully accomplish long-range sea rescues. U.S. Air Force rescue squadrons with PJs, HC-130 aircraft, and helicopters capable of in-flight aerial refueling represent the pinnacle of global rescue capabilities.

There are two ways to carry out open-ocean rescue missions. Rescuers can use helicopters, or if helicopters are unavailable or impractical, rescuers can deploy medically equipped parachutists. When using helicopters is not feasible, air force rescue units use HC-130 aircraft and PJs. The HC-130 is a large four engine cargo plane outfitted for rescue operations and has large internal tanks to carry extra gas. These two tanks each hold eighteen hundred gallons of extra fuel, extending the plane's range and providing gas for thirsty helicopters. The rescue enhanced HC-130 also has color radar and state-of-the-art communications gear. Loadmasters, crewmen in charge of the cargo compartment, can configure the interior of the plane for various types of personnel and cargo parachute drops. They can also drop illumination flares, life rafts, and other survival gear to needy sailors.

Three PJs form the parachutist contingent of the HC-130's flight crew. After flying hundreds of miles to rendezvous with a ship at sea, the PJ team leader talks with the pilot and guides the plane to a calculated parachute drop point thirty-five hundred feet above the ship. In order to reach a patient isolated on a ship at sea, the PJs parachute from the HC-130 with a large bundle, called a RAMZ (riggable alternative method Zodiac), containing an inflatable Zodiac boat, and land in the ocean near the ship. After inflating the boat, the PJs scramble into the Zodiac and drive it to the ship where the crew winches them onboard. Once on deck the PJs use their medical skills and equipment to stabilize the patient until the ship reaches shore or comes within helicopter range. Jump missions are extremely complex operations with a lot of moving parts. Imagine doing a jump mission at night with high winds and twenty foot waves! The slightest miscalculation or mistake can be disastrous. That's why jump missions require the most expert PJs and air crews.

The second type of sea rescue uses helicopters with refueling probes. For this type of mission the air force will simultaneously launch a helicopter and an HC-130. The HC-130 will refuel the helicopter in midair with its fuel hoses and drogue chutes. If a helicopter cannot refuel for whatever reason, it will crash-land into the ocean, a catastrophe called ditching. Mechanical failure can also force a helicopter to ditch. In case of ditching each crewmember carries a small bottle of compressed air. This miniature scuba bottle allows crewmen to breathe for a short time underwater like a scuba diver. Hopefully, they can breathe long enough to escape from the aircraft before it sinks into the ocean depths. To increase their chances of survival after ditching all helicopter crewmembers have to undergo underwater escape training. During the training crewmen practice escape procedures on a helicopter mock-up. With flight crew inside, a mock aircraft slides down rails, splashes into a large pool, and flips over. Blind-folded and held upside down by their seatbelts, trapped aviators must establish a reference point, find an exit, and swim clear of the aircraft. Safety divers equipped with scuba tanks look on ready to rescue unsuccessful escapees.

Ditching is a last resort, a controlled crash landing into the sea. If refueling is successful and the helicopter does not experience mechanical difficulties, the rescue is on. Once on scene, a flight engineer will lower a PJ to the ship using the rescue hoist. Mission success depends on the flight engineer's skill. There are two hundred feet of usable cable and the flight engineer controls the rate of decent with a lever. During the hoist operation the engineer constantly talks to the pilot, passing instructions to adjust the hover or move the aircraft left or right. The crew must also remain vigilant to keep the aircraft clear of a sea-tossed ship's masts and antennae.

Once on deck, the PJ will treat the patient's life-threatening injuries and prepare him for recovery into the hovering chopper. Back onboard the aircraft the PJ will treat patient's injuries, administer IV fluids and medications, and monitor vital signs during the return flight to the hospital. On the way back to base the helicopter will dodge rough weather and refuel as necessary. Sometimes the injured sailor is on a submarine. On submarine missions the PJ lowers onto one of the fins that jut from the sub's conning tower. With a submarine rocking side-to-side and rising and falling on ocean swells, this is a difficult and dangerous proposition. Because submarine pickups are so challenging they are much sought after by PJs.

Many nations sail the seas around Iceland, and we frequently launched aircraft to rescue distressed seamen. These were humanitarian missions, and we rescued any and all needy sailors, no matter their nationality. Hoist missions at sea are very exciting, but they can also be very dangerous. In

July 1992 I was on alert and was scrambled for a shipboard rescue attempt. Our mission was to recover a critically ill seaman from a Lithuanian trawler 265 miles out at sea and transport him to a hospital in the Iceland's capital city, Reykjavik. I was not exactly clear on what type of illness I would be treating, because the trawler's radio operator only spoke broken English. When our helicopter lifted off from Keflavik, the sun was hidden by a solid deck of gray clouds. Our Pave Hawk helicopter flew over dark choppy seas, and the flight crew wore anti-exposure suits in case the helicopter had to ditch. These suits are designed to help a person survive in freezing water. Hopefully the suit will keep a person alive long enough to be rescued. Without some type of protection from the thirty-nine degree water a person only has thirty minutes of useful consciousness.

Instead of an exposure suit, I wore a rubber dry suit. PJs use dry suits in order to scuba dive and operate in very cold arctic water. Snug neck and wrist seals keep water out of the one-piece rubber suit. Underneath, I wore thick, synthetic insulation. Over the dry suit I wore a standard survival vest with radio and other survival gear. On the off chance I ended up in the drink, I preferred the superior protection of the dry suit over the anti-exposure suit.

Our refueling operations were very tense because of low clouds, poor visibility and gusty winds. The HC-130 reeled out fuel hoses and slowed down in preparation for our refueling rendezvous. At the end of the fuel hose the drogue chute flapped in the turbulent air. The drogue chute resembles a cloth funnel stiffened with metal spokes to help it retain its shape and provides a somewhat stable target for the helicopter pilot. Our pilot skillfully positioned our helicopter to guide the refueling probe into the drogue chute. We slowly inched forward, the helicopter jerking up and down in the rough air. Finally the pilot committed to the maneuver and the chopper lurched forward. A miss! The probe bounced off the side of the drogue and for an instant, it fluttered around the cockpit threatening to tangle in the helicopter's rotors. Unfazed, the pilot quickly backed the aircraft into clear air and prepared for another attempt. Like a jousting knight our helicopter charged fearlessly towards the drogue, and this time I could feel the satisfying "thunk" of the lance-like probe, spearing the drogue and connecting to the fuel hose. We gratefully took on precious fuel and pressed on with our mission.

Hours later we arrived on scene where the trawler, mottled with rust and flaking paint, rocked side-to-side on the black waves. The deck of the Lithuanian ship was festooned with nets, masts, and cranes. The forlorn looking vessel tossed left and right, rising and falling on dark ocean swells, its mast a shifting obstacle and constant danger to our hovering helicopter. While we planned details of the recovery, the HC-130 circled overhead and acted as airborne mission commander. The HC-130 with its superior radios and radar relayed communications to shore, provided our crew with weather updates, and coordinated other rescue assets. Our pilot talked to the trawler and directed it to orient its bow into the wind and to prepare for hoist operations.

The flight engineer connected a rescue strop, also known as a horse collar, to the end of the hoist cable. I slipped the collar around my upper body and fastened the strap under my arms. The rescue strop, is a device that securely connects and suspends a PJ from the hoist cable. The strop wrapped around my chest but allowed my legs to dangle free, essential for ship operations. A PJ must have free use of his legs in order to successfully land on the deck of a moving ship. I moved to the open cargo door and braced myself. I carried a small, streamlined medical kit specially designed for hoist operations. The small kit contained the bare medical essentials necessary to stabilize my patient. My primary medical kit was heavy and bulky and I left it onboard the helicopter.

I gave the engineer a "thumbs up signal" and eased out the door into empty space. The helicopter was in a high hover above the trawler in order to remain safely above the gyrating masts and antennae. Besides the obvious danger that masts pose to an aircraft they are also a severe hazard to a PJ hanging from the end of a thin cable. Modern ship masts are not the smooth timber poles that graced the decks of the wooden sailing ships of yore. They are made of steel with struts and metal crosspieces welded onto their surface. With the ship rising and falling on the waves I had to take care not to get dragged across the mast and its metal rungs and girders. On a previous mission one of my men Rogo Sheppard was lowering to a deck when the ship's mast swung menacingly towards the helicopter. The pilot instinctively jerked the aircraft to the side to avoid a collision and in the process whipped Rogo, who was dangling from the end of the cable, into the mast with its tangled rigging and jutting steel rods. The rising helicopter ripped Rogo up the length of the mast, tearing his survival vest from his body, snapping his ribs, and bloodying his face. The concerned crew hoisted Rogo back into the helicopter to assess his condition and fine tune their plan. Rogo was not to be denied and descended a second time, successfully reaching the ship's deck where he completed his mission and saved a seaman. When he returned to base, we first celebrated with some champagne and dinner, and then checked him into the hospital.

Another bad outcome was for the hoist cable to be caught on a ship's rigging. Imagine a PJ and steel cable snagged on a mast with thousands of tons of ship tossing on the waves, tightening the cable, and threatening to yank the helicopter from the sky. If this situation ever develops the crew can cut the cable with an explosive powered guillotine system. This can save the aircraft and crew, but means almost certain death for the PJ. Every PJ knows that concern for the multiple souls onboard the aircraft outweighs considerations for the single PJ dangling at the end of the cable.

I looked below at the tossing ship, gave the go-ahead signal, and the engineer began to lower me. I could fend off obstacles with my hands if necessary, but I relied on the flight engineer's skill and the pilot's steady hand at the flight controls. For the PJ, the most dangerous part of the hoist operation is landing on the ship's deck. For one thing, the steel deck is usually slippery with water and oil. There is also a matter of timing. The ship is rising and falling on the waves. While the ship's deck is rising the engineer has to be careful he doesn't lower the PJ too fast. The PJ has to stay focused with knees slightly bent to maintain footing and absorb the shock of the landing. A mistake can result in a broken leg or spine. This time when I landed I hit the steel deck hard, but kept my balance. The engineer quickly played out a few feet of cable, ensuring enough slack to prevent me from being jerked back off the deck as the ship dipped into the trough of the next wave. I quickly disconnected from the cable, but held on, maintaining control. As the flight engineer reeled in the cable I made sure it did not entangle with the ship's infrastructure. With the cable retrieved, the aircraft flew clear of the ship, and I established radio contact, telling them I'd update them on the situation as soon as possible.

The helicopter orbited the ship in wide circles, waiting for my next radio transmission. Without the whine of the chopper's turbine engines and the blast of the rotor wash it was suddenly quiet on the deck of the ship. A seaman approached and I shook his hand. He led me below deck to the patient. The man looked to be about thirty-five years old and did not speak English. He was very pale and his rapid pulse and respirations indicated he was in shock; he had severe abdominal pain and tenderness. I examined him closely and suspected he had a bleeding ulcer, but I couldn't make a definitive diagnosis. The best thing I could do for him would be to get him on the helicopter, keep him stable, and transport him as quickly as possible to a hospital.

I radioed the helicopter and requested they lower a Stokes litter. The Stokes litter is a metal, basket-type litter that connects to the rescue cable. We use it when a patient is too ill or injured to use a rescue strop. The Lithuanian crew used one of their litters to move the patient topside. The helicopter hovered overhead and tossed me one end of a tagline. A tagline is a two hundred foot length of line used to control and guide rescue devices. The flight engineer attached one end of the tagline to the foot end of the Stokes litter. The helicopter hovered off to one side while the flight engineer carefully lowered the litter. With the aircraft offset and safe from masts, I pulled the litter towards me using my end of the tagline. A firm hold on the tagline also prevented the unweighted litter from spinning in the rotor wash. The cable and litter angled towards me through the air until I finally pulled the litter onto the deck. Next I moved the patient into the litter and secured him with straps. I made sure he was comfortable with ear plugs and eye protection.

I made eye contact with the engineer in the door of the hovering helicopter and gave him the signal to raise the litter. As the litter lifted off the ship's deck and rose towards the helicopter, I guided it with the tagline, keeping it away from the ship's masts and rigging. I watched as the engineer hoisted the litter and patient into the aircraft. Now it was my turn. With the litter safely inside the engineer disconnected it from the cable and lowered the hoist hook. I snapped the hook to my rescue strop and signaled to be raised. I waved to the sailors huddled on the ship's deck as I lifted into the air. While I rose into the crisp salt air I mentally reviewed my medical duties. When I arrived at the door the engineer pulled me into the helicopter and I disconnected from the strop. Recovery complete it was time to focus on my patient. The engineer and I helped the sailor out of the metal litter and onto a more comfortable canvas litter suspended from webbing and brackets in the rear of the aircraft. I strapped him onto the litter so he could not fall off if we hit turbulence. I already had my medical equipment pre-positioned for convenient access and immediately began medical treatment.

During the hours long return trip I accomplished complete medical assessments and treatment, conducting a complete exam and monitoring the patient's vital signs. I started an IV to treat shock and to provide a route to administer medications if necessary. I also had an oxygen unit and placed a constant flow mask on the seaman. My patient was stable and I periodically rechecked his vitals and monitored his condition. Our return flight and refueling went smoothly. An ambulance met us after we landed and I handed over my patient with a written record of medical treatment. The ambulance took him to the hospital, and I later received word that he had survived and would recover.

PJs have successfully rescued thousands of sailors from ships far out at sea. Still, there are a lot of variables and bad things do happen. I lost two PJ friends to disasters during these types of operations. PJ Mark Judy died when his helicopter crashed into the Atlantic Ocean fifty miles off Cape Canaveral, and PJ Rick Smith lost his life when his helicopter ditched after impossible weather prevented aerial refueling. Rick's mission was part of the rescue operation immortalized in the book and movie, "The Perfect Storm." I was thankful our mission was successful. We had a skilled crew and our guardian angels were watching over us.

CHAPTER 8

KHOBAR TOWERS

PARARESCUE CREED
It is my duty as a pararescueman to save life and to aid the injured. I will be prepared at all times to perform my assigned duties quickly and efficiently, placing these duties before personal desires and comforts. These things I do, that others may live.
—*Lieutenant Colonel Richard T. Kight*

IN AUGUST OF 1992 I WAS ASSIGNED TO THE 71ST RESCUE SQUADRON at Patrick Air Force Base. Patrick is located on Florida's east coast, nestled between the cities of Cocoa Beach and Melbourne. Although I had enjoyed my time in Iceland I looked forward to warm weather and different types of rescue missions. My son and I arrived in August and checked into the base hotel. Only a few days later the base commander ordered everyone to evacuate inland due to the imminent arrival of hurricane Andrew. This record storm made landfall in South Florida and was the fourth most intense hurricane to ever strike the United States. Andrew wiped out Homestead and Florida City, caused thirty billion dollars in damage, and killed fifty people, but Patrick Air Force Base was north of the storm and escaped significant damage.

Despite the turmoil caused by Andrew, I eventually settled into my unit and bought a house in Melbourne. I initially worked in the standardization and evaluation shop, but soon took over PJ operations which included scheduling and training functions. We had a lot of great operators on our team, including SMSgt. Bob Lapointe. A Vietnam War hero, Bob was known for his extensive PJ experience and activism. He constantly fought to modernize and expand PJ and air-rescue capabilities. Bob's blunt approach sometimes ruffled feathers and he often found himself in hot water with higher-ups who wanted to stifle the logical path of PJ evolution. Some Vietnam-era flying officers in positions of command stubbornly clung to an antiquated view of a PJ as mere extensions of a rescue helicopter. Bob was one of the visionary PJ leaders who lobbied for more PJ autonomy to increase rescue capabilities. Bob led our first PJ deployment to Southwest Asia and set the tone and tactics for subsequent PJ deployments.

In the 1990s air force rescue units almost exclusively used HH-60 Pave Hawk helicopters. Large rescue units that operated both rescue helicopters and HC-130s had gone the way of the dinosaurs in the latest wave of air force reorganization. The 71st Rescue Squadron was the only active-duty rescue unit that still had large turbo-prop HC-130 aircraft as part of the unit. In January 1993 our unit began to deploy our aircraft, flight crews, and support personnel to King Abdul Azizz Air Base in Daharan, Saudi Arabia. The air force ordered our squadron to the desert to provide a rescue capability to coalition forces deployed in the area. After the first Iraq war the United Nations established no-fly zones in northern and southern Iraq. Surrender terms and U.N. resolutions prohibited Iraqis from operating their combat aircraft in these zones. This limited the amount of military force the Iraqis could visit upon the Kurds and others who revolted against Saddam Hussein. American, British, and French combat jets conducted daily flights over Iraq enforcing the no-fly zones. Iraq remained belligerent and frequently focused targeting radars and and even launching ground-to-air missiles at coalition aircraft. Our rescue unit could recover any friendly pilots who were forced to bail out over Iraq due to mechanical problems or a lucky Iraqi missile strike.

Rescue crews and PJs were excited about the deployments and possible rescue missions. Our squadron flew its own HC-130s to Saudi Arabia. It's a massive undertaking to deploy multiple aircraft and more than a hundred people halfway across the globe. In addition to stuffing our own planes with men and equipment, additional personnel traveled by commercial jet airliners known as "rotators" because they rotated people in and out of

Southeast Asia. Huge C-5 cargo planes, larger than 747 jumbo jets, also transported hundreds of tons of equipment and supplies. American military units constantly practice and prepare for deployments and at a moment's notice can pick up and "move out of Dodge." Very few countries can rapidly project power to anywhere on earth, and none can match the magnitude, speed, efficiency, and finesse of the United States of America.

Our flight route to Saudi Arabia required a two day stop-over in Crete. Crete separates the Aegean and Libyan Seas and is the largest of the Greek islands, measuring 160 miles long by 30 miles wide. In Greek mythology Crete was home to the Minotaur, a half-man and half-bull monster who feasted on human flesh. People have lived on Crete since 6,000 BC, and the island boasts cultural rarities and important archeological digs. Of course the PJs had a very narrow focus of interests: booze, women and food. Our final destination was Saudi Arabia, an Islamic country where alcoholic is banned. To mollify the Saudis, our top military commanders issued "general order number one," prohibiting the import or consumption of alcohol. Anyone caught smuggling booze faced court martial. The Saudis are also very strict on pornography. Under their draconian rules even People magazine is too risqué. By western standards Islamic culture is very oppressive. While in public women must wear black robes that conceal every inch of skin. Male relatives chaperone women wherever they go. In Saudi Arabia it is even against the law for women to drive cars. Religious police called *Muttawa* patrol the streets and enforce Islamic dress codes. They also prevent single men and women from socializing. The *Muttawa* are so strict that they once prevented school girls from escaping a burning building because they had no chaperones and were not wearing head scarves and robes: fifteen young women burned to death. In Saudi Arabia it is virtually impossible for foreigners, and especially infidels—anyone who is not Muslim—to socialize with local women. Among deployed military personnel men outnumber women ten-to-one. For Americans living in Saudi Arabia women are scarce and alcohol is scarcer . . . life is hard. This rest stop on Crete was our last opportunity to kick up our heels, and we planned to make the most of our stay.

After a long and tedious flight on our HC-130 crowded with passengers and cargo, we finally landed at Souda Bay Air Station, Crete. We locked up our plane, boarded buses, and drove to our seaside hotel in Chania, pronounced "hahn-ya." We quickly checked into our rooms, tossed our bags on the bed, and hit the town. We wasted no time in sampling local culture and slugging down Greek ouzo and beer. Our hotel was near the harbor in Old Town, the most beautiful part of the city. Old Town is a maze of winding, narrow streets with interesting and unique bars and restaurants. The nightlife is amazing with bars staying open till daylight.

Old Town still shows scars from World War II and you can still visit the skeletal remains of devastated structures. Our group's first stop was a bombed-out building that had been converted into a restaurant and bar. There was no roof, and the large central dining area was open to the warm Mediterranean breezes. We were surrounded by picturesque ruins and beautiful women, a stimulating combination. The streets bustled with party-goers, barhopping or buying food from street vendors. My favorite street foods were lamb kebabs with fiery chili sauce or shawarmas. A shawarma is a gyro wrap, a Middle-Eastern sandwich made from a combination of meats, such as lamb, chicken or beef. The meat is stacked vertically on a large skewer, and a rotisserie turns the stack in front of an electric burner. The meat is roasted all day and slabs of fat placed in the stack keep the meat juicy. The vendor uses a razor sharp knife to shave off thin slices of meat onto flat bread. Spicy sauces and condiments complete the sandwich. Shawarmas are a staple food, Middle Eastern counterparts of tacos or hamburgers.

As night wore on towards morning, I hung out with PJs Brian Higgins and Pat Harding as we drank our way back towards our hotel. Eventually we gravitated to the beach and stood on ancient sands watching waves roll in. We inhaled the crisp salt air and savored our buzz. In the distance a jagged black rock jutted from the dark water. Surf crashed against it forming geysers of sea spray, silver fountains in the moonlight. Fortified by alcohol, Brian decided he would swim to the rock. Before we could stop him, he stripped off his clothes and bounded into the cold, foamy surf. We drank beer as we followed Brian's progress while he swam towards the rock, a mile distant. Finally, we saw him on top of the rock, waving his arms and leaping around to ensure we took note of his daring accomplishment. When he was sure we had seen him, Brian plunged back into the water for the return swim.

When Brian finally straggled back onto the beach he was nearly frozen.

He was so cold, his shivering reflex had shut down and his penis had shrunk to nothing. At first I thought a hungry fish had ended his sex life. He looked like a cross between a naked Ken doll and a bedraggled department store manikin. We draped Brian's arms around our necks and carried him to his room and placed him in a hot shower. He eventually warmed, recovering his senses and regrowing his penis; a lesser man would have died. We made the most of our time on Crete, partying till we puked, and spending most of our money on whiskey and women—the rest we wasted.

After a couple of days we left Crete and finished our journey, finally landing in Saudi Arabia. After several years of deployments to Saudi Arabia our squadron was deeply integrated into the structure of the expeditionary group. We kept aircraft and aircrews on rescue alert twenty four hours a day. Our tours of duty lasted three months, after which our home unit back in Florida sent fresh crews to replace us. We referred to these ninety day stints in the desert as "rotations." Each member of our unit could expect to spend two rotations, or half of each year in Saudi Arabia. Rescue forces were designated as low density/high demand (LDHD) forces. Translated, LDHD means there is a *small number* (low density) of operators with special skills, such as PJs, that many generals want to have under their command (high demand). LDHD units spend more time deployed than regular forces because there are not as many people to share the burden. Our unit was deployed almost constantly with the Arabian Desert our home away from home.

Our rescue squadron was not the only military unit based at Daharan; we were only a small part of a very large operation. At any one time, there were literally thousands of American airmen and soldiers working there. An entire air base had been created in Daharan complete with dining and recreation facilities, transportation, communication, supply, and administrative offices. There were large numbers of military aircraft on base along with the mechanics and equipment needed to keep them flying. It was a coalition of forces from numerous countries including Britain and France. There were also battalions of U.S. Army Patriot missile air defense artillery.

All of the coalition servicemen lived just outside the air base in Khobar Towers, a semi-modern apartment complex consisting of approximately fifty high-rise buildings. Rumor had it that the Saudis originally built the apartments to entice Bedouins to settle there, but the tribes preferred their tents and nomadic way of life and refused to move into the city. During operations Desert Shield and Desert Storm the Saudi government decided the vacant apartments were the perfect place to house thousands of coalition airmen. The buildings were four to eight stories high with three suites of rooms on each floor. Each suite had a living room, kitchen and four bedrooms. Between the buildings were volleyball courts, barbecue grills, and the occasional above-ground swimming pool. The Saudis employed workers from the Philippines and Pakistan to maintain the grounds.

Concrete jersey barriers and steel fencing topped with razor wire surrounded the rectangular shaped compound and isolated Khobar Towers from the local community. Just inside the barriers was a narrow, mile long road that ran around the perimeter of the complex. At night regularly spaced sodium street lamps illuminated the road with glaring yellow light. Military police continuously patrolled the perimeter in humvees mounted with .50-caliber machine guns; security was tight. There was only one entrance into the compound, and it was heavily guarded and fortified. Anyone wishing to enter Khobar Towers had to slow their vehicle to a crawl in order to negotiate a maze of concrete obstacles. Armed guards with military working dogs checked identification cards and carefully inspected each vehicle entering the compound. They used mirrors attached to long poles to examine the undersides of vehicles for bombs.

Our rescue unit shared building 133R with another squadron from Hurlburt Field, Florida. Our building was located adjacent to the perimeter road on the northeast corner of the Khobar Towers compound. It was eight stories high with two elevators and a stairwell. Our seven man PJ team lived on the fourth floor in two suites. Each living room had sliding glass doors that opened onto a small balcony. Our balconies overlooked a Saudi park on the other side of the jersey barriers and security fence. The building was only twenty yards from the park, the width of the concrete barriers and road that encircled our compound.

For the past three years numerous rotations of PJs had continuously occupied the fourth floor suites. Over the years each PJ team made their unique contributions to the décor of the rooms. Inexpensive throw rugs with oriental designs covered the marble floors, and maps, photographs, bulletin boards, and paintings decorated the walls. One wall sported a large hand-painted mural of the pararescue emblem and motto, "That Others

May Live." We proudly displayed a large American flag and a black and white POW/MIA flag on another wall. Each PJ had his own small room with a bed and dresser. The suites were furnished with plenty of old furniture and a TV and VCR in the living room. In one suite, we built a planning room complete with computers, tables and wall-maps. Deployments are always a hardship, but life at Khobar was much more comfortable than living in a tent.

During this rotation to the desert I was the senior PJ in charge of six others. Since I began deploying to Saudi Arabia in 1993, I had spent about a year total in Khobar and was very familiar with the daily routine and typical range of rescue missions. Some of my teammates were fresh out of the PJ school and this was their first desert rotation. For two weeks we overlapped with the team we were replacing. During this "hand-off" we spent much of our time configuring our gear and training on our radios, weapons, and rescue procedures. We attended intelligence briefings and rigged our aircraft for parachute operations. We practiced navigation, map analysis, parachute jumps and desert survival and rehearsed realistic mission simulations. We kept our medical skills honed by working shifts in the clinic, and many of the flight surgeons and medical technicians became familiar with our faces and medical capabilities. When my team was ready to assume rescue alert responsibilities, the other PJ team returned home to their families.

Saudi Arabia is ridiculously hot in the summer. During the day temperatures often soared to a blistering 115 degrees Fahrenheit. The runway baked under a searing sun, and heat waves rose from the tarmac roiling the air. Occasional sand storms assaulted the airfield making it impossible to see and forcing everyone to take shelter so they could breathe. Daharan is located on the coast and high humidity multiplied the effects of the heat. Off duty entertainment was very limited: there was a recreation center with pool tables, dart boards, and a place to rent movies, but women were scarce and alcoholic beverages were banned. Despite decent living conditions, we were still separated from our families. A deployment to Khobar was a hardship tour.

To boost morale leadership occasionally granted us passes to travel a few miles off the coast to Bahrain. Bahrain, its name means two seas, is a small island country of a little under three hundred square miles and is connected to Saudi Arabia by a man-made causeway. Bahrain is famous for its pearls and oil reserves, and some claim it was the original site of the Garden of Eden. Bahrain has a Formula One race track, a drag strip, and one of the largest water parks in the world. Bahrain is a Muslim country but manages to balance western and Arab traditions.

Alcohol is legal in Bahrain and there are many large hotels that cater to tourists. My crew chose to party in the Gulf Hotel, drinking pints of Guinness in the Sherlock Holmes pub and smoking expensive Cuban cigars. Many of the pub's patrons were Arabs. To my surprise, they seemed to ignore the Islamic restrictions against alcohol. During one of my excursions to the pub I gulped down a few pints of beer and made my way to the restroom. I stared straight ahead as I relieved myself at the urinal. A huge Arab dressed in a white, Kaftan-style robe and red-checked headgear stood next to me. He was sinister looking, with dark eyes, a bushy black beard, and huge flowing mustaches. While I was in midstream he scowled at me and said, "Beer just goes right through you, doesn't it?" I was totally caught by surprise.

He spoke perfect English and we continued our conversation back in the bar where he bought us all drinks. He'd attended college in the United States and was a mechanical engineer. He was very thankful for the American military action against Iraq. He said that if it wasn't for America he thought Iraq would have invaded the kingdom. I had similar encounters whenever I visited that pub—so much for stereotypes. I don't know if it is a hundred percent true, but I heard that Saudis think that when they're outside the Kingdom they are invisible to Allah and can get away with having a few beers. The Saudis I met in Bahrain were not religious fanatics; they were more like Americans who go to church on Sunday, but stray a bit during the week. From my conversations with Arabs in Bahrain, I gather that many Saudis also engage in amateur home brewing and wine making.

In Daharan we occasionally drove downtown and shopped for souvenirs in one of the many markets. Twenty-two carat gold jewelry is relatively inexpensive, and intricately designed silk and wool carpets are fantastic bargains. The malls are very modern and even have American hamburger stands. There was a lot to do, but by far the most popular pastime at Khobar was exercise. Many people jogged in the evening when temperatures dipped below a hundred degrees, and there was an excellent gym with state-of-the-art exercise machines and barbells. Everyone developed a routine and each day was pretty much the same as the day before.

25 JUNE 1996, KHOBAR TOWERS, SAUDI ARABIA

The PJs:
>Master Sergeant Bill Sine
>Staff Sergeant Matt Wells
>Senior Airman Mike Atkins
>Senior Airman Greg Randall
>Senior Airman Rich Dixon
>Senior Airman Dan Williamson
>Senior Airman Eric Castor

The day started off just like every other day: breakfast in the dining hall, routine work and training, blazing sun and scorching heat. Early that evening I drove to town with a couple of friends. We ate dinner and shopped for bargains. When we returned to the compound, I changed into my gym clothes and went for a three-mile run around the perimeter road. Afterwards, I went up to my room to cool down before going to the gym to lift weights. I took the elevator to my fourth-floor suite and slumped into an overstuffed chair set in front of sliding glass doors that led out onto our balcony. I drank some water, watched TV, and enjoyed the air conditioning. A few minutes before ten o'clock, I dragged myself off my chair and got up to go to the gym. As I left, I saw my teammate Eric Castor working at the computer in the common room. "I'll see you later. I'm going to the gym." I told him. I felt no premonition of danger.

Shutting the door to the suite behind me I walked towards the elevator. After only a few steps I heard a muffled boom; then a battering ram of debris pounded into my back. In the split second before the blast slammed me to the floor, I realized that a bomb had exploded outside my building. Instinctively, I thrust out my arms to break my fall as the shock wave smashed me face first onto the unyielding marble floor.

I lay on my stomach in the darkness: it was black as a cave. The palms of my hands stung from slapping the tile floor when I was knocked down. My body felt numb and tingly, as if I had received a powerful electric shock.

That strange sensation flashed me back to a Fourth of July incident in my childhood. A cherry-bomb firecracker had exploded too near my hand and my fingers had felt this same electric, paralyzed sensation. This time not only my hand, but my whole body felt numb and vibrating. I moved my limbs experimentally; my right arm and leg throbbed painfully with mysterious, unknown injuries. When I moved my arms and legs I didn't feel any bones grating together—at least I didn't have any compound fractures. I ran my hands over myself in the dark. Parts of my body felt wet, "*Could that be blood?*" I thought. I wanted to look at my injuries to see how badly I was hurt, but it was too dark to see. The silence was thick and oppressive, and my ears were ringing. I thought I heard human voices, but they sounded faint and far away. I called out, "Can anyone hear me?" My voice sounded dry and cracked, and ridiculously loud. There was no answer. The silence was eerie. The only sound was the occasional tinkle of falling glass and the dull scrape of stone on stone as rubble shifted and settled. Dust floated thickly and I craved cool fresh air. I tried to push myself to my hands and knees and discovered that I was pinned beneath debris, imprisoned by rubble, and I experienced a moment of panic in the stifling heat. With a frenzied burst of activity I frantically struggled to free myself. Rough stone scraped my skin, but I finally staggered to my feet.

I had an overwhelming desire to look at my injuries to see how badly I was hurt, but there was no light. I resolved to escape the building and groped my way in the dark past the twisted elevator doors to the stairway. Grabbing onto the handrail I began to descend. The marble stairway was an obstacle course of jumbled and broken stone. I was limping badly on my injured leg, and my right arm throbbed; I felt like Quasimodo. Time felt distorted and slow. It seemed like I had been picking my way down the stairwell for a ridiculously long time. Something was wrong. I thought I had traveled down enough flights of stairs to reach the ground floor and the exit, but I was still lost in a dark limbo. I was confused and shouted into the darkness, "Have I gone too far? Is this the basement or the ground floor?" There was no answer. Then I remembered that there *was* no basement in this building! How could I have forgotten that? On and off, I had lived at least a year in this building. I resolved to continue down the never-ending steps. I struggled through the broken marble slabs for what seemed forever and finally stumbled onto the ground floor.

Pale yellow light streamed feebly through broken lobby doors and I could feel a faint breeze on my face. Even though it was a hundred degrees outside the air felt cool and delicious. I hobbled out of the ravaged foyer onto the sand courtyard and quickly looked myself over. The muscles of both my calf and my forearm looked weird, crushed and twisted. I wondered why the muscles hadn't popped back into their normal shape. My damaged limbs pained me, but at least I could still use them. I had a lot of cuts and abrasions, but didn't find any squirting arterial bleeding. My back hurt and it was hard to move, but at least I *could* move. Overall, I thought I was in good shape—I would live.

I heard someone calling for help. I scanned the surrounding area and saw a man lying motionless on the ground, about fifty feet away. I went over to him and asked him what was wrong. He had been outside when the bomb exploded and the blast had flung him through the air. He was scared and disoriented and told me he couldn't move his legs. He was afraid he was paralyzed for life. I examined his injuries and checked his spine, but I couldn't find any physical reason for his paralysis. Although he couldn't move his legs he could feel me squeeze his toes. I told him I thought his condition was temporary, probably caused by the shock wave from the bomb and reassured him he would recover the use of his legs. I saw two people approaching, and motioned them over. I told them that I had a person who couldn't walk and asked them if they could get a litter and some people to help carry the man to the clinic. They jogged off towards the clinic and I reassured the injured man telling him more help would soon arrive.

I turned back towards the building and spotted Mike Atkins, one of my PJ teammates, rounding the corner. Mike looked like he had only just now stumbled out of the building. He was covered in dust and bled from numerous cuts and scrapes: he looked like hell. He kept one hand pressed to the side of his head and blood trickled from beneath his palm and dripped down the side of his face. I intercepted him by the entrance to the building, "What the hell happened?" he asked. "Obviously, a bomb went off!" I joked. Mike was taken aback by my flippant response. I laughed at the expression on his face, "What happened to you?" I asked. Mike told me he had just walked into his bathroom when the bomb exploded and he had been crushed pretty hard. He thought he might even have fallen through to the floor below. A large spear of wood impaled his calf and shrapnel had sliced him in numerous places. A spray of glass shards pierced his muscles and would take months to find and remove.

Mike and I decided to walk to a central area to get an overall view of the scene. Although our building had absorbed the brunt of the explosion the adjacent buildings were also severely damaged. For the first time I looked around and realized the full extent of the carnage. Suddenly, the whole panorama zoomed into focus; people were staggering out of ravaged buildings, many of them bleeding and ripped-up by shattered masonry; victims were screaming and crying out for help; a lot of people had been sliced by flying glass from the hundreds of glass windows and sliding patio doors. It was pure pandemonium, a scene from a Hieronymus Bosch painting—. There were so many wounded it was hard to know where to start helping. We spotted Darcy, a medical technician whom we knew from the clinic. She knelt over a wounded man, bandaging his leg. We walked up to her, and I said something brainless like, "Hey Darcy, how's it going?" She looked at me quizzically and turned back to what she was doing. I shrugged, and Mike and I started to walk the short distance back to our building. We must have looked a mess, covered with dirt and blood.

Looking back on these surreal events, I now realize that I must have suffered a concussion. During my escape from the building, I thought I had descended too far and was in the basement, later remembering there was no basement. My inappropriate greeting to Darcy was further evidence of my confused mental state. But the most puzzling aspect of my behavior was that I had totally forgotten about Eric, who had been in our suite during the attack. Eric was at ground zero and must have taken the full force of the explosion. Unbelievably, up until this moment, Eric's fate had never crossed my mind. I suddenly realized that there still could be other teammates and friends trapped and dying inside building 133.

As Mike and I limped back towards our building, it was as if God suddenly lifted a veil from my eyes. I must have been recovering from my concussion. I stopped and grabbed Mike by the arm. "Mike! We have to go back in the building. Eric's still in there!" I quickly explained that Eric was in the suite working, only seconds before the explosion and there were probably other people trapped inside. My revelation seemed to galvanize Mike, who was badly beaten up and also suffering from a concussion. With an urgent sense of purpose we determined to search our building.

When we arrived at the entrance of the building, we found a security policeman on guard who wouldn't let us inside. He could see we were injured and insisted we go to the casualty collection point. He said it was too dangerous for all but rescue personnel to enter the building. There was no way Mike and I were going let this cop stop us from entering the building. We knew that a few minutes could mean the difference between life and death for our friends. I told the cop that we *were* the rescue personnel! We were PJs and we would not let him stop us from going inside. He was taken aback by our confident aggression and quickly stepped out of our way. I added a symbolic exclamation point to our demands when I grabbed his flashlight. He didn't object. Mike and I must have been a pretty scary sight.

We picked our way through the debris on the stairway and made our way up to the fourth floor. The door to our suite, and portions of the wall were missing. The entire front of our building was gone, and we looked down on the Saudi park and huge bomb crater. It didn't take long to search for Eric, because there was nothing left of our rooms. Even the floor was gone, collapsed down to the levels below. I felt a sick feeling in the pit of my stomach. It seemed like there was no possibility that Eric could have survived. The room where I had last seen him was gone. The grim implications of our failed search for Eric went unspoken: he was probably dead. Mike and I were stunned.

I heard some noise from the stairwell and moved to investigate. I was surprised and relieved to discover two of my PJ teammates SSgt. Matt Wells and Amn. Greg Randall. Matt told us that when the bomb exploded he and Greg had been in the center of the compound exercising at the gym with airmen Rich Dixon and Dan Williamson. The blast blew the mirrors off the walls, but the structure survived and they were unhurt. When my PJs left the gym, they saw hundreds of injured people streaming out of buildings in chaos and confusion. Their PJ training kicked in and they began directing people to an open area between the clinic and dining hall, establishing a casualty collection point. Airmen Dixon and Williams stayed at the collection point to help the doctors and medical technicians deal with the overwhelming numbers of wounded. They saw Eric Castor brought into the collection point white as a sheet from loss of blood, but

Postmission: PJs who made the night jump in Afghanistan to rescue an Australian SAS trooper, from left to right: Randall Cunningham, Rich Carrol, and Bill Sine.

Author Bill Sine in front of Kandahar, Afghanistan, airport.

Military and civilian applicants taking part in the 306th Rescue Squadron pararescue screening hoist a wooden log while lying in a mud pit at Davis-Monthan AFB, Arizona, on 21 April 2006. Applicants must pass a timed 3-mile run, 1,500-meter swim, calisthenics and other tasks before proceeding to the pararescue indoctrination course at Lackland AFB, Texas.—*Airman 1st Class Veronica Pierce (USAF), af.mil*

Staff Sergeant Chris Uriarte monitors pararescue applicants during a push-up exercise. Sergeant Uriarte is a pararescueman with the 306th Rescue Squadron.
—*Airman 1st Class Veronica Pierce (USAF), af.mil*

Pararescue applicants simulate a freefall in a mud pit during screening.
—*Airman 1st Class Veronica Pierce (USAF), af.mil*

Airman Basic Matthew Bernard and other pararescue trainees endure water-filled masks while performing more than a thousand flutter kicks The airmen had already completed twenty hours of nonstop physical training during their extended training day at the pararescue indoctrination course. The ten-week course is the first hurdle of intense physical and mental training for pararescue hopefuls. It prepares them for the twelve to fifteen months of extreme training they must pass to become Air Force pararescuemen.
—*Tech Sergeant Cecilio M. Ricardo Jr. (USAF), af.mil*

Airman 1st Class Brian Pajor treads water with 16-pound weights on his belt during pararescue indoctrination training.
—*Tech Sergeant Cecilio M. Ricardo Jr. (USAF), af.mil*

Students recover after completing a 40-meter underwater swim in the pararescue indoctrination course.
—*Robbin Cresswell, af.mil*

Hell Week: Airmen "stack up" in a pond during the Air Force Pararescuemen Indoctrination Course. During Hell Week airmen simulate a real-world mission involving air, ground, and water survival.
—*Staff Sergeant Vernon Young Jr. (USAF), af.mil*

Bill Sine as a goodwill ambassador in Korea.

Airman 1st Class Kevin Freyre carries Airman 1st Class Nathan Greene to safety at a simulated helicopter crash scene after performing self-aid and buddy-care techniques during a mass-casualty incident exercise at Kirtland AFB, New Mexico. The exercise is part of the pararescue recovery specialist course.—*Tech Sergeant Cecilio Ricardo Jr. (USAF), af.mil*

PJs who participated in recovery mission in Ethiopia, from left to right: Ken Bollinger, Mike Fleming, Bill Sine, Mike Grahm, Maurice Sweet, Jerry Sowles, Rick Weaver, and Scott Copper.

Right: An HH-60G Pave Hawk helicopter from the 64th Expeditionary Rescue Squadron comes to pickup pararescuemen in Iraq.
—*Staff Sgt. Aaron Allmon II (USAF), af.mil*

Below: Pararescuemen from the 304th Rescue Squadron are hoisted up to an HH-60G in Iraq.
—*Staff Sergeant Shane A. Cuomo (USAF), af.mil*

Tech Sergeant Sean Pellaton guides SSgt. Adam Vanhaaster and his patient into a Pave Hawk rescue helicopter on 4 February 2012, two hundred miles off the coast of California. When a 54-year-old male suffered stroke-like symptoms aboard the cargo ship MSC *Beijing,* air national guardsmen with the 129th Rescue Wing provided medical assistance and airlifted the patient to the San Jose Regional Medical Center in San Jose, California. Pellaton is an aerial gunner assigned to the 129th Rescue Squadron and Vanhaaster is a pararescueman assigned to the 131st Rescue Squadron. Both squadrons and the wing are at Moffett Federal Airfield, California.—*Senior Airman Jessica Green (USAF), af.mil*

Pararescueman SSgt. Bill Cenna (212th Rescue Squadron) prepares to move a patient on a litter while an HH-60G lands during training on 21 September 2011 at Joint Base Elmendorf-Richardson, Alaska. The training focused on quick-care under fire and also gave training to Baker Company, 3rd Platoon, 509th Infantry Regiment (Airborne) on how to react when pararescuemen arrive.
—*Staff Sergeant Zachary Wolf (USAF), af.mil*

Airmen from the 346th and 342nd Training Squadrons perform a high-altitude, low-opening (HALO) parachute jump over Lackland AFB, Texas. The proficiency training exercise had combat controllers and pararescuemen exiting the aircraft at 9,500 feet, traveling at 130 knots, and landing on a precise target at the drop zone.—*Master Sergeant Lance S. Cheung (USAF), af.mil*

Pararescuemen jump from a HC-130P/N for a HALO freefall drop from 12,999 feet over Iraq. The Airmen are assigned to the 38th Rescue Squadron and the 58th Rescue Squadron from Nellis AFB, Nev. The HC-130P/N "King" is the only dedicated fixed-wing personnel recovery aircraft in the USAF inventory.—*Staff Sergeant Jeremy T. Lock (USAF), af.mil*

PJs over Afghanistan: The extreme terrain and altitude of much of the country make it a very difficult operating environment.

Right: Staff Sergeant William Lawson, a pararescueman with the 129th Expeditionary Rescue Squadron, keeps an eye on the countryside as he cares for a wounded Afghan National Army soldier from Hemland Province, Afghanistan. *—Staff Sergeant Shawn Weismiller (USAF), af.mil*

Below: Pararescuemen of the 66th Expeditionary Rescue Squadron provide medical attention to an Afghan who has suffered gunshot injuries. PJs are able to rescue patients who need medical attention from virtually any situation. *—Staff Sergeant Angelita Lawrence (USAF), af.mil*

Air Force pararescuemen flank Astronauts Neil A. Armstrong and David R. Scott, sitting in the Gemini 8 space craft, while awaiting the arrival of the recovery ship, the USS *Leonard F. Mason* after splashdown in the Pacific Ocean March 16, 1966, in the Philippine Sea. PJs have a long history of supporting NASA activities.—*NASA, af.mil*

Air Force Reserve Command's 920th Rescue Wing pararescuemen prepare to position an inflatable flotation collar around a mockup of the Orion four-astronaut space capsule during recovery testing on 8 April 2009 near Cape Canaveral Air Force Station, Florida. The collar stabilizes the capsule after water landing and provides a platform for recovery personnel to stand on. The Orion was part of the now-cancelled Constellation program that had been the follow on to the Space Shuttle.—*Tech Sergeant Paul Flipse (USAF), af.mil*

The facade of the undamaged side of the severely bomb damaged building in the Khobar Towers complex. The explosion of a fuel truck set off by terrorists at 2:55 p.m. EDT, Tuesday, June 25, 1996, outside the northern fence of the Khobar Towers complex near King Abdul Aziz Air Base, killed 19 and injured over 260. The facility housed U.S. armed forces personnel and served as the headquarters for the 4404th Wing (Provisional), Southwest Asia.—*Senior Airman Sean Worrell (USAF), defenseimagery.mil*

An overall view of the north side of the building that was severely bomb damaged in the Khobar Towers complex.—*Senior Airman Sean Worrell (USAF), defenseimagery.mil*

A close-up of the PJs' suite on the fifth floor of Building 133.

The PJs of Khobar Towers: Willy Williamson, Rich Dixon, Eric Castor, Mike Atkins, Mat Wells, Bill Sine, and Greg Randall.

The bomb crater in front of the severely bomb-damaged north side of Building 133.
—Senior Airman Sean Worrell (USAF), defenseimagery.mil

PJs fast rope from a HH-60G.

The PJs's office: Inside a Pave Hawk's cramped interior.

Right: PJs prepare a Stokes litter for raising.

Above: PJs Matt White (left) and Rob Disney (right) in front of their crashed helicopter.

Right: Rob Disney after being shot through the face.

Above: Dan Houghton front and center, back row left to right: Chris Trisko, Matt Leigh, Tim Brauch.

Left: Remains of helicopter in which PJ Dan Houghton was riding.

Below: Airmen flying a Pave Hawk during a pararescue training mission perform a brown-out landing during a training mission at Bagram Airfield, Afghanistan. The pararescuemen are assigned to the 33rd Expeditionary Rescue Squadron. Due to the thick dust in many areas of Afghanistan, helicopter takeoffs and landings from unimproved positions, particularly at night, can be very hazardous.—*Staff Sergeant Christopher Boitz (USAF), af.mil*

PJs Bill Cenna and Zack Kline.

Bill Cenna next to crashed U.S. Army Kiowa helicopter during a recovery mission with Zack Kline in Afghanistan.

Under fire: Zack Kline during the Kiowa recovery mission with Bill Cenna in background.

The author with his son Billy.

Staff Sergeant William D. Sine is a reconnaissance specialist in the Marine Corps.

Author Bill Sine with his wife Debra.

alive and conscious. I could not fathom how Eric escaped the building without me seeing him. The answer would have to come later.

We started to methodically search our building and almost immediately found two of our squadron mates sprawled in the stairwell between the fifth and sixth floors. Greg and I stayed to attend to them while the others continued upward to look for more survivors. One of the men appeared to be badly injured and was only semi-conscious. He was lying on his stomach and replied groggily to my questions as I examined him. We discovered he was bleeding heavily from a badly lacerated arm. I took off my tee shirt and used it to bandage his arm and stop the bleeding. The other man was disoriented. We examined him but couldn't find any obvious external injuries, but he appeared to have a fractured pelvis and internal injuries; very serious injuries.

Greg and I carried the victims out of the building and placed them by a nearby picnic table. We went back into the building to look for more survivors and met Mat Wells coming down the stairwell with more injured people. Greg and I helped the additional victims out of the building and put them with the other injured. Greg went to help search for more wounded people in the building, and I realized I needed to start treating some of the people we had pulled from the high-rise. As my friends brought down more maimed and wounded comrades I started to realize the full extent of the damage and the gruesome injuries the bomb caused throughout the building. I also received the dreaded news that some of our friends were killed in the blast.

Our Humvee was parked a short distance away from the building and sustained heavy damage, but our medical kits survived. We retrieved the kits, which each contained about forty pounds of medical supplies. I dug into my medical kit and began treating people with the most serious injuries. The next hours were a blur of punctures, lacerations, and squirting blood. I focused on stopping serious bleeding, bandaging wounds, and splinting fractures. Flying glass and debris from the explosion caused horrendous injuries. I worked on one man whose legs were shredded by flying glass. It was as if glass shards had scooped out holes in his flesh. His legs were covered with shallow wounds, like small potholes filled with blood. Luckily no arteries were cut, and I was able to stem the flow of blood with pressure bandages. Semi-conscious, he moaned as I covered the wounds with gauze and wrapped elastic bandages around his legs, tightening them until the bleeding stopped. Early on all of our uninjured squadron mates arrived and clamored to help. They were a godsend! They scrounged pole litters and blankets and provided desperately needed manpower. When I finished treating a patient they moved him onto a litter and carried him to the casualty collection point to get more definitive medical care. It was an amazing team effort. We had never practiced this scenario, but we naturally organized using common sense and compassion to get the job done. My squadron mates were awesome!

While I was bandaging a man's wound, Mike Atkins walked up, and asked if I could take a quick look at a cut on his head. He was still pressing a shirt to the side of his skull, but blood continued to stream down his face. He told me blood in his eyes was hindering his efforts to function and help people. When he removed his makeshift pressure dressing, blood squirted from a dime-sized hole in his temple. Blood pulsed from the wound in time to the beating of Mike's heart. He had obviously severed his temporal artery, a serious life threatening injury. I pressed a whole roll of fluffy gauze over the wound and wrapped an elastic bandage very tightly around his head. When I finished, Mike wiped residual blood from his eyes, waited for a few seconds, and when he realized the bleeding was finally stopped he nodded his head as if thinking, "All right! Now I can get back to business!" He thanked me, grabbed the other medical kit, and took off. Despite his impaled calf and bandaged head, Mike continued to carry people from damaged buildings until there was no one left to rescue. Then he treated patients at the casualty collection point until the doctors stopped him. When the doctors finally got around to examining Mike and removed my bandage from his head, blood started to pump from the wound. Surgeons had to sew his temporal artery back together to staunch the flow of blood once and for all.

After taking care of Mike, I went back to work treating other wounded; they were scattered around me awaiting their turn. I would bandage a patient and others would cart them off on a litter. I felt like I was inside a dream; nothing seemed real. I don't know how long I worked on patients near the building, but suddenly I looked around and there were no more people to treat. With no more patients to treat my adrenaline wore off and I felt myself mentally and physically slump. My injuries were stiff and agonizing, and I could hardly walk. For a time, two security policemen supported me between them and carried me over to wounded airmen who needed medical attention. They carried me from one wounded person to another until my medical supplies were exhausted. Finally, the cops took me to the casualty collection point.

There were hundreds of wounded people milling about at the casualty collection point. Doctors worked on patients with the most serious injuries while those with less critical wounds stoically huddled on the ground and waited their turn. When the doctors finished working on someone, volunteers would place them on a litter and carry them to an awaiting ambulance. Hours had passed since the explosion and all of the really critical patients had been evacuated to local hospitals. My PJs had set up a secondary clinic in the dining hall to handle overflow, treating minor injuries and stitching lacerations. I felt emotionally poured out and empty and sat in a daze among the press of injured people awaiting treatment and evacuation. Word spread that I was a PJ and soon I was once again helping to treat some of the wounded around me. Good Samaritans carried me over to a man whose leg was badly cut. No one had been able to stop the bleeding, so I took care of it and helped treat other wounded airmen as best as I could. Eventually it was my turn for treatment and Dan Williams, one of my own PJs, splinted my arm and leg and loaded me onto an ambulance.

When I arrived at the Saudi hospital, doctors x-rayed my injured limbs and determined I had no broken bones. I was taken to a room and plopped exhausted onto a bed. I was filthy and drained from the day's ordeal. My arm and leg were badly swollen and throbbed painfully; I had no pain medication. I was also covered with minor cuts and bruises. Despite my pain and the lack of medicine, I immediately fell into a dreamless sleep. Very early in the morning I was awakened by the sound of someone moving in my room. A slightly built, swarthy man nervously approached the foot of my bed. He told me he was a reporter for the Associated Press out of Bahrain. I asked him how he had gotten into the hospital, and he told me he had approval from the staff. He asked me questions and I briefly told him about some of my personal experiences of the previous night. I was groggy and still suffered effects from the bomb blast and cut short his questioning. After he left I examined my surroundings and discovered I shared the room with a few other injured Americans. I dropped off to sleep, not realizing, that the reporter's story would be the first to hit the wire.

A phone ringing near my bed woke me up. When I answered, there was someone on the other end asking for me by name. It was a London affiliate of the Today Show. They had read the Associated Press story and tracked me down. I was amazed, because I didn't know the name of my hospital or even what city I was in and no officials from the base had yet visited. The *Today Show* wanted to interview me over the phone. I felt uneasy and told them they had to clear it through air force public affairs. A few minutes later the news hounds called again and connected me to a representative from air force public affairs who told me I could do the interview. They cautioned me to talk only about my personal experiences and to avoid making statements about policy. "Are you satisfied?" the reporter on the phone asked. "Yes," I replied

The voice from London continued, "I'm going to connect you to the *Today Show* and someone will explain things to you." Soon I was talking to a man who gave me instructions. I could hear the TV show in the background. He told me to listen for my name, and shortly after I heard my name mentioned, I would be talking to the host Bryant Gumbel. I listened to the show over the phone and heard them lead into my interview. Suddenly, I was talking to Bryant Gumbel, answering his questions.

Gumbel: "On the phone with us now is MSgt. William Sine of Warren, Ohio. Following yesterday's blast, he's in a hospital bed at King Fahd Hospital in Daharan. Sergeant Sine, good morning."

Sine: "Good morning."

Gumbel: "First of all sir, how are you and what's the extent of your injuries?"

Sine: "I have just minor injuries, no broken bones, cuts, bruises, so forth."

Gumbel: "Talk to us about what happened last night. Where were you when the blast went off?"

Sine: "I was in the building closest to the blast. I was thrown onto the floor and the power went out; it was dark. After I struggled out of the building, I went back in to search for people and the whole side of the building was gone."

Gumbel: "How much general panic was there, Sergeant Sine following the blast?"

Sine: "I wouldn't say it was panic. People were trying to find their way in the dark. They were calling out, other people were answering. Initial reaction was just to make our way outside the building and once we did, we got our bearings and then a lot of us went back in to try and find other people to bring out."

Gumbel: "Was there adequate rescue and medical assistance at hand?"

Sine: "Yes, that portion of it went really well. Everyone in the compound pitched in, all the injured personnel were moved to a central area and prioritized and evacuated to the various hospitals."

Gumbel: "Since the blast, we've since been made aware that there were threats made against the U.S. facility prior to the blast. Were you aware of such threats?"

Sine: "Not personally. There was heightened security. It was really good, tight security on the compound. There was a danger, but nothing specific."

Gumbel: "What can you tell us about the attitude in and around the base and the hospital now, in the wake of this blast?"

Sine: "Everyone has a pretty good attitude. A lot of people just want to get back to work and . . . I think with a little further increase in security, everything will be fine there."

Gumbel: "Master Sergeant William Sine, as we say thank you, anybody at home you want to say hello too?"

Sine: "Yes, I have a son named Billy and he's staying with my father right now in Melbourne Florida, and also my mother in Warren, Ohio."

Gumbel: "I'm sure they're glad to hear you're well. Sergeant Sine, thank you very much sir, appreciate it."

Sine: "OK. Bye."

I hoped my parents would hear about the interview and know I was OK, but my role as an interviewee was far from over. After my appearance on the *Today Show*, the phone started ringing off the hook with various radio and TV shows wanting to conduct interviews. One radio station in Cleveland hooked me up on a conference call with my mother, and another station in Florida let me talk with my father and son. I don't remember how many people I talked too, but eventually the phone stopped ringing.

The next afternoon, we started getting visits from base officials and, at one point, some high ranking Saudi dignitaries came and expressed their remorse for the tragedy. My injuries were very painful: my calf was swollen to twice its normal size, my lower back was injured, I had six broken ribs, and bruises covered my back and legs from when the blast sent rubble crashing into my back. I was finally getting pain medication and I wanted to return to the base and reunite with my team. The hospital wanted to keep me for one more day before releasing me back to the U.S. base. An air force representative told me that once I returned to the base, I was going to be evacuated, along with my teammate Eric Castor and other victims, to a military hospital in Germany.

The next day, an ambulance took me to a large hangar on the air force base. The interior was crowded with injured airmen awaiting evacuation, well-wishers, and medical personnel. Later that day I would board a hospital plane and fly to Germany. It was nearly impossible for me to walk, so I was on a litter. All my teammates arrived, and they congregated around Eric and me. I looked around. All the PJs had survived, but nineteen other airmen had not. Five of our friends and squadron mates had been killed. Everyone was sad and dejected. I knew that our team had made huge contributions in the immediate aftermath of the attack. They should be proud of the way they performed.

I gathered them together. They knew many of the men who were killed, yet they had maintained their composure and used all their training, saving lives practically around the clock. These guys were young, and I knew they felt conflicted. Many of them had only recently graduated from PJ School and had never been on a rescue mission. They were feeling intense conflicting emotions, grief for the dead, but also the pride and satisfaction of saving lives and performing perfectly under pressure. As PJs, they had survived their baptism by fire and now knew they had the right stuff. Some were probably feeling guilty about feeling good about themselves, especially amid all the sadness and death. I needed to change that; I needed to get their minds right. "I know many people were killed, some of them friends." I said. "But this is not all about sadness. You guys did a hell of a job and saved a lot of lives. I'm proud of all of you. Hooyah PJs!"

I could see their faces light up as they realized I knew how they felt and that it was OK. And then the stories began to jumble out, the things they had done, the lives they saved. A skilled surgeon does not rejoice in the circumstances that led to his involvement, but he lives to do lifesaving surgery because it is his calling. The surgeon knows he has the special gift of lifesaving abilities and is uniquely suited to save lives. He knows that not everyone can do what he does. Like a surgeon operating on a patient we PJs had not caused the devastation, but we helped to limit the extent of the damage. Despite the sadness and grief of losing comrades, it was OK to feel good about the lives they saved. If you can't master that attitude, you can never be a PJ.

It was during this reunion that I learned of everyone's exploits and also the solution to a mystery that had been puzzling me from the beginning. Eric had barely survived the blast, which had blown him through the air. Glass shredded his back and splinters had speared his neck. Bloody and struggling to remain conscious, he laboriously crawled to the stairwell. On the way he noticed someone covered in debris near the elevator, but was too injured to render assistance. Listening to his story, I suddenly realized that I was the person that Eric saw under the rubble. Suddenly, everything made sense. I never realized I had been knocked unconscious! I thought I was knocked down by the blast, but instantly regained my feet. The reality was that I was probably unconscious for at least fifteen minutes.

Doctors decided to evacuate Eric and myself, along with other seriously wounded, to the regional medical center in Landstuhl, Germany. Medical technicians loaded us onto a special jet outfitted for aerial medical evacuation and flew us to Germany. We settled into our rooms in Landstuhl and I was finally getting pain medication and other treatment. Then news agencies announced that President Clinton would deliver a memorial speech on 30 June at Patrick Air Force Base. I decided I had to be there. Obviously some people were too severely injured to travel, however, I was not a total invalid and many of my fellow squadron mates were also not so severely injured that they couldn't travel to Florida. I thought it was important to attend this memorial honoring our comrades who died in the attack, so I began a campaign to convince the powers-that-be to arrange a flight so we could attend the ceremony. I talked to those in charge and even threatened to escape from the hospital and travel on my own. Finally, hospital administrators capitulated and arranged for a plane. After a long flight over the Atlantic we dropped off patients at Hurlburt Field and continued on to Patrick.

When we landed, there was a large crowd to greet us. My father, brother, and son met me on the tarmac, along with many friends and squadron mates. As the many wounded slowly made their way off the plane, there was much hugging and crying as airmen were reunited with their loved ones. I was able to walk unassisted and even answered a few questions from local reporters before being driven to my house. Some good friends from out of town Mike and Cheryl Moore were at the house to meet me along with more news media. Reporters interviewed me, my son, and even my neighbors. With the liberal use of pain killers the next morning I was able to squeeze into my service dress uniform and attend the memorial. President Clinton spoke. It was a sad, heart-wrenching occasion, but one I wouldn't have missed for the world. My fallen comrades deserved that much at least.

Our unit immediately sent other PJs and crew to replace our killed and injured squadron mates and they quickly reconstituted the rescue squadron. The replacement PJs, Art Boyd, Mike Ziegler (Z Man), John Shiman, and Chad Evans, also assisted the FBI in their investigation, using their technical rescue skills to access the unstable, bomb damaged building. My PJ friend, Z Man sent me a letter written on yellow-lined notebook paper that I still have:

5 July 96
Dear Bill and the guys,
We sorted through the rubble the best we could. Sorry we weren't able to get more, but I think you all understand. We couldn't even find the 90210 tape. Oh well.

John, Chad & I are doing good. We're busier than hell. We've managed to scrape together most of the regs and armory shit, even one safe. We'll be moving into more permanent quarters shortly & to top it off the whole squadron has to move from the property we have now. Saudi directed. Probably somewhere at the end of the flight line we'll call home.

If you're wondering about Art Boyd, he's still cleaning his room in Khobar and singing songs about fat ladies while playing his guitar. Enclosed is the only porn we managed to find in the mess. The Saudis, SPs, & FBI might be holding the rest for evidence.

All for now
Love
Z-Man xoxo
HOKA-HEY
[Hoka-Hey is a Sioux Indian battle cry shouted by Crazy Horse.]

My PJ buddy John Shiman roped up and crawled onto a narrow, crumbling ledge, four stories high to recover my beret. The metal PJ flash is bent and the beret is battered, but like me, they survived.

CHAPTER 9

TROUBLE COMES IN THREES

The woods are lovely, dark and deep.
But I have promises to keep
And miles to go before I sleep,
And miles to go before I sleep.
—*Robert Frost "Stopping by Woods on a Snowy Evening"*

ROB DISNEY WAS ONE OF MY OPERATORS WHEN I WAS THE PJ OPERA-tions superintendent at Moody Air Force Base in Georgia. When I think of Disney I'm reminded that life and death is sometimes only a matter of a fraction of an inch. I'm also reminded of John Dillinger. John Dillinger was one of the toughest gangsters of all time. He robbed two dozen banks, escaped from jail twice, and was the FBI's most wanted killer: public enemy number one. A special FBI taskforce eventually ambushed Dillinger and shot him with a thirty-eight special handgun. The bullet tore a bloody path through John Dillinger's neck and face, and public enemy number one died a violent, painful death.

Master Sergeant Rob Disney survived the almost identical wound that killed John Dillinger. Instead of FBI agents, Islamic insurgents ambushed Sergeant Disney and shot him through the face with a high powered Russ-ian assault rifle. The speeding bullet smashed into his right cheek, drilling a perfect tunnel through muscle and bone, before exiting out the back of his neck. But unlike Dillinger, Sergeant Disney was back on his feet within days. Survival in combat is often a matter of inches—shrapnel that barely misses, the position of your body, or in Sergeant Disney's case, a quarter inch difference in the trajectory of a bullet.

Today, a jagged scar crosses Sergeant Disney's face: a warrior's badge of honor. Despite his close brush with death and the lingering aftereffects of his injury, Sergeant Disney continues to battle the jihadist enemies of our country. The violent ambush and near fatal gunshot wound capped a series of three dramatic incidents that Sergeant Disney experienced during a period of a few short months. When it comes to tragedies, pararescuemen have a saying, "Trouble comes in threes." This phenomenon is usually spread over the entire pararescue population worldwide. Sometimes months or years pass without a significant tragic episode. Then suddenly in short order, a PJ dies in a parachute mishap, on the other side of the globe pararescuemen are involved in a plane crash, while elsewhere a PJ is hurt on a mountain. But it is unheard of for a single PJ to be involved in a quick series of three major traumatic events. Depending on your point of view, Sgt. Rob Disney is one of the luckiest or unluckiest men alive.

Rob Disney was born in Decatur, Illinois, in 1977 and grew up with his younger sister Jennifer. His father Robert served four years in the Marine Corps, but when Rob was born he left the marines and accepted a job at a chemical plant. Rob's mother Barbara taught in the local elementary school system. Rob was a gifted child. Intellectually ahead of his peers, he skipped the third grade and went on to graduate from high school when he was only sixteen. After high school Rob enrolled in college with the goal of becoming a medical doctor. Meanwhile, his younger sister enlisted in the air force as a Russian linguist. Craving adventure, Rob visited his local military recruiters in 1996. After closely examining navy SEALs and other commando units, he ultimately chose to enlist in the U.S. Air Force with a guaranteed chance to become a PJ. Pararescue appealed to Rob because its special operations heroics blended with the challenge of lifesaving emergency medicine. He wanted to be like MSgt. Mike Maltz, the impressive-looking PJ on the cover of the pararescue recruitment pamphlet.

Rob proved to be mentally and physically up to the PJ challenge, and after almost two years of grueling training he graduated PJ school and reported to his first duty station at Moody Air Force base in May of 1998. I was a senior master sergeant working under CMSgt. Don Shelton. At the time our PJ team was a component of the 41st Rescue Squadron, flying

HH-60 Pave Hawk helicopters. Our PJs would later split-off to become the 38th Pararescue Squadron in 2001. I supervised day-to-day PJ training and operations at the unit. Newly assigned PJs like Rob are expected to train diligently to gain operational experience and perfect their rescue skills. As I got to know Rob, I discovered he had a lot of potential. Rob laughed easily and a wide grin often split his baby-face. He was interesting and talented, but most impressively, many of his skills were warrior centered. His mastery of weapons was nothing short of uncanny. He was a champion archer and a competition-level marksman with both rifle and pistol. At the gun range, he easily out-shot all the other PJs. Rob's talents were not limited to marksmanship. He was also an accomplished song-writer musician and frequently hung out at my home and taught my son how to play guitar.

In his first combat deployment, Sergeant Disney went to Afghanistan and operated out of Kandahar. The PJs there worked in conjunction with the 41st Rescue Squadron saving coalition soldiers wounded in battle. On 12 August 2002 PJ Sergeants Rob Disney and Matt White scramble on a rescue mission. At 9:00 P.M., their two-ship Pave Hawk formation lifts off from Kandahar. Their mission is to rescue two Afghan soldiers who have been shot. The helicopters take-off despite bad weather and thunderstorms and fly to the pick-up site. Once on scene, Sergeant Disney's helicopter circles overhead, providing machine-gun cover fire while the other helicopter, carrying PJs Donovan Chapman and Gabe Ruff, lands and collects the casualties.

With patients onboard, the choppers continue on to an army special forces forward operating base (FOB). In total darkness, they touch-down on a helicopter pad paved with flagstone. Just outside the shale landing pad the ground is twelve inches deep of fine, talcum-like dust. The field hospital and army surgical team is set up in a large goat barn a short distance from the pad. The PJs unload the patients and hand them off to the surgeons. One victim's intestines are exposed, the result of a bullet slicing through his abdominal muscles.

Their missions complete, the helicopter crews decide to return to home base. It's 0200 hours and the night is black as tar. The crew wears night vision goggles on their helmets, but it is so dark that it's hard to see even peering through these latest generation devices. To increase elbow room in the small helicopter cabin and make it easier to work on patients, mechanics stripped the seats from the interior of helicopter. The PJs sit on empty ammo cans facing towards the rear of the aircraft. Miniguns extend from the open windows locked into position and ready to fire. The lead aircraft takes off without incident. Sergeant Disney's helicopter tries to enter a hover in preparation for forward flight, but there in an unexpected problem. The weather is hot and the chopper is heavy with fuel. The Pave Hawk doesn't have enough power to hover and begins to falter. One way to cheat and gain aerodynamic lift is to increase forward airspeed. The pilot moves the helicopter forward, trying to gain speed to take off. After traveling a hundred yards, the chopper has moved off the shale and the gale-force rotor wash whips up the fine sand. Dust engulfs the helicopter in a "brown out" and reduces visibility to zero. The pilot and crew can't even see the fiery green halo that normally sparks off the tips of the titanium capped rotor blades.

Fixed reference points on the ground normally help the pilot to recognize aircraft drift and prevent disorientation while hovering. The pilot tries to land, but in the "brown out" there are no visible ground references, and they are flying blind. The flight engineer comes up intercom, "The rotors are drooping!" he yells. Drooping rotors signal a loss of power—a serious problem. Although both doors are open, Sergeant Disney can barely see Sergeant White in the swirling murk. The left gunner yells, "Stop left drift!" The pilot tries to correct, but the helicopter backslides into the five-foot-high berm of earth that surrounds the FOB. The earthen barrier is topped with razor wire and the tail rotor tangles in the concertina. The job of a helicopter's tail rotor is to counter the torque of the main rotor blades and keep the aircraft flying straight. Without a tail rotor to steady the aircraft, a helicopter will spin out of control and crash. The razor wire shatters the tail rotor blades, and the helicopter rolls to the left. Someone yells, "Hang on!" One-by-one the four main rotor blades flash into the ground like thunder claps, churning earth and violently snapping off in all directions. As the crippled chopper rolls on its side, gravity slams the left door shut. Sergeant Disney careens into the door and ends up sprawled on the ceiling, which is now the floor. His night vision goggles break off his helmet, and he is truly blind in the dark.

With no blades to turn, the rotor head spins faster and faster, whining incredibly loud. The escalating scream of the engines seems a prelude to an inevitable explosion and Sergeant Disney thinks, "This is the end." But the pilot manages to shutdown the engines and finally there is silence. Sergeant Disney yells out, "Is everyone OK?" Sergeant Matt White chimes in, "Count off by crew position." One-by-one the crew responds, pilot, copilot, flight engineer. Miraculously, everyone is alive. "Let's get out." someone yells. The PJs are first to escape the aircraft and quickly pry open the cockpit door to help get the rest of the crew out.

The special forces troops in the FOB hear the crash and soon arrive on scene. The pilot is injured and they help put her on a stretcher. Meanwhile, the other Pave Hawk returns, and Sergeant White gets on the radio and calmly directs them to a landing on the pad. After all that has happened further flight operations are out of the question. Both helicopter crews decide to stay the night at the FOB. The next day, dawn reveals the full extent of the near fatal crash. The stricken helicopter lies on its side in the dirt. Its tail and main rotor systems are totally destroyed. The violent forces involved in the crash are immense and it's a miracle no one was killed. Later that day the undamaged helicopter returns to home base, but it is another three days before an army helicopter finally ferries Sergeant Disney and his crew back to Kandahar. To Sergeant Disney the crash is a grim reminder that when you least expect it, life can pitch you a curve ball.

When Rob's tour ends he returns to America, but it's only for six weeks. He realizes that all the rescue action is in the combat zone, so he volunteers to go back as soon as he can. Rob spends a festive Thanksgiving holiday with me and Billy and leaves for Pakistan the next day. This time he flies combat missions on HC-130s based at Jacobabad, nicknamed Jbad and pronounced jay-bad. When his three months are up, Sergeant Disney volunteers to stay for a second tour. This allows the PJ slated to replace him to remain in the United States to deal with a family emergency.

On 23 March 2003, an HC-130 takes off from Jbad and hours later lands at Karshi Kanabad, Uzbekistan, called K2. Onboard is CRO Lt. John Shoemaker. Lieutenant Shoemaker is a prior enlisted PJ and has great skills and experience. The PJs onboard are Sergeants Rob Disney, Craig Fitzgerald, and former army ranger turned PJ Ross Funches. It's a routine transport mission for the rescue crew, although the weather is bad with thunderstorms and poor visibility. On their landing approach to K2 a bolt of lightning strikes their plane and sizzles over the aluminum skin of the aircraft, but they are still able to land safely. Afterwards mechanics crawl over the entire plane but can find no serious damage. The crew decides to eat at the dining hall while their plane takes on gas for the return trip to Jbad. Then they get the word; there is a possible rescue mission. While the pilot gathers data at the command post the PJs set up their portable satellite radio on the tarmac and listen in on the radio chatter.

The mission is to pick up two seriously injured Afghan children who have fallen down a hill. The PJs immediately nickname them Jack and Jill. Two HH-60 Pave Hawks from the deployed 41st Rescue Squadron take off from Kandahar to rescue the children. Jack and Jill are in the northern part of the country, hundreds of miles away. En route to the pickup location the helicopters will need to refuel. That's when the HC-130 becomes indispensable. The Hercules, carrying Sergeant Disney and the other PJs will gas up the helicopters mid-air. Onboard the first chopper, call sign Komodo 11 (pronounced Komodo one, one) are two PJs, MSgt. Mike Maltz, a twenty-four year PJ veteran and twenty-one-year-old SAmn. Jason Plite. On board Komodo 12 are PJs Matt Leigh and Josh Johnston.

Before this deployment Master Sergeant Maltz had worked closely with me at Moody. Over the course of seventeen years we have occasionally been stationed together and are good friends. Mike is an imposing figure, well over six feet tall; he has a bodybuilder's physique and is incredibly strong. At forty-years old he still has washboard abs, which he flaunts at the younger PJs. Mike truly has a unique personality that stands out, even in a profession peopled with unusual characters. He is hyperactive—nonstop energy. His New York accent and unusual mannerisms are well known throughout pararescue. He is possibly the most impersonated man in pararescue. In a nut shell, Mike is a piece of work but in a good way.

For the past few months Mike has been preparing to retire but suddenly decides to put in a couple more years. He comes to my office and tells me his decision. He is an experienced team leader. He has rare and valuable skills that take many years to develop. Since his retirement was imminent, he has been off limits for deployments. I tell him that now that he's staying in the air force, I need to send him on the next deployment to Afghanistan. "No problem man." he says. "I know it's my turn. I want to go."

Sergeant Maltz's team member Jason Plite typifies the new generation of PJs. He is only twenty-one years old and this is his second combat deployment. Born in Grand Rapids Michigan, Jason is tall and athletic. He is a wicked fast runner, always the first pick when we choose teams to play ultimate frisbee. He is also very smart, winning academic achievement awards during PJ training. Jason is good at everything he does. Moody is his first PJ assignment, and he immediately fits in. I get to know Jason when we both attend two weeks of rescue training in New Hampshire. He is magnetic, impossible not to like.

Sergeant Rob Disney is flying onboard the HC-130, which is tasked with providing vital fuel to the choppers. It is incredibly dark outside, and the crew wears night vision goggles. The goggles allow them to see in the night, but the trade-off is a lack of depth perception. The pilot must dodge numerous thunderstorms and lightning continues to pose a danger to their plane. There is fog on the mountain peaks, but the air is clear down low in the valleys. Before they leave K2 the HC-130 Hercules and helicopter crews plot a refueling rendezvous point on the map. To avoid flying through clouds the crews plan to refuel in a long valley at only four hundred feet above the ground. Even wearing goggles and flying at this low altitude, it is so dark the crew can barely make out surface features. During training missions the minimum refueling altitude is one thousand feet. This is a real-world lifesaving mission, and normal altitude restrictions do not apply. The low refueling altitude should be safe given the skill and experience of the crews.

The HC-130 will refuel the helicopter in midair by reeling out long fuel hoses from pods mounted under its wings. The hoses end in funnel-like baskets called drogues. Rescue helicopters capable of aerial refueling have an extendable tube mounted on the front of the helicopter, called a probe, making them resemble a giant mosquito. The probe can telescope to a length that extends beyond the whirling rotor blades of the helicopter. To take on fuel the pilot guides the helicopter probe into the center of the drogue. The probe locks into place and fuel flows from the HC-130 through the hose and probe into the helicopter's gas tanks. Aircrews always preplan specific rendezvous points to refuel the helicopter en route to a rescue scene, in this case a valley. Low clouds and rough weather can jeopardize aerial refueling, so there is a huge element of risk. If a helicopter cannot aerial refuel it will run out of gas, and if the terrain is too steep to land, the chopper will crash.

The HC-130 is already at the re-fueling point when the helicopters arrive. The crews decide to refuel both helicopters simultaneously. The HC-130 Hercules reels out its right and left fuel hoses from its wing-mounted pods. The choppers are thirsty for gas and the fluttering drogue chutes beckon in the wind. Komodo 11 is piloted by Lt. Col. John Stein and carries PJs Mike Maltz and Jason Plite. They choose the left hose, and Komodo 12 takes the right hose. During refueling, the Hercules flies with both its paratroop doors locked open. A loadmaster stands in each open door and keeps his eyes focused on the helicopters, relaying information to the pilot. Komodo 12 quickly spears the drogue with its probe and begins to take on fuel. Turbulence makes maneuvering sketchy and Komodo 11 has multiple misses on the left hose before finally connecting. As Komodo 11 locks onto the fuel hose, the planes approach the end of the valley. At valley's end, jagged mountains thrust into the cloudy sky, an impassable barrier. Still connected by the refueling hoses, the three aircraft begin a slow turn to the left to reverse their course back down the valley and finish refueling. The helicopters remain attached to the hoses during the gradual turn.

The planes fly through low-hanging clouds as the terrain begins to rise. Halfway through the turn the Hercules crew feels a sharp tug as Komodo 11 inadvertently disconnects from the fuel hose. The helicopter moves off to the left in a descending turn. Moments later, a blinding flash lights up the sky and illuminates the mountains. A huge fireball rises into the night, colored brilliant green by the crew's night vision goggles. On the ground, a trail of fire points to the main inferno. The loadmaster standing in the left paratroop door begins to scream over and over, "Oh my God!" At first, Sergeant Disney thinks they are under enemy missile attack, but it soon dawns on him that Komodo 11 has crashed. The wreckage is spread over a large area, and green flame is smeared over a prominent ridge

The screaming loadmaster is inconsolable and can no longer perform his duties. The second loadmaster seats his grieving friend and takes over. The intercom is eerily quiet, everyone is absorbed in their own thoughts and no one knows what to say. Komodo 12 lands as close to the wreckage as is safe. PJs Matt Leigh and Josh Johnston run to the fire-blackened heap of twisted metal that was Komodo 11 and begin the grisly search for survivors. Sergeant Leigh gets on his radio and relays a situation report. Sergeant Disney is struck by Leigh's composure and professionalism. Sergeant Leigh reports, "Found two crew, no survivors. We'll look till we find them all." Left unsaid is the condition of the crewmen. These crash victims are friends and the sight of their lifeless bodies is traumatic and heartbreaking. A short time later, Leigh radios an update, "Found three, still no survivors." He also reports approaching vehicle lights in the valley a mile and a half away. The Rescue Coordination Center says there are no friendly forces in the area and recalls the PJs. Sergeants Leigh and Johnston reluctantly abandon their search and return to their helicopter.

Despite the fatal refueling catastrophe, Komodo 12 will still need to refuel in order to return to Bagram Air Base. This time the Pave Hawk turns on its infrared spotlight and refuels at one thousand feet. Despite all that has happened, the crews of both aircraft maintain calm professionalism and successfully gas the helicopter. When Komodo 12 lands at Bagram, the PJs hurry over to lobby the commander of the army's quick reaction force (QRF). The QRF is firing up Chinook helicopters to carry soldiers to the crash. They will have the manpower and firepower to secure the area and recover the crash victims. Leigh and Johnston insist on accompanying the QRF, and when the mission commander hears their story he lets them onboard. In minutes the Chinook is speeding to the crash site.

In the sky above the wreckage Harrier jump jets drop illumination flares to light the area and help speed the search and recovery effort. The Harriers carry Maverick air-to-ground missiles and sport wicked five-barreled 25mm Gatling-style cannons and thousand pound bombs. The show of force prevents Islamist fighters from interfering with the operation. The vehicle that had earlier ended the PJs' search quickly flees the area. The QRF recovers all the fallen heroes and returns to Bagram. The HH-60 crash is a costly accident. Six airmen die: two PJs and four crewmembers from the 41st Rescue Squadron.

On 24 March friends and comrades-in-arms pay tribute to the crew of Komodo 11 at a memorial ceremony at Moody Air Force Base. Members of the 41st and 38th Rescue Squadrons honor the six heroes, with friends relating personal accounts of their lives and characters. There are hundreds of people present who fill an entire aircraft hangar. I give the eulogy for Sergeant Maltz. It is a heartbreaking occasion.

The fallen heroes of Komodo 11:

Lieutenant Colonel John Stein, 39
First Lieutenant Tamara Archuleta, 23
Staff Sergeant Jason Hicks, 25
Master Sergeant Michael Maltz, 42
Senior Airman Jason Plite, 21
Staff Sergeant John Teal, 29

JACOBABAD, PAKISTAN, APRIL 2003

Sergeant Rob Disney is once again deployed to a war zone, eating dehydrated rations and flying combat missions. During this deployment he acts as a PJ team member on a three-man HC-130 rescue team. Combat Rescue Officer Lt. John Shoemaker (Shoe) leads this deployment and occasionally stands in as a PJ team leader. The other team leader is TSgt. Louis Distelzweig, nicknamed D-10 for obvious reasons. The team members are Staff Sergeants Ross Funches, Craig Fitzgerald, Jason Rusoff and SAmn. John Griffin. An alert team consists of a team leader and two team members who are on-call for three days, able to scramble on a rescue mission at a moment's notice. The two teams alternate alert responsibilities, three days on and three days off.

One day Sergeant Disney meets another American flyer at the gym. This pilot is unconnected to Sergeant Disney's deployment and flies Russian-made Mi-17 Hip helicopters with the Pakistanis. The Mi-17 Hip multi-purpose helicopter is an improved export version of the ubiquitous Mi-8 Russian transport helicopter. Russia supplies this chopper to many different countries, and it's specifically designed to operate at high altitudes and in hot weather. Hot weather and high altitudes describe much of Pakistan and the country owns twelve of the Hips.

Disney hits it off with the Hip pilot and floats the possibility of having PJs fly on the Russian bird. This will take coordination, but the pilot is agreeable to the plan. This is something new and interesting for the PJs to sink their teeth into; PJs are always looking for new training opportunities. Lieutenant Shoemaker ultimately guides the plan through the myriad bureaucratic wickets and finally schedules PJs on the Hip. During their down time, the PJ team that is not on alert can fly on the Russian-made helicopter. At 1630 on Good Friday, 18 April 2003 a Hip takes off for a survey mission with three PJs onboard.

Two pilots, one American and one Pakistani, sit in the cockpit. A duo of U.S. and Pakistani flight gunners occupy the left and right-side doors, which are located just behind the cockpit. The interior of the aircraft is equipped with inward facing seating. Sergeant Disney sits on the rearmost seat on the right, just a few feet from the wide-open rear of the helicopter. PJ Craig Fitzgerald sits forward, to the rear of the right door. An extra pilot, a lieutenant colonel, sits on the left side, just behind the left door. Sergeant Funches also sits on the left but further towards the rear. The crew's mission is to mark and evaluate a new landing pad near a deserted village in the Bugti region of Baluchistan Province. The plan is to land at the prospective helicopter landing zone (HLZ), drop-off the PJs and depart. The PJs will mark the exact position of the HLZ with a handheld GPS. Afterwards, the aircraft will return, pick up the PJs and deposit them on the far side of the ghost-village. The PJs will patrol through the motley sprawl of twenty five crumbling mud huts on their way back to the HLZ.

The landing pad is easily visible from the air; it is a large sandy circle outlined in light colored gravel. The circle is a hundred feet in diameter and has a large gravel "H" in the center. Outside the dun colored circle, the cracked earth is rock-hard dirt disfigured by a morass of wadis and jagged fissures. When the PJs arrive back at the HLZ the Hip will land on the pad for a second time, pick up the team and depart.

The Hip takes off from Jacobabad and begins the forty-five minute flight to the HLZ. For a while the aircraft cruises over lush green fields, then suddenly the landscape changes to a bleak tortured wasteland completely void of vegetation. The cabin is small and cramped, only eight feet wide. Everyone has their rucksacks clipped to metal rings on the floor. The space is congested; it's almost impossible to move about. Light streams through round, porthole-shaped windows that line the sides of the chopper. This is only a survey mission, so the aircraft is unarmed and has only one VHF radio. The PJs in the back do not even have intercom with the flight crew and have to communicate with hand signals. This mission is considered low threat. Nonetheless, the PJs and crew are prepared for the unexpected and carry normal combat accoutrements: M4 rifles and body armor. Their flight route is over tribal areas and radical elements of the population are extremely hostile.

The abandoned village is perched on a bluff overlooking the HLZ. A predator drone has overflown the village for the past week and detected no movement. If any of the crew spots people near the landing pad or village they plan to scrub the mission. The helicopter nears the landing area and slowly descends to make a low observation pass over the HLZ. The PJs in the cargo compartment, peer out the gaping opening where the helicopter's rear clamshell doors used to be. Earlier that day, mechanics removed the doors specifically for this flight to allow the PJs quick exit and entry.

The aircraft flies an approach a half mile to the right of the HLZ. Sergeant Disney and the others in the back of the chopper eyeball the area and are shocked to see four people dressed in local garb standing in the center of the landing zone. The PJs immediately try to alert the pilots to the presence of people on the HLZ. This is supposed to be a show stopper, but the PJs' yelling is drowned out in the ear-splitting whine of the helicopter's engines and communication fails. Things are happening fast and the chopper banks hard to make its landing. The intruders have disappeared from the HLZ, and the PJs prepare to jump out the back after the aircraft touches down. Disney can see the dilapidated mud huts off to his left on the ridge. The gunner holds up an index finger and signals "One minute!" The Hip is only twenty feet above the ground, moving at a snail's pace.

Sergeant Disney hears a loud pop. The sound is reminiscent of a helicopter launching defensive flares to counter heat-seeking missiles, but the PJ quickly remembers he is on an unarmed Hip, not an HH-60 rescue helicopter equipped with flares. Sergeant Ross Funches remembers the first shot sounding like a blacksmith's hammer hitting an anvil. The gunners look up at the ceiling like they think there might be a mechanical problem with the transmission. Disney hears the second shot like the crack of a bull whip, and suddenly there is no doubt that the sounds are gunfire. They are being attacked by men armed with AK-47 assault rifles. Disney looks forward and yells, "Lock and load!" but the others are already reacting to the attack. The helicopter is only a few feet from the ground and preparing to land. While Sergeant Disney raises his weapon to return fire the pilots swing the Hip's tail towards the threat and pours power into the engines to escape the ambush. With the open rear of the aircraft pointed towards their attackers only yards away, the PJs and crew are sitting ducks. Fully exposed to enemy fire and with complete disregard for his own safety, Disney raises his rifle, pinpoints rifle flashes on the ground, and sights down his barrel to return fire. Sergeant Funches is dumbstruck and later refers to this remarkable event as a "Medal of Honor" moment.

Sergeant Disney's defensive actions are abruptly cut short when a 120 grain AK-47 bullet slams into his face below his right eye. The bullet is traveling at twenty-three hundred feet per second and hits with fifteen hundred foot pounds of energy. He feels the impact on his face and then his entire body is racked by a shockwave (hydrostatic shock) creating devastating effects. Hydrostatic shock is a wave of destructive force that radiates out from the point of impact of a high-velocity bullet. The force ripples through flesh and bodily fluids which make up 60 percent of the human body. Hydrostatic shock can explode a head with a direct hit, and an impact to a shoulder can cause a victim's lungs to fill with blood.

The bullet smashes Sergeant Disney onto the metal floor of the chopper. He doesn't immediately grasp the entire nature of his injury: his face is laid wide open. He experiences double vision. He can still see enemy rifle flashes, but now there is two of everything. He thinks he can adapt, he'll just shoot between the two flashes. But it's hard to focus and it feels like something is pulling on his eyeball. It's his hanging, face-stretching muscles connected to his eye. He yells out, "I'm hit!" Sergeant Funches quickly yells, "Shoot back!" Sergeant Funches watches Rob Disney raise his rifle to return fire. The butt of the weapon disappears into the bloody hole that is the right side of his face. Later it will take Ross Funches hours to clean the blood and flesh from Rob's rifle. Funches also aims his rifle, looking for targets. He can't see any enemy muzzle flashes to shoot at and resists the urge to fire blindly, fearing he may accidentally hit the tail rotor and shoot down his own helicopter.

It is incredibly fortunate that the pilots are not killed in the initial attack. Despite the chaos and flying bullets, they keep their composure and steer an escape route. Suddenly, the helicopter crosses over a hill that shields the aircraft from further hostile fire. The pilot pours on the throttle and makes top speed for Jacobabad. The entire fire fight lasts less than sixty seconds. Sergeants Funches and Disney experience time distortion, and during the short duration of the attack they experience a bewildering onslaught of thoughts and events. It's the "life flashing before your eyes" phenomenon, but on steroids.

Rob Disney enters survival mode. His whole fight for life plays out on a small patch of helicopter floor. He removes his helmet and combat gear, and has the presence of mind to put his rifle on safe. He has no idea what's going on with the rest of the crew, although others have also been shot. He is lying on the floor of the chopper with his legs dangling out the back of the aircraft, connected to a floor tie-down ring with a lanyard, fearing that the aircraft is about to crash. Rob thinks that a bullet has punctured the aircraft's hydraulic system. PJs have a name for the red-colored hydraulic fluid: helicopter blood, and it is crucial to the aircraft's flight-control systems. Without hydraulic fluid the pilots cannot control the helicopter.

The reason for Rob's alarm is that hot, red fluid seems to be spraying onto his arm and leg from somewhere behind him. He reaches up to locate the source and feels his face hanging down from his skull. He is stunned to realize that what he thought was hydraulic fluid spraying under pressure is really his own blood. His face is splayed open from his eye to his ear. The bullet exited from the back of his neck only a quarter of an inch from his spine. He feels the back of his neck and his fingers find the bloody exit hole. Sergeant Funches locks eyes with him and yells, "Hang on!" Sergeant Rob yells back, "I'll be OK." But he's not feeling OK at all.

When Sergeant Funches sees Disney's face up close he grimaces. An experienced paramedic, Ross quickly goes to work. Rob tries to help and uses his hand to apply direct pressure to his face to stop bleeding. Sergeant Funches is dismayed to see Disney's hand disappear into his face. Rob's facial nerves are not working, and he can't feel what's going on. Funches removes Disney's hand, repositions the flap of hanging face to its correct anatomical alignment, and places Sergeant Disney's own hand on the best spot to apply pressure and stop the bleeding. This quick, simple procedure probably saves Rob's life. Unknown to both PJs, the bullet partially severed Sergeant Disney's jugular vein. The jugular vein is one of the largest vessels in the body and carries large volumes of blood from the brain to the heart. A person with a cut jugular can quickly bleed out and die. When Rob presses his hand to his face, he pinches off his jugular and slows the gushing torrent of blood.

Sergeant Funches moves to the front of the cabin to check on the other wounded, but he keeps tabs on Sergeant Disney even as he treats the other crewmen. Funches works frantically on PJ Craig Fitzgerald. Sergeant

Fitzgerald has been shot through his wrist and took a second bullet in the side of his chest, as well. Ross quickly applies a tourniquet to Fitzgerald's arm to stop the bleeding; he has to twist the tourniquet extremely tight to make it work. Sergeant Disney sees Craig on his back, spasmodically thumping his heels into the floor. Sergeant Funches is bending over Fitzgerald, working feverishly. Sergeant Fitzgerald is in a huge amount of pain and is not sure he will survive. He makes Funches promise he will tell his wife he loves her.

Sergeant Funches is under enormous mental pressure. His teammates are yelling in pain, hideously wounded—blood is everywhere. And, he only has a limited amount of medical supplies and IV fluids. He tries to ration his medical gear, using fluids and morphine only where it is most needed. But there is a lot going on; he is experiencing sensory overload. When the screaming and the sight of raw, bleeding wounds threaten to derail his mental composure, he flashes back to his medical training when he practiced treating traumatic injuries on drugged goats.

During PJ school, the long months of medical training culminate in a live-tissue lab. Doctors recognize this type of practice as the most realistic and valuable lifesaving medical training. The lab begins with administering general anesthesia to a live goat. Once the animal is completely knocked out and can feel no pain, instructors inflicting on the goat injuries that mimic commonly seen combat trauma. PJs treat the wounds, stop bleeding, start IVs, and strive to keep the goat alive, as if it were a human patient. While the broken bones and squirting blood in the lab are real, no training can truly duplicate an actual combat situation. Missing is the fog and confusion of war, the screaming and human emotion, and the threat of enemy attack. Sergeant Funches mentally shuts out the mayhem and bedlam and does what he needs to do. He methodically treats the gunshot wounds, refusing to be affected by the horrific sights and sounds. He does this by repeating a phrase over and over in his mind, "It's only a goat. It's only a goat."

When he has stabilized Craig Fitzgerald, Sergeant Funches rushes over to attend to Shawn Swift, the left door-gunner. Sergeant Swift has been shot twice and is down, totally unconscious. While he was scanning out the door for enemy activity, a bullet glanced off his pistol holster and penetrated his body armor just below the titanium plate. The bullet proof vest is made of Kevlar with titanium plates inserted in pockets centered over the chest and back. Kevlar fabric alone will only stop low velocity projectiles, such as shrapnel or handgun bullets. The titanium plate is the only part of the vest that is truly impervious to a high-velocity rifle bullet. In this case the bullet missed the plate, ripping a livid path through the muscle beneath his armpit. The bullet also dragged tatters of Kevlar fabric through the flesh. The speeding bullet created a gruesome purple wound. The second bullet exploded Swift's bicep, and Sergeant Funches tightly binds the muscle, which has quickly swollen to the size of a football. For a time, Funches moves back and forth between Fitzgerald and Swift, reacting to their changing medical situations.

When he is satisfied that Sergeants Fitzgerald and Swift are stable, Funches returns to work on Sergeant Disney. He packs rolls of fluffy gauze into Rob's face wound and stuffs another roll in the neck wound to staunch the raging river of blood. On top of the gauze, he places a large pressure dressing and ties the cloth retaining strips behind Disney's head. Rob grabs Sergeant Funches's arm and asks if his right ear is shot off. He suddenly realizes he can no longer feel his ear or hear from the right side of his head. Ross reassures him that only his earlobe is missing. The rest of Sergeant Disney's ear is intact, although it is positioned off-kilter on the side of his head: he looks like a mutant.

Rob presses the bandage to his face while Sergeant Funches inserts an intravenous line into the large vein in the crook of Disney's right arm. This successful IV stick is quite an accomplishment in itself. It takes a lot of skill to stick a needle into a tiny vein with all the movement and vibration caused by a helicopter in flight. Afterwards, with his feet raised and life-giving IV fluids pouring into his circulatory system, Sergeant Disney is feeling good about his situation, but he is quite a spectacle. He is drenched in blood, his face is covered in bandages, and the long bandage ties flutter out the rear of the aircraft like streamers—a surreal sight. It's just too weird, so Sergeant Funches trims the fluttering bandage ties with scissors.

He then moves to the front of the cabin to check on Sergeants Fitzgerald and Swift. While he's examining them he glances over at Sergeant Disney who is lying on the deck with his feet propped-up on a bench. Then, Rob struggles to his feet and immediately lies back down—over and over again. What is happening is that he feels better with his feet propped up on the bench, higher than his heart. Gravity helps force the life-giving fluids into his body's core and brain. The IV fluids along with his elevated feet counteract the shock brought on by his blood loss. As soon as he starts to feel better his instinct to help others kicks in and he tries to get up and assist his wounded friends. But as soon as he gets up, blood drains away from his brain, the shock returns, the world begins to spin and he nearly passes out. Sergeant Disney's instinct for self-preservation reasserts itself and he quickly lies down and puts his feet back up on the bench. Soon he begins to feel better, and once again rises, only to be forced back down by dizziness. Funches yells at Disney to stay down, but Rob's up and down antics continue until Ross returns to his side.

As the helicopter speeds through the air, Disney briefly passes out. When Sergeant Funches glances over to check on him, his eyes are closed and he appears to be dead. Sergeant Funches goes ballistic and immediately screams at Disney. Sergeant Disney is abruptly startled awake. Sergeant Funches is beside himself, extremely upset. "What are you doing? I thought you were dead! Don't do that to me. I love you man!" It is crucial that patients with head injuries stay awake. If a patient is goes to sleep it is impossible to detect changes in their mental state that may indicate worsening brain damage. Closed eyes can also mean the patient is dead. Sergeant Funches is so distraught that Disney struggles to stay conscious out of a sense of guilt; he doesn't want to upset his teammate any further.

The helicopter lands at Jacobabad and a fleet of emergency response vehicles with flashing lights immediately surround the aircraft. During their escape, the pilots pushed the Hip's engines to the max, making a normally forty-five minute flight in only twenty-eight minutes. The first responders casually walk towards the helicopter, perhaps thinking this is merely a training exercise. Sergeant Funches leaps from the aircraft covered in blood, frantically waving his arms like a madman. The responders belatedly realize this is a real emergency and begin sprinting to the helicopter. Funches barely has time to stop an overzealous fireman running towards the rear of the helicopter. The fireman holds a litter vertically in the air and nearly runs into the spinning tail rotor.

Somehow communications from the helicopter back to base were garbled, and the emergency responders are expecting burn patients, not gunshot victims. The medical technicians soon sort things out and begin evacuating the wounded on stretchers. Sergeant Disney insists on leaving the helicopter under his own power, and two men help him to walk to where an ambulance awaits. On his way to the ambulance, he passes by the base commander, and salutes him. is Stunned speechless, the colonel just stares.

The medics take Rob and the others to the Expeditionary Medical Support tent where a doctor meets them. Craig Fitzgerald is badly hit and mostly out of it. During the transport to the clinic, a firefighter holds Craig's hand—the firefighter is shaking badly. Sergeant Funches is also distraught, because when he arrives at the medical tent he finds the patient stations are rigged to treat burn victims. At first there is confusion and a scramble for proper medical supplies. Finally each patient has a doctor and nurses tending to their wounds. Ever the PJ, Sergeant Disney concisely briefs the doctor on his own medical condition and requirements, "I need fluids, whole blood, and morphine." Other PJs from the deployment soon arrive to console and support their wounded comrades. Even amid these grim circumstances, the wounded PJs and their teammates still joke around. D-10 hovers over Sergeant Disney and murmurs comforting PJ words. "Your face looks like a bloody pussy." he says.

The doctors evacuate Sergeant Disney and the other wounded airmen to Al Udeid Air Base in Qatar. When Rob is wheeled into surgery, the doctor asks, "Who are these guys?" Someone says, "They're PJs." Before he fades out under anesthesia, Rob remembers the doctor motivating his surgical team, "This is high-priced real estate, people!" The doctors perform necessary surgeries, suturing, and postoperative care. Afterwards, Sergeant Disney and the others remain in Qatar for two days before specially equipped medical transport jets take them to Ramstein Air Base in Germany.

The transports take Rob Disney and the others to Landstuhl Hospital, which is just outside the air base. Landstuhl is the initial clearing house for serious combat casualties in Southwest Asia. Sergeants Disney and Fitzgerald spend five days in Landstuhl. During his stay in Germany, Rob gets a new wardrobe and a visit from the Speaker of the House Dennis Hastert who presents him with an American flag. Rob also gets a morale-boosting phone call from MSgt. John Kingsley. Master Sergeant Kingsley is a former force recon marine turned PJ. When Kingsley tells Rob that the guys back at Moody are proud of him, it is a life-changing event. It's hard to make your mark in pararescue, but if you do, you automatically become a role model for fledgling PJs. The question becomes, do you rise to the occasion and take your game to the next level?

After spending five days in Germany, a C-141 flies Rob Disney to Walter Reed Army Medical Center in DC, while Craig Fitzgerald travels to Wilford Hall Medical Center in Texas. While at Walter Reed numerous PJs and CROs visit Sergeant Disney along with his family and dignitaries, such as Chief Master Sergeant of the Air Force Gerald Murray. But the highlight of his five-day stay is when Chief of Staff of the Air Force Gen. John P. Jumper and the Secretary of the Air Force James Roche present him with a Purple Heart.

When the hospital finally releases him, an HC-130 from the 71st Rescue Squadron picks him up and takes him back to Moody. This is not a good time for Rob to be totally alone, so he agrees to stay with my son Billy and me for awhile. His wound requires regular maintenance, dressings, and bandage swap-outs. When I repack Rob's injury I'm struck by the perfection of the bullet wound. Rob has a tunnel bored through his neck muscles and face that looks as if it was created with a power drill—flawless. The bullet missed all major arteries and nerves, but it did cut Rob's jugular vein and nicked a salivary gland. As a result Rob has a temporary drooling problem. Rob's face and ear are also numb from nerve trauma, although doctors tell him he will eventually regain sensation. But for the time being his face is temporarily paralyzed and stiff.

With his stiff, botox-like face, Rob talks a bit funny, lisping slightly. Billy and I have endless fun at Rob's expense, exploiting his disabilities. Billy likes to sneak up behind Rob and play with his numb ear. Rob senses something is not quite right, but it always takes him a few moments to catch Billy in the act. When he does catch on, he yells, "Billy, cut that out!" Billy rolls on the floor laughing. Sometimes Billy attaches a potato chip bag clip to Rob's ear which he only discovers later when he looks in the bathroom mirror. There's no telling how long he has been walking around with that clip on his ear. If laughter is the best medicine, then Rob has state-of-the-art medical care.

EPILOGUE

Sergeant Ross Funches was the only combat medic in the back of the helicopter who wasn't shot. The entire burden of treating three critically wounded casualties rested entirely on his shoulders, and he rose to the occasion. Ross stayed calm and maintained his professionalism, despite the chaotic circumstances, and provided life-saving medical treatment to his comrades. When his team needed him most, he was there for them. His heroic actions under fire were in-keeping with the highest standards of PJ composure and bravery. For this event he was decorated with an Air Medal for heroism.

In 2012, Sergeant Funches lives on Kirtland Air Force Base with his wife Wendy and his four children and teaches at the PJ and CRO School. Although he escaped gunshot wounds, the ambush took a mental toll, and Ross struggles with symptoms of post-traumatic stress disorder. PTSD not only affects the individual, it affects their entire family. It is a complex condition with consequences that ripple outward through the sufferer's circle of friends and loved ones. By openly seeking treatment, Sergeant Funches continues to display uncommon courage.

When PJ Craig Fitzgerald returned to Moody Air Force Base from his time at Wilford Hall Medical Center he has an external-fixator attached to his wrist and arm. The bullet which traveled through his arm required the doctors to fuse his wrist bones. As a result, Sergeant Fitzgerald is no longer medically qualified for pararescue duty. Sadly, he has to find another job. Ultimately Craig is medically retired from the air force, and at the time of this writing is attending the Harvard Business School.

In November 2004 Sergeant Disney accepted a three-year assignment to England. During his time there he participated in the largest evacuation of American civilians and foreign nationals since World War II, removing more than thirteen thousand noncombatants from Beirut, Lebanon, in 2006 during the Israel-Hezbollah War. On Christmas day Rob proposed to Tess Lovein, a girl he met online. She accepted, and Rob mailed her an engagement ring. Rob returned to the United States on 1 May 2005 and the couple married only seven days later. In 2012 MSgt. Rob Disney is the superintendent for pararescue standards and evaluations for Air Combat Command at Langley Air Force Base, Virginia. Rob and Tess have two dogs, a Pomeranian a Yorkie, and two horses. He is also on the executive board of the Langley Saddle Club as their facilities manager.

Master Sergeant Rob Disney has had other close calls and other injuries over the years. These experiences come with the pararescue territory. He knows that people in positions of responsibility need to lead by example. When young PJs are confronted by the inevitable adversity and danger inherent in their chosen profession, they will emulate others who have come before them and who have triumphed over similar circumstances, people they respect, PJs like Rob Disney, Ross Funches, and Craig Fitzgerald.

CHAPTER 10

CASUALTIES OF WAR

What doesn't kill us makes us stronger.
—*Friedrich Nietzsche*

ONE DAY I RECEIVED A PHONE CALL FROM PAT SINON, A RETIRED PJ and old friend. Pat is a contract civilian in charge of boats and engines for the 38th Rescue Squadron at Moody Air Force Base in Georgia. A retired PJ himself, Pat has been working with PJs at Moody since 2002. In the fall of 2005 I accepted a job as the lead mountain rescue instructor at the Guardian Angel Training Center at Kirtland Air Force Base, New Mexico, and have been teaching there ever since. One day Pat phoned and told me they had a young sergeant named Dan Houghton who was heading my way for an assignment as an instructor. Pat said that Dan was a very sharp troop and wanted to teach mountain rescue. This was high praise from one of my mentors, so I told him I would pull some strings. At the time I was a one-man shop and really needed someone capable to help share the load.

I talked to my leadership about assigning Dan to the mountain block and they agreed. Everyone who knew Dan had high praise for him. I also learned that Dan had survived a helicopter crash in Afghanistan and was recovering from serious injuries. Many others on the helicopter died in the crash, including PJ Scott Duffman. Dan arrived at Kirtland in December of 2008 with his wife Marjorie and immediately set about getting qualified to teach mountain rescue. Mountain rescue is one of the most complex blocks of training and is difficult to master, but it was obvious from the start that Dan had a knack for technical rescue.

Dan is six feet tall with black hair and a slim build. His dark brown eyes glint with intelligence and energy. Dan is mechanically inclined and is well known among his peers for his ingenuity and talent for improvising. Even in a profession where operators are famous for their ability to adapt, improvise, and overcome, Dan stands out. He is the MacGyver of PJs. Dan is unique, and other instructors good-naturedly poke fun at his quirks. A typical exchange: "Has anyone seen Dan?" Another PJ replies, "I think he's making a boat engine from some wire and buttons he found." Dan is famous for his cleverness and enthusiasm. With students Dan the instructor does not tolerate sloppiness; his mantra is attention to detail.

Dan still struggles with the lingering aftereffects of the injuries he received in the helicopter crash. Six months after he arrived at the PJ School he entered the hospital to have a steel rod removed from his femur. When the surgeon took out the hardware he discovered a massive infection in the bone. It was a major operation and Dan was in a hospital bed with his leg swollen to twice its normal size and tender to the touch. To combat the infection, doctors administered massive doses of intravenous antibiotics. On 22 June 2010, at this fragile moment in his life, Dan received word that his older brother, Captain George "Ice" Houghton died during an aircraft crash in Utah. Captain Houghton, a prior T-6 jet instructor pilot, had recently transitioned to flying F-16 fighters with the 421st Black Widow Fighter Squadron. At the time of the mishap, Captain Houghton was piloting an F-16 Viper on a night training mission, preparing for his upcoming deployment to Afghanistan.

The 388th Fighter Wing scheduled a memorial service for Captain Houghton on 26 June at Hill Air Force Base, Utah. Despite Dan's painful and precarious condition, only days after major surgery, he resolved to attend his brother's memorial. Dan was restricted to a wheelchair, so the PJ School sent an escort to assist him and his wife with the necessary air travel. Dan ignored his great pain and overcame all obstacles in order to honor his brother's memory. During his stay in Utah, his serious medical condition forced him to visit the local emergency room, but he persevered. Dan's mental and physical toughness are unquestioned.

Dan Houghton was born in Ashville, North Carolina in 1984. Dan was the first person in his family to officially enter the military, although at the time his brother George was only one year away from graduating from the prestigious Air Force Academy. With his parent's blessing, Dan joined the air force under the delayed enlistment program when he was only seventeen years old. He carefully considered his decision and actually signed up before the attacks on 9/11 with the intention of becoming a PJ to serve his country and save lives.

Dan proved his mettle during a grueling year and a half of training, and excelled in all blocks of PJ training. Upon graduation from PJ School, he reported to his first assignment at the 38th Rescue Squadron in September 2005. Dan was a quick study and, after only six months, he deployed to a combat zone. After years of physical and mental preparation it was finally time to put his skills into practice. In April 2006 he arrived in Balad Air Base, Iraq. At the air base PJs operated out of two trailers and a large tent; conditions were austere. PJ team members shared Lilliputian-sized rooms and flew rescue missions on Pave Hawk helicopters. On 16 June Dan and his PJ teammates launched on an early morning rescue mission near Fallujah, a notorious insurgents' nest.

The PJs flew to the scene of a firefight on the outskirts of the infamous hot spot. Pilots yanked and banked their helicopters less than a hundred feet above the ground to avoid hostile fire. At their destination, well-armed insurgents had earlier attacked three 101st Airborne Division soldiers who were guarding a checkpoint. The Screaming Eagles had come under withering enemy fire and fought bravely, but they were overwhelmed by superior numbers. When American reinforcements arrived they found one man killed and two soldiers missing. PJs were brought into the mix to perform an underwater search for the body of one of the missing soldiers. The PJs' three helicopters landed two hundred meters from the checkpoint. A small force of fifteen Screaming Eagles met the PJs at the landing zone. The soldiers' commander, a no-nonsense sergeant major, organized security and briefed the situation and objectives.

There was clear evidence of a violent struggle at the scene of the firefight. Blood soaked the ground, and brass shell casings littered the area. It looked as if the victorious attackers had dragged a wounded American to a nearby bridge that spanned the Tigris River—there was an obvious blood trail. It looked like the insurgents had executed the soldier and tossed his body into a nearby canal.

The PJs decided to use scuba gear to search the bottom of the canal to recover the soldier. In addition to Sgt. Dan Houghton, the Search and Rescue (SAR) force consisted of 1st Lt. Matt Arnold and Sergeants Brian Tharp, Brian Zmijeski, and Trevor Nordin. Airmen Hatzidakis "Hatz" and Joe George rounded out the team. Sergeant Houghton and Airman Hatzidakis prepared to do a hasty search in the canal under the bridge. A hasty search is a quick look at the most likely place to yield results. If that failed they would conduct a more methodical search.

The PJs dressed in waterproof dry suits to protect their skin from the filthy water, but even with all their precautions they could not completely avoid exposure. Their heads would be drenched with sewer water because they only had standard face masks and scuba regulators, not watertight helmets. Dry suits are designed for diving in icy cold water and are uncomfortably hot, even in mild temperatures. In the blazing sun and one hundred degree temperature in Fallujah the dry suits were suffocating. Heat stress and exhaustion were tangible hazards.

The canal was thirty-five feet wide and fifteen feet deep. The contaminated water contained raw sewage and rotting garbage, a toxic brown soup of amoebas, bacteria, and fungus. The slimy mud bottom was littered with discarded trash. Visibility in the opaque water was less than two feet. While Dan and Hatz fruitlessly searched the canal the other PJs, wary of further attacks, pulled guard duty along with the American soldiers. After twenty-five minutes of futile hunting the PJ divers surfaced to plan a more thorough search along the edge of the canal.

The PJs divided the search area into a grid of small sections they could methodically check. This time they attached Sergeant Houghton to a rope, and he entered the water alone. He searched the sludge for thirty minutes until he felt urgent tugs on his line, the signal to surface. Sergeant Houghton wondered why his tenders wanted him to come up after only a half hour. His curiosity was answered when his head broke the surface of the water. His team was under attack. Machine gun bullets whizzed through the air and a mortar exploded only a hundred yards away. As Sergeant Houghton stroked for the bank, he heard someone yell, "Shoot those bastards!" One of the soldiers spotted a two-man enemy mortar team, and American snipers took aim to ruin the enemy's day. As Sergeant Houghton scrambled out of the canal the army lit up the insurgents with .50-caliber machine guns and automatic grenade launchers. Devastating American firepower quickly obliterated the enemy mortar team. Caught in the open, Sergeant Houghton and his teammates dashed to take cover at the base of the bridge and proceeded to exchange fire with their attackers. After fifteen minutes of intense fighting the surviving jihadists fled the scene.

With the area once again secure, Sergeant Houghton slid back into the canal to resume the hunt for the missing soldier. He searched the poisonous water for an additional forty five minutes but only found rusty cans, trash, and an unexploded mortar. When it was obvious the canal was barren, the sergeant major called off the operation and moved the PJs a few hundred yards away to a helicopter landing zone for pickup. Rangers led the patrol on a circuitous route back to the helicopter pad, because they suspected insurgents of placing an improvised explosive device (IED) on their back-trail. While the PJs searched underwater, ranger observers saw insurgents surreptitiously kick out an IED from a car. If not for the eagle-eyed rangers the IED would have wreaked havoc on the Americans returning to the landing zone. With the soldiers providing security, three Pave Hawk helicopters landed and picked up the PJs.

An army patrol later found the missing soldier in a nearby power plant. Jihadists had executed the soldier and stuffed him into a booby-trapped barrel. The ambush and booby traps confirmed that the enemy had orchestrated a search-and-rescue (SAR) trap. In some ways Americans are very predictable. Our enemies know we will always send a force to save besieged fighters or rescue wounded Americans, and oftentimes the bad guys set a trap for the rescuers. That's why PJs and aircrews always go in prepared for the worst. During this rescue operation the SAR trap failed, and Sergeant Houghton escaped with only a chronic skin fungus he contracted during his dive in the toxic canal.

After his tour of duty in Iraq Sergeant Houghton returned to the United States, but after a short hiatus he volunteered for another four month combat deployment. In December of 2006, Houghton deployed to Bagram Air Base in Afghanistan. During this deployment, he flew with the army's 160th Special Operations Aviation Regiment (SOAR), the Night Stalkers, on MH-47E Chinook helicopters. These warbirds specialize in covertly delivering and extracting special operations forces. A Chinook is a wicked looking helicopter, long and black with a set of rotor blades mounted at each end. With their two powerful engines, these aircraft are particularly effective in the Hindu Kush Mountains of Afghanistan, because they can fly and hover at high altitudes. The Night Stalker's helicopters are highly customized and come equipped with aerial refueling probes, advanced night flying optics, a .50-caliber machine gun, and miniguns for defense. A crew of five operates the Chinook which can carry up to forty-four special operators.

On 17 February, Sergeant Houghton is at Kandahar with a SAR security team poised for an assault mission. The helicopter is slated to carry three PJs, a combat controller, twelve rangers, and the aircrew: twenty-two men in all. The three day lead-up to this mission is so intense that no one even has a chance to shower. As occasionally happens, circumstances beyond the control of the operators causes the mission to be scrubbed at the last minute. After the adrenaline charged run-up to the mission the cancellation is a big psychological let-down. The operators shift into a different mental gear and prepare for departure. The Chinooks take off after dark, beginning the three-hour flight back to home base.

To prepare the aircraft for the mission, mechanics had stripped down the passenger compartment and removed the seats to make more room. As the helicopters drone through the night sky, the special operator passengers sprawl on the bare metal floor sleeping on their rucksacks and combat gear. After days of focused preparations, the lack of sleep and adrenaline let-down finally takes its toll. Sergeant Houghton sits on his rucksack near the center bubble window and dozes. With all the seats removed from the aircraft cabin the passengers use specially designed tethers to clip-in to metal tie-down rings riveted to the aircraft floor. Houghton has no premonition of danger and in a rare lapse in his disciplined routine does not snap-in to a floor tie-down ring.

Sergeant Houghton's helicopter is third in a three-ship formation flying through a heavy snow storm. The flakes fall so thick that the pilots experience a whiteout. Whiteouts occur when blizzard-like conditions makes the view from the cockpit windshield a solid, uniform white. Snow obscures the horizon and there are no reference points. With no visual orientation pilots must rely on their instruments to fly the aircraft. To make matters worse, the night is ink black; it's so dark outside that even looking through night-vision goggles everything looks dim and grainy. About two hours into the flight, Houghton wakes up and looks around the gloomy cabin. Things are so relaxed and uneventful that he thinks to himself in passing, "It is times like these that Murphy strikes." The PJ is thinking about Murphy's Law: "If anything can go wrong it will." Murphy's Law is particularly notorious for rearing its ugly head during complex military operations. Seconds later, Dan's thoughts of Murphy prove prophetic.

Even though he is wearing a noise-canceling headset, Sergeant Houghton hears a loud pop. He is a trained aircrew member and the unusual noise sets off internal alarm bells in his head. He looks around; the rest of the passengers remain oblivious, but Sergeant Houghton notices flight engineers moving around, nervously referring to their checklists. And then he hears the ominous sound of an engine winding down and losing power. He flips up his night vision goggles and mentally takes stock of his situation. Word quickly circulates around the cabin—hold on!

Sergeant Houghton grabs onto a cargo strap attached to the wall and momentarily regrets not being clipped into the helicopter floor. Seconds later the malfunctioning engine completely stalls. The stricken helicopter tilts nose-down to the left, and Dan feels a falling sensation in the pit of his stomach. Four hundred feet above the ground the Chinook completely loses power and falls from the sky. Events happen quickly. When investigators later recover the helicopter's black box the elapsed time from engine stall to impact is only forty-eight seconds. The snowstorm is so severe and the vertical terrain is so dangerous that the other two helicopters in formation are unable to turn around and assist.

Sergeant Houghton's helicopter crushes into the ground, crumpling and breaking into pieces. Powerful impact forces violently rip him from his hold. He barely has time to think, "Holy shit! We just crashed!" before the wind is knocked out of him and he can't breathe. Suddenly, his entire body is numb with fresh blood pouring down his face. He takes off his helmet. There is eerie silence; the helicopter's turbine engines are quiet, destroyed. Houghton thinks the gravitational forces of the crash may have sliced his liver and ripped his aorta away from his heart. The aorta is as big around as a finger and pumps blood away from the heart; it is the largest blood vessel in the human body. Dan is an accomplished paramedic and knows this type of injury is common during rapid-deceleration events such as helicopter crashes. A torn aorta is almost always fatal He sets his stop watch; if his aorta is torn he only has a short time to live. Five minutes tick by, and he's still alive. He shifts his attention to his leg which is painful and tingling and begins to check his lower body for injuries. Something about his leg looks weird. It takes him a few seconds to figure out what he's looking at. Somehow he is sitting on his own leg, impossible even for a circus contortionist. The thigh bone, or femur, is the strongest bone in the body, and it takes a tremendous amount of force to break it. The PJ finally figures out his femur is snapped in half, and his leg is folded back underneath him.

Initially Sergeant Houghton had the wind knocked out of him, but now he realizes he can breathe, although with pain and difficulty. He calls out the names of his PJ teammates . . . no response. His senses are heightened and the helicopter reeks of fuel, urine, and blood. He will remember this combination of odors forever. With his snapped thigh bone bent underneath him, Houghton is pinned to one spot. In order to move about, he will have to straighten his folded leg. He reaches down and twists his leg straight out—bone ends grate together. The pain is excruciating and he blacks out. When he comes to, he checks the pulse in his foot. His pulse is strong which means that despite his broken femur, his foot is still receiving blood. If he survives this ordeal, at least he will not lose his leg. Dan is on his back and can't turn over in the close confines of the wreckage. He awkwardly wiggles and claws his way towards a small opening. He can smell fresh air, but the way is blocked. He manages to reach his knife and continues on, cutting through a tangle of wires that blocks his way. He manages to drag himself halfway out of the small tunnel before he becomes stuck.

It has stopped snowing and Sergeant Houghton now has a clear view of his surroundings. He spots the dangerous orange glow of fire in the rear of what's left of the chopper. His heart sinks. Fuel is splashed everywhere; a fire is the worst possible development. His survival instincts kick in and his adrenaline ratchets his physiology to high alert. He has to act fast or everyone will be burned alive. He calls out for anyone who can still walk— this is all important. The flight engineer responds but says his legs are paralyzed. Dan finally gets the attention of a ranger who is standing upright, dazed but relatively uninjured. He urgently directs the ranger to fight the fire. Despite Houghton's injuries and immobility, his voice carries authority. The ranger scrambles to do the PJ's bidding and tries to fight the fire. Houghton hears others regaining consciousness, screaming, moaning and crying out. He painfully drags himself back into the wreck. His partner, Sgt. Chris Trisco comes to, but his legs are pinned by their teammate, PJ

Scott Duffman. Sergeant Trisco whispers, "Scotts down." His meaning is clear, Sgt. Scott Duffman is dead.

Miraculously, two rangers are healthy enough to move about and fight the fire. The ranger that Sergeant Houghton ordered to fight the fire is having difficulties. There is nothing to fight the fire *with*. "Hoo-ah sergeant, shall we use our hands?" the soldier asks. "Use anything you fuckin want!" yells Sergeant Houghton. The rangers use snow, mud, anything they can scrape off the ground. The situation with the fire is getting desperate. At any second fuel fumes can ignite, sending flames flashing through the wreckage and roasting everyone alive. The rangers suddenly find a Halon fire extinguisher, part of the helicopter's emergency equipment. Halon will put out most kinds of fires, especially electrical fires, and the rangers are finally able to defeat the blaze.

The helicopter has crashed in a war zone. With the fire out, Sergeant Houghton directs the ranger's activities towards establishing an armed guard against enemy attack and providing first aid to crash survivors. Sergeant Tim Brock, an air force combat controller, regains consciousness and asks what happened. Sergeant Brock has a fractured pelvis and broken jaw. Splintered bones are jutting out of his lower leg. He also displays classic symptoms of a concussion, lapsing back and forth into unconsciousness. He comes to every five minutes and asks the exact same questions, before nodding off into oblivion.

Forty minutes have elapsed since the crash. Sergeant Trisco complains that his arm is trapped and he can't move. Somehow Sergeant Houghton finds a metal rod in the debris and uses it as a lever to free Trisco's arm. He frees Chris's arm, but can feel that it is broken in many places. Scott Duffman is draped across Trisco's legs. A ranger medic named Yassi is also trapped inside the wreck, struggling with a broken pelvis. He tries to move Duffman off Trisco's legs and accidently kicks Sergeant Houghton's broken leg in the process. The pain is excruciating. After all this exertion and pain Sergeant Trisco still can't move.

Sergeant Houghton's paramedic training asserts itself. It is time to reassess his own medical condition. He's in terrible pain and it's getting harder to breathe. He's thirsty and drinks some water from his CamelBak, a small bladder of water with a plastic drinking tube. It's freezing cold. Things are fuzzy and Dan fades in and out of consciousness. Occasionally he says a silent prayer. He knows he's badly injured and is in a battle against the clock. He will not quit. If he doesn't make it, it won't be because he gave up.

He finds his handheld survival radio but the antenna is broken. He asks around for a working radio. A dazed crewmember sprawls against the wreckage. He says, "I think mine is somewhere inside." no help there. No problem: Dan grabs some wire and strips off the rubber insulation with his knife. He improvises an antenna for his busted radio. This occupies his time for a while, but afterwards the radio still refuses to function.

Sergeant Houghton has another idea. He locates his handheld GPS and turns it on; this will give him his exact location. He needs to place the device where there's a clear view of the sky so it can acquire satellites. He attempts to put the GPS on top of the fuel cell, struggling to slide it into place, pushing it slowly across the metal skin of the aircraft. It's almost there when inexplicably, the GPS tumbles out of reach. "Damn it!"

Another distraction: Sergeant Houghton feels an urgent need to move his bowels. With his broken thigh bone and other injuries, this will be a very complicated and inconvenient procedure. Dan devotes serious thought to the problem but doesn't come up with any solutions before he passes out again. When he regains consciousness, he is stripped down and shivering in the twenty-degree cold. Somehow he has pulled himself back through the hole. He lies halfway out of the tunnel, wedged between wreckage and a fuel tank. He doesn't remember how or why he did this; it's a mystery. Maybe severe hypothermia, also known as exposure, is affecting his thought processes, or it could be severe blood loss or a concussion.

Sergeant Houghton puts his clothes back on as best he can and suddenly notices his kick-ruck. Every PJ flies with a rucksack packed with survival gear. When a helicopter puts a PJ on the ground during a rescue mission, it may have to leave the scene due to enemy attack or mechanical failure. If the chopper has to abandon the PJ a crewmember will kick-out the PJ's rucksack so he is not stranded without gear. Sergeant Houghton's discovery of his kick-ruck is a Godsend, because there is a sleeping bag inside. Houghton says, "Hey Chris. Look what I found—a sleeping bag!" Sergeant Trisco says, "I bet that's gonna be warm!" Dan folds the bag and cuts it with his knife. He gives half the sleeping bag to Chris and then loses consciousness.

Once again, when Sergeant Houghton wakes up, half his body is out-side the aircraft, and it's snowing. Cold, white flakes settle on his face as he raises his exasperated gaze to the heavens. His mental conversation is with God, "*Really? After all this, now snow?*" Instantly the weather clears; it stops snowing and the moon comes out, hopeful and bright. Wow! Houghton laboriously pulls himself back inside the wreckage. Three-and-a-half hours have passed since the crash. He hears the distinctive sound of an aircraft flying overhead. Someone says, "Helicopters are coming! They're only a few minutes away!"

It's now a painful struggle even to suck air into his lungs. Sergeant Houghton knows something bad is going on inside his chest. He has some kind of internal damage that he knows will get progressively worse. That's one bad thing about being a paramedic and a victim. You've seen it all and can diagnose yourself. He figures he doesn't have long to live. His pain is unbearable now. He tells Sergeant Trisco, "I'm going to use my morphine injector." PJs carry morphine autoinjectors that deliver twenty milligrams of the powerful narcotic. To use it Dan will remove the safety, press the injector against his thigh, and, voila, a needle will shoot into his quadricep delivering instant relief. Chris talks him out of it. Morphine will ease the pain but might depress Dan's breathing and have other adverse effects. Morphine might kill him. In the midst of his mental debate—to inject, or not to inject—Dan passes out. When he awakes, the drama repeats with Trisco arguing against morphine and Houghton's unbearable pain arguing for the drug. It's as if Sergeant Houghton has a little Trisco angel perched on one shoulder and a horned morphine devil perched on his other shoul-der. They both whisper into his ears, each making their case. Once again the argument is resolved when he passes out. This time when he wakes up he hears that the helicopters are definitely on their way in.

Sergeant Houghton fades in and out more often now. He is in very bad shape. He hears boot steps crunch nearby and, suddenly, someone drags him out of the wreckage. PJs deployed from Davis-Monthan Air Force Base are the first rescuers to arrive. PJ Sergeants Chris Tellsworth, John Lane, Brian Kimble, and Joe Piccolli are on scene. Dan knows all the Davis-Monthan PJs. He spent time with them while preparing for this mission and he trained with many of them during paramedic school. PJs often end up saving other PJs—the guys from DM are a welcome sight. A

short time later a quick reaction force arrives and, with additional manpower, the evacuation of dead and wounded begins in earnest. Of the
twenty-two operators on the Chinook, fourteen are still alive. But like Sergeant Houghton, most of the survivors are seriously wounded. PJ Scott
Duffman is among the eight dead.

The rescuers sort their patients according to the severity of their
wounds. This process is called *triage* and focuses attention on those with
immediate life threatening injuries that can benefit the most from treatment. Rescuers place Sergeant Houghton on a backboard to stabilize his
spine and move him to a casualty collection point. They label him a category one patient: someone in need of fast, lifesaving intervention. Sergeant
Houghton's breathing has become progressively more labored to the point
where he can hardly inhale. He is also in shock from internal bleeding and
his broken thigh bone. A PJ places a traction splint on Dan's leg. The splint
stretches the leg, pulling it straight and relieving pressure. Traction immediately alleviates his agonizing leg pain; the soothing effect is dramatic; it's
as if a healing light from heaven shines down on his leg. He thinks angels
must have designed the traction device, and then loses consciousness.

Sergeant Houghton wakes up on a Chinook helicopter flying through
the air. The sky is brightening as morning dawns over Afghanistan. The
helicopter speeds towards Kandahar and a fully equipped hospital. Dan is
in great pain. He grabs a passing crewman and yanks him close; he has to
yell to be heard over the loud engines, "I need morphine!" The man pulls
away, "There's a lot of guys more fucked up than you!" which makes him
feel selfish, but his pain is intense. Regretting his harsh words, the crewman
returns a moment later with a fentanyl lollipop. Fentanyl is a painkiller
eighty-one times as potent as morphine. Dan savors the lemon lime flavor
while his cheeks greedily absorb the painkiller. The drug immediately starts
to banish his pain; his new focus is on the source of warm air. He sees an
aircraft heater vent close by on the floor. How convenient. Dan manages
to unstrap from his litter, roll to the vent, and jam his frozen hands into
the warm air. It's the last memory he has of his ride to Kandahar.

Moving in and out of consciousness Sergeant Houghton next awakes
on an operating table with his wrists tied together. Robed doctors and
nurses surround him, looking down at him with unblinking eyes. They
look creepy in the bright fluorescent light. Dan asks, "What are you going

to do?" A doctor tells him they are going to put in a chest tube. As a paramedic, Sergeant Houghton knows all about chest tubes. A doctor pokes a hole through the side of your chest, between your ribs, and inserts a large plastic tube. They position the mouth of the tube in the space between the lung and the chest wall. The tube drains out blood and air that can cause pressure and collapse the lung. Of course, the part where they poke the hole through the chest wall is very painful. Dan asks, "Are you going to knock me out?" no one answers and he feels them begin to burrow through his chest. He passes out.

Dan wakes up in a hospital bed with a framework of metal rods around his leg. Some of the rods pierce his skin and screw directly to his leg bones. This construct of bolts and rods is called an *external fixator*. It's a very fancy splint for his shattered femur. While doctors perform extensive surgical operations, they keep Sergeant Houghton in a drug-induced coma. He is at the Walter Reed Army Medical Center in Washington D.C. and has been unconscious for eleven days.

Awake and conscious, the doctors finally talk to Dan and he learns the full extent of his injuries. He is lucky to be alive. A lesser man would probably have died. He received four chest tubes to drain off blood and air. The tubes siphoned off a liter-and-a-half of blood that was pressing on his right lung and relieved an air pocket that was collapsing his left lung. He has multiple rib fractures, a lacerated liver, and, in addition to his broken femur, a broken bone in his right, lower leg. He has compressed vertebrae, and six of his spinal processes—the pair of bones that stick out from the vertebrae—are snapped off. He also has abdominal compartment syndrome, which can have fatal consequences.

Dan's fiancée Marjorie visits while he is still sedated. The surgeons have fitted Dan with a bewildering array of tubes, wires and medical paraphernalia, but to Marjorie he still looks beautiful. She is thankful the man she loves is alive. On this, her first of two visits, Marjorie stays with Dan for two-and-a-half weeks. Dan needs to be close to her, so sometimes Marjorie lies next to him in the hospital bed. In this intimate setting Dan opens up and tells Marjorie about the crash. A few minutes pass, and Dan says, "Marjorie, have I told you about the crash?" she says no. She feels that she should encourage Dan to speak. She hopes this will have a therapeutic effect.

Somehow, she instinctively does the best thing she can do to help Dan:

she encourages him to talk. Dan's psychological floodgates open wide. His next telling reveals more details and deeper emotions. This is an intense, heart-wrenching experience for both of them. A few more minutes pass in silence, and then Dan asks, "Marjorie, have I told you about the crash?" and once again she says no. Dan relives his ordeal five times in a row. With each telling he remembers more about the crash. His recollections are short, vivid episodes loosely strung together, each one a mental film clip of a life-and-death drama. Each new revelation exposes deep feelings and vulnerabilities. It is a long night, but most nights are long during this visit.

Dan is out of it during much of Marjorie's visit. He experiences frequent hallucinations and lucid dreams where he relives the crash. Despite the medication Dan does remember most of his hospital stay. He has a second surgery to replace the external fixator on his thigh with an internal device. His doctors cobble his femur together with a metal rod and screws and put a walking cast on his leg, but Dan is restricted to his bed and can't walk. The heavy cast presses his leg into the mattress and he develops a painful bed sore on his heel. Marjorie helps as best she can. She lifts his leg to take pressure off the sore. She uses towels and odds-and-ends to elevate his leg. It is an ongoing ordeal.

Sergeant Chris Trisco, also a patient at Walter Reed, is one of the first people to visit. "How many chest tubes did they stick you with?" he asks. "Four," says Dan. Chris's face falls. "You've got me." he says, "I only had three." Secretary of Defense Robert Gates also visits. He orders his security detail to stay outside and closes the door and has a private conversation with Dan and his family.

Marjorie, who is a college student, has to return to Valdosta to attend to school issues, but returns five days later. Once again she spends nights in Dan's room. Dan's new focus is on physical therapy. Specialists work with him to increase the range of motion in his damaged limbs. He learns to get in and out of bed and use the restroom. His goal is to progress from bed to wheelchair to walker to crutches to one-hundred yard dashes. The process is slow, extremely difficult, and humbling. In the blink of an eye, Dan has gone from physical stud to near helpless cripple. But his determination burns bright, and he is resolved to make a full recovery.

Sergeant Houghton is extremely gaunt. His metabolism is expending prodigious amounts of energy to repair his ravaged body, actually cannibalizing itself to get energy for repairs, burning all his fat reserves . . . and then his muscles. Dan should be eating like crazy to fuel his runaway metabolic engine, but he isn't. For some unfathomable reason—maybe a side effect or interaction between his many medications—everything he eats tastes like battery acid, so he refuses to eat. The only things that still taste good are Coca Cola and Dr. Pepper. He drinks so much Dr. Pepper that Marjorie worries it may shut down his kidneys.

With all the trauma, medications, and strain, Dan's sleep patterns go haywire. At night he talks in his sleep, blurting out disjointed sentences. Once he tries to convince Marjorie he is needed urgently on an important rescue mission. He wants to label the beds and organize for the rescue; he is a sleepwalker who can't walk. Doctors prescribe powerful potions to knock him out and counter the vivid dreams and sleep-talking.

In the the daytime Dan is mostly lucid and concentrates on achieving daily physical therapy goals. He constantly pushes himself to improve in some way each day, but he is also taking powerful pain medications that lower his inhibitions; he makes occasional gaffs. One day he is surrounded by his entire family; his room is full of loved ones and Marjorie and her future sister in-law are cleaning Dan's fingernails. Dan's family really doesn't know Marjorie very well; she is an unknown quantity. Marjorie has been trying to make a good impression. In the midst of his manicure, Dan blurts out, "Hey everybody! If you guys weren't here, Marjorie would be doing this topless!" While Dan punctuates his statement with a silly grin, Marjorie turns beet-red, mortified and embarrassed. She knows it's the drugs talking, but still . . .

Dan checks out of the hospital and returns home to Moody Air Force Base on convalescent leave. In nearby Valdosta, he shares a house with two other PJs, Trevor Nordine and Dave Wilcoxin. Dan is still very weak and Marjorie practically moves in to take care of him. She arranges her entire schedule around him. At night Dan endures great pain and suffers from night sweats. Marjorie often replaces soaked sheets. She tries to make everything accessible to Dan, meals and all the everyday necessities. Above all Dan wants to reclaim his independence, and Marjorie is careful to give him his head. She continues to demonstrate the same psychological insight she displayed at the hospital. She lets Dan do his thing, which being a prideful PJ often involves biting off more than he can chew. As a result, there is a lot of spilled food and minor accidents. She quietly follows behind Dan making things right. Dan's drive for normalcy is implacable and he slowly regains mobility.

After a month of recuperation Dan is finally self-sufficient. He returns to light duty at work as a scheduler. Flight surgeons have removed him from flight status. To be a PJ on flight status you must be in good health with near perfect vision and with no metal rods and bolts holding your bones together. His next goal is to get headquarters to grant an exception to the rule that bars airmen with internal hardware from being on flight status. Dan needs a favorable decision because in order to be a PJ you have to be able to fly. On 16 February 2008 Dan returns to flight status, although doctors will eventually need to remove the metal rod.

Dan's life is not exclusively focused on his injuries. He makes a life decision and decides to pursue a new goal, setting a complicated scheme in motion to achieve his ends. He takes Marjorie on a trip to North Carolina for a visit with his family and some recreational hiking and makes elaborate plans to walk to a famous landmark. Partway through their winter trek they discover a key section of the trail is closed. Dan is upset out of all proportion to the event. Marjorie is surprised at Dan's temper, which is uncharacteristic of his usual unflappable personality. She finally calms him and talks Dan into detouring down a little-used section of trail. The side trail proves to be an excellent hike. After walking three miles they arrive at an unusually beautiful area in the forest. Dan stops and sets up a camera tripod. It is 28 Dec 2007 and, in a pristine wilderness setting, Dan proposes marriage. On 12 April 2008 Marjorie and Dan tie the knot.

Dan and Marjorie arrive at their new assignment in New Mexico in December of 2008. Kirtland Air Force Base is located in Albuquerque, a fantastic city with a population of about 850 thousand people. The PJ School has been located in Albuquerque since 1976. While he completes his recovery, PJ instructor Sgt. Dan Houghton passes his knowledge onto the next generation of PJs. When surgeons remove the rod from his femur and discover massive infection they doubt Dan will ever regain flying status. But of course Dan beats the odds and is now almost one hundred percent. On 27 July 2010 flight surgeons permanently return Dan to flying status. An American hero, Dan has returned to the fight to save lives and live the motto, "That Others May Live."

CHAPTER 11

TO BOLDLY GO

To boldly go where no man has gone before.
—*Star Trek*

ON 28 JANUARY 1986, ONLY SEVENTY THREE SECONDS AFTER LIFT-off, the space shuttle Challenger exploded at the top of a towering column of smoke. When *Challenger* disintegrated in the skies above the Atlantic Ocean all six astronauts and school teacher Christa McAuliffe were killed. At the time of this national disaster I was stationed at Eglin Air Force Base near Fort Walton Beach, Florida. My unit, the 1730th Pararescue Squadron, took part in the massive aerial search and recovery operation that followed the tragedy. After the accident, NASA suspended shuttle launches for thirty-two months, conducted an accident investigation, and developed procedures to cover every conceivable emergency scenario. NASA also modified the fleet to allow astronauts to bailout from a space shuttle.

To begin the bailout sequence, the pilot slows the shuttle, allowing it to descend. Once at the proper altitude and airspeed the crew opens the main door and extends a hydraulic escape pole out the hatch. Each astronaut snaps a connector link from their space suit around the pole and jumps from the orbiter. Suspended from the pole by their connectors, they slide down and off the pole and exit below the left wing. Last to leave, the pilot engages the autopilot to keep the orbiter stable while he bails out. Astronauts free fall to ten thousand feet where their parachutes automatically open. They eventually land in the sea, strung-out in a line about a mile apart from each other.

The new bailout capability generated additional requirements. NASA plans called for an astronaut recovery at sea, but they had no concept of how to execute the pick-up. In the spring of 1986 NASA project officers met with PJ MSgt. Malcom "Chuck" Hassler to discuss open-ocean astronaut recovery. Master Sergeant Hassler ran the PJ branch of the Test and Evaluation Center, at Hurlburt Field, Florida. Hassler's mandate at the test center was to explore new technology and develop better equipment and tactics for special operations and rescue forces. Pararescue has a historical connection with NASA. PJs supported NASA from 1962 until 1974, and had parachuted into the ocean and recovered Aurora 7 Mercury astronauts in 1962 and Gemini astronauts in 1966. As a result, NASA was very familiar with PJs and was interested in one of Master Sergeant Hassler's test projects.

NASA was intrigued by Hassler's plan to improve pararescue's open-ocean recovery capability. When a sick or injured person is on a ship hundreds of miles from shore, PJs can parachute to their rescue. Using special parachuting techniques PJs land in the ocean as close as possible to the vessel. Once in the water PJs rely on their swimming ability or a ship's launch to reach the side of the boat. PJs climb a rope ladder or a crane lifts them onto the deck so they can attend to their patient. Parachuting into the ocean without a motorized boat is extremely hazardous, especially in high winds and rough seas, but that was the way PJs operated before the 1990s. PJs had successfully followed this sea-rescue blueprint hundreds of times, despite the obvious dangers.

The potential for disaster became actual disaster on 11 April 1983. On that date, Staff Sergeants Steve Rodman and Jeffrey Y. Jones, two PJs from McClellan Air Force Base, California, parachuted into the Pacific Ocean to rescue a pair of navy aviators who had ejected from their aircraft. During this rescue mission, Sergeant Jones was lost at sea and presumed drowned. His death and the subsequent accident investigation provided the spark that led to the concept of using a boat system capable of being parachuted from a rescue plane. Since April 1983 Master Sergeant Hassler had been working on ways to airdrop inflatable motorized boats to better conduct ocean rescues. He explained the concept to NASA planners and suggested that PJs could use the same system to recover astronauts. NASA embraced the idea and even agreed to fund a portion of the testing.

Master Sergeant Hassler modified a system the navy was testing for SEALS and Marine Corps force recon. He added a fifteen foot inflatable, rubber Zodiac boat to the system, and riggable alternate method Zodiac was born (RAMZ). After laying the groundwork for the project, Master Sergeant Hassler left for a new assignment in 1987. His handpicked successor, MSgt. Bob Holler, took over and conducted the operational tests of the RAMZ system. His office was located only a few miles from the 1730th PJ Squadron at Eglin Air Force Base, so Master Sergeant Holler used those PJs to test-jump the RAMZ in nearby Okaloosa Bay. I was one of the test jumpers for the program and had a lot of fun helping to perfect a historical new rescue capability.

The RAMZ system consists of a fifty-five horse power boat motor placed in an open-topped, wooden box. PJs attach a deflated Zodiac's transom to the boxed engine and accordion fold the rest of the boat on top of the motor and box. The padded wooden box is designed to protect the motor during parachute descent and impact with the ocean. Next, the PJs encase the boxed motor and folded boat in a large canvas "diaper." PJs strap a sturdy harness made from thick, nylon webbing around the entire bundle and cinch the package into a compact four foot cube. Next they use a fork lift to load the RAMZ cube into the open back of an HC-130 Hercules. They position the cube onto steel rollers bolted to the plane's floor and attach a large cargo parachute to the RAMZ bundle.

To deploy the RAMZ, the Hercules flies at thirty-five hundred feet and 130 knots airspeed. The pilot steers to fly directly over the bailed-out astronaut floating in the ocean. When deployment is imminent loadmasters open the back of the plane and disconnect the cargo straps that hold the cube in place. At the appropriate time a PJ gives a signal and both loadmasters slide the one thousand pound RAMZ bundle over the rollers and push it out of the plane. The four foot cube tumbles out of the back of the aircraft and through the air until its cargo parachute opens. The bundle floats slowly towards the surface of the sea, suspended beneath its huge parachute canopy. A few seconds after the RAMZ leaves the aircraft, three PJs wearing free-fall parachutes and small scuba tanks, called spuds bottles, dive out the back of the plane. The first PJ falls for five seconds before pulling his ripcord, the second PJ counts three seconds, and the last PJ out of the plane pulls his ripcord as soon as he is clear of the aircraft and is falling stable. These staggered openings create altitude separation between the PJs and helps them to avoid midair collisions. As the RAMZ slowly descends under its massive cargo chute, the PJs follow in their faster, more maneuverable sky-diving parachutes.

When the cube splashes into the sea a hydraulic device automatically releases the billowing parachute so the wind can't drag the RAMZ across the water and away from the pursuing PJs. Using skills honed during countless training missions the PJs steer their parachutes to land in the ocean within arm's reach of the RAMZ. The PJs quickly release their parachute harnesses and unwrap the bundle, which is now floating partially submerged in the ocean swells. One PJ scrambles onto the cube and disconnects straps while the other two use their scuba gear to work underwater, unpacking the boat. Once unpacked, the PJs carefully inflate the rubber boat using compressed air. Once inflated, the PJs connect rubber bladders full of gas to the engine. Approximately ten minutes after splashing into the ocean, the PJs have transformed the half-ton cube into a sleek rescue craft streaking across the sea to the rescue!

At the culmination of RAMZ testing we ran a full-mission scenario, complete with volunteers playing the roles of bailed-out astronauts. Afterwards, Master Sergeant Holler certified the RAMZ as operational and notified NASA we were ready to support shuttle launches. In anticipation of the next launch, PJs from the 1730th PJ Squadron staged all the RAMZ packages and associated rescue gear at RAF Woodbridge, United Kingdom. When space shuttle launches resumed in September of 1989, PJ teams were ready for action. PJs also supported shuttle launches with helicopters near Cape Canaveral and with HC-130s equipped with RAMZ at emergency, overseas transatlantic abort landing sites (TALS).

In the mid-1990s, while I was stationed at Patrick Air Force Base, Florida, we moved the forward-staged RAMZ gear from England to a NASA compound in Rota, Spain. Naval Station Rota has a seaport and airfield and is strategically located near the city of Cadiz. Prior to every space shuttle launch, eighteen PJs traveled from Patrick to Rota to prepare for their role in the massive operation that surrounded each space shuttle launch. Two days before shuttle liftoff, two C-130 cargo planes from Ramstein Air Base, Germany, flew to Rota and loaded nine PJs and three

RAMZ packages each. The planes also carried firemen, doctors, and a host of other support personnel. One plane usually flew to the emergency landing site at Zaragosa, Spain while the other plane flew to the landing strip at Ben Guerir Royal Moroccan Air Base or a site in Banjul, Gambia.

RAMZ parachute jumps present unique hazards. During RAMZ, PJs jump from the aircraft at relatively low altitudes, twenty-five hundred to thirty-five hundred feet above the water. These low altitudes do not allow a lot of time to deal with parachute malfunctions. Normal freefall parachute jumps take place at thirteen thousand feet, allowing forty seconds during freefall to deal with emergencies. During RAMZ jumps PJs only have a couple of seconds to resolve any high-speed parachute malfunctions. An ironic bit of parachuting lore: If your parachute doesn't open you have the rest of your life to fix the problem. RAMZ missions also require PJs to land very close to the cube in order to unwrap the packing and inflate the boat. If jumpers fail to land close enough to swim to the bundle, especially during high wind and high sea conditions, they are stranded in the open ocean with only an emergency one-man life raft to preserve them.

I experienced some of the unexpected hazards associated with RAMZ jumps when I moved from Patrick Air Force Base, Florida, to Moody Air Force Base, Georgia. Our unit was the primary PJ Squadron responsible for space shuttle rescue and often practiced open-ocean parachute jumps. Moody is only a short flight away from the Atlantic, which means increased opportunities for ocean rescues. Because open-ocean parachute jumps are such an important capability in our rescue tool bag, we practiced constantly to be expert in all things RAMZ. I was one of the most experienced RAMZ jumpers at our unit and trained our younger PJs to be expert as well. On one of our routine ocean training jumps I was acting as an instructor and jumpmaster. The training mission involved a night jump into the Indian River Lagoon near Patrick Air Force Base, which is just south of Cape Canaveral. As jumpmaster I was responsible for delivering all voice commands and hand signals and for determining where the RAMZ cube and PJ jumpers would exit the aircraft. It was February and the weather and water temperature were cold enough to justify wearing a dry suit. Dry suits are custom fit to each individual. The suit has rubber wrist and neck seals which must be trimmed with scissors to fit snugly enough to keep out water, but not so snug as to restrict blood flow, especially the neck seal. A tight neck seal will reduce blood flow to the brain and cause a person to pass out. As I performed jumpmaster duties I didn't think my neck seal was too tight, because I had been moving around comfortably in the back of the aircraft for at least an hour with no problems.

It was pitch black outside the plane as we flew towards our goal. Our target was a one-man life raft floating in the river. The small raft was lit up with strobe lights and chemical light sticks. I knelt on the left side of the plane's ramp and craned my head outside the aircraft, peering towards the front of the plane to see the target raft far below. I steered the plane by proxy, telling the pilot over the intercom to turn left or right. The pilot followed my instructions and steered over the target. I repeatedly thrust my face outside the plane into the 130 knot wind while I lined up the aircraft. As I stretched my head outside I didn't realize that my neck seal was putting pressure on my carotid arteries, slowly cutting off the blood supply to my brain. The fierce wind of the slipstream continuously battered my face like invigorating slaps, masking the symptoms of the onset of hypoxia. As we passed over the target I quickly stood, intending to begin my series of parachute commands. If a person is lying down and then jumps to their feet very quickly, it sometimes causes a condition known as postural hypotension. Most people experience this condition at some time in their lives, feeling lightheaded, even almost fainting when they get up too fast. In my case, the effects of postural hypotension were intensified by the dry-suit neck seal pressing on my carotid arteries and restricting the blood flow to my brain. After I leaped to my feet from the plane's deck I stopped dead in my tracks, suddenly mesmerized and transfixed by colorful swirling stars . . . then everything went black.

For a second I teetered on the edge of the open ramp with my back to the night sky. One foot behind me yawned a black abyss and the river, thirty-five hundred feet below. I collapsed unconscious, and toppled out of the back of the plane. The other jumpers were caught totally by surprise and stunned into temporary paralysis. When they were watching me, they expected me to rise from my kneeling position, walk towards them, and give jump signals. Loadmasters would then push the RAMZ off the ramp into the sky. I would normally have waited a few seconds before diving out of the plane after the package. My team would have immediately jumped out after me. Instead, the other jumpers watched me tumble off the ramp, limp as a rag doll. They stood transfixed, frozen in shock and disbelief. I would reach terminal velocity in seconds. If I didn't regain consciousness and pull my ripcord, I would smash into the lagoon at 125 mph terminal velocity for a human in free fall. There was not a lot of time to play with: I fell from only thirty-five hundred feet giving me about six seconds to impact. I was not thinking of *any* of this; I was unconscious and totally oblivious to what was going on. When a conscious skydiver jumps from a plane it is a smooth controlled experience. When an unconscious jumper falls limp out of an aircraft flying at 130 knots, his limbs and body are whipped akimbo and twisted violently by the gale-force slip stream: it's an eye opening experience. And that's what saved me. Tumbling chaotically through the sky, the vicious somersaults revived me just long enough so that I instinctively pulled my ripcord.

Full awareness slowly returned as I hung suspended under my parachute in the silent night. When I revived I was momentarily bewildered. I looked around in the night sky and there were no other jumpers and no RAMZ package. I was floating in the air alone and descending towards our support boat. I quickly deduced what had happened and let out a mental groan. When my parachute ride ended and I splashed into the river, my guardian angel smacked me hard on my forehead leaving crimson slap marks. When the support boat picked me up, I was embarrassed to tell them what happened. Annoyingly, the red marks on my face gave me away—served me right. The silver lining around this cloud is that when PJs survive the unexpected, we pass on the lessons learned; we don't make the same mistake twice.

All of our RAMZ training served a practical purpose: to prepare us to support space shuttle launches. Before every shuttle launch we deployed eighteen PJs to Rota, Spain, who then split up and moved on to the emergency shuttle landing sites in Morocco, Gambia, or Zaragoza, Spain. Zaragoza is located in Aragon, northern Spain. It is the fifth largest city with a population of six hundred thousand. Zaragoza was founded on the river Ebro in 14 BC as a Roman settlement. The center piece of the city is a huge baroque cathedral, the Basilica Cathedral of our Lady of the Pilar. Most of the current cathedral was built in 1681, but original structures date back to the first or second century AD. The basilica is Roman Catholic and was built to honor the Virgin Mary. During the Spanish Civil War three bombs fell on the cathedral but miraculously none exploded. Visitors can still see two of the bombs and a hole in the ceiling. Visiting the cathedral is an awe inspiring experience. The cathedral is huge, built on a massive scale, and the architecture and interior design is incredibly ornate. Its open spaces are decorated with fantastic statues and rare oil paintings; magnificent works of art are visible everywhere in the church.

The NASA contingent stayed at a hotel in downtown Zaragoza. The hotel was ultra-modern and within walking distance of many city attractions. During shuttle launch delays we had plenty of free time to explore the city. Sometimes we watched live soccer matches at the stadium. Europeans refer to soccer as football, and Zaragoza had a top notch team. The atmosphere at a Spanish football match is totally different than the ambiance of an NFL game. Because of soccer hooligans, fans of the opposing teams are separated from each other by chain link fencing; horse-mounted police patrol the area. Fans constantly chant and sing slow, monotone, dirge-like tunes—the vibe is alien to an American. Spaniards take their football seriously.

Night life in Zaragoza is fantastic. We often barhopped across town to party in the tubes. The tubes are a bewildering labyrinth of narrow, winding streets with hundreds of bars. At all hours of the night the tubes are packed with a multitude of boisterous people scurrying through the maze of streets dressed in all manner of colorful clothing and displaying varying degrees of sobriety. Everyone smokes cigarettes. There is no political correctness when it comes to smoking. Spanish people smoked in airports, elevators, and hospitals.

The food in Spain is good but different from what we are used to in America. The best thing about eating dinner in Spain is that you never have to eat dinner; you can eat tapas instead. Tapas are small tasty appetizers. Many bars will serve you tapas with every drink you buy. Tapas can be a slice of bread and piece of ham, a few olives and cheese, or maybe a couple of meatballs. Many tapas pubs prominently display a cured pig leg on the bar. Spain is famous for these Serrano hams. Many gourmets acknowledge the cured Iberian pig haunch as the best ham in the world. The leg is secured in a special "ham stand" and the bartender slices off thin pieces with a specially designed knife. There are hundreds of different types of tapas and even restaurants that specialize in tapas. Many times we skipped sit down meals and barhopped, eating tapas at each establishment.

During a stay in Zaragosa some PJ buddies and I visited a bullfighting ring called the Plaza Del Torres. Bullfighting is the preeminent iconic cultural tradition associated with Spain. Bullfighting dates back to the eighth century and is still hugely popular with Spaniards. When I learned I would be traveling to Spain, I looked forward to experiencing a real Spanish bullfight. In America, politically correctness has run amuck and any sport involving animals is controversial, even horse racing. I expected to see protesters when I attended a bullfight but, pleasant surprise, there were no PETA representatives in sight. Zaragosa's bullring, one of the oldest in Spain, was built in the mid seventeen hundreds and can seat about ten thousand spectators. The arena is circular and has a diameter of a hundred meters. Zaragosa's bullring was the first in Spain to have a roof. From the outside, the arena looks like a smaller version of the Roman Coliseum. The arena is a circular battlefield of dirt and sand where matadors fights bulls. The interior of the arena is surrounded by tiers of benches to seat spectators.

During a fight the bullring is crowded with men and women from all walks of life. People smoke cigarettes and pass around suede leather bags of red wine. A small orchestra sits in the topmost tier and plays traditional music to liven up the proceedings. I took a seat with my fellow PJs and settled in to watch what I thought would be a classic bullfight. A gate opened in the side of the ring and a small press of men led a large bull onto the field. The stomping bull was hundreds of pounds of rippling muscle and wicked sharp horns. He was securely chained and chafed at his bonds. This was not what I expected to see. My friends and I looked at each other and shrugged, this was different.

The bull had a metal framework mounted on the top of his head. Straw was packed into the lattice and around the bull's horns. Suddenly a man with a torch approached the bull and lit the straw on fire. The men quickly released the bull and scrambled over the barrier wall. The bull charged and bucked around the ring, furious that his head was on fire. People from the stands hopped the short wall and streamed into the ring. *"What the heck is going on?"* I wondered. *"Where is the matador with his suit of lights? Where are the picadors and banderilleros? Where is all the pomp and ceremony?"* I watched in amazement as people from the stands, many who had been drinking, waved towels to capture the bull's attention. People leaped and scampered about trying to touch the bull, while others tried to entice the animal into charging their makeshift capes.

The bull was confused, not sure who among the crowd to attack next. But the angry bull was deceptively fast and caught a careless matador wanna-be on his horns and tossed him cartwheeling into the air. The bull kicked its razor-sharp hooves and bucked like a whirling dervish, scattering people left and right. It was chaos, confusion and anarchy, but it was exciting, especially when the bull caught someone who ventured too close and flung them into the air like a rag doll. The action was nonstop, and the crowd relentlessly pursued the bull. Eventually the bull seemed to tire, his head drooped and his chest heaved. Sweat ran in rivulets, lathering the bull's flanks. Just as he slowed to a walk firecrackers buried deep in the flaming straw, started to explode atop the bull's head. The animal was immediately infuriated and reenergized. The crowd roared their approval as the bull attacked with renewed vigor.

I soon realized this was not a traditional bullfight. We had picked an unusual night to attend our first fight. This night was a special fiesta known as the *Toro Embolado* (fire bull). This fiesta normally takes place at midnight. Sometimes the bull is set free on the street where young men dodge and run away from the charging animal. However, this Fire Bull Fiesta took place in a bull ring. Eventually, the fire in the bull's horns burned down and the bull hung his weary head. Workers led a large cow into the ring and the exhausted bull dutifully followed her, ambling out of the ring.

Subsequent bulls were introduced into the ring through a wide gate, but their heads were not set on fire. Amateur night continued. At one point I decided I would give bullfighting a try and vaulted over the wall that encircled the ring, intent on touching the bull. Many would-be matadors milled and jostled in the ring. As I began to thread my way through the crowd the bull was goring people on the other side of the arena. From across the dirt field the bull looked my way and we locked eyes. I froze in place, recognizing intelligence and malice in its eyes. Like ancient gladiators, we faced each other from across the ring. I instantly knew this was a clever, hostile beast. He sensed my challenge and trotted towards me, his sharp hooves thudding into the dust. Suddenly, the bull lowered his horns and galloped towards me, an evil red gleam in his eyes. A strategy quickly began to take form in my head, but I had to act quickly. I turned and sprinted to the edge of the ring and leaped over the wall to safety. The bull snorted in deri-sion. I didn't care; bullfighting was way scarier than I thought it would be.

Once the bull visibly began to tire from tossing people into the air, it was led out of the ring. Before they released the next bull I joined a group of twenty people gathered in front of the gate and foolishly sat in a clump a few yards in front of the doors. We sat bunched close on the ground. I bent over and grasped the man in front of me. We resembled a giant turtle shell positioned just outside the bull-pen gate. We sat rigid as statues, deter-mined not to move or raise our heads no matter what happened. Without warning the gate slammed open and a fresh bull thundered directly at us. Moving only my eyes, I nervously watched the bull charge towards us, dirt sprayed up from its hooves. The bull was tricked by our brilliant ruse and mistook our motionless, clump of humanity for an inanimate obstacle. He charged full speed and leaped over us. I felt the air ripple as a half ton of bovine fury hurtled overhead. If anyone had moved, the bull would have lowered his head and plowed through our midst. Once the bull was clear, we quickly regained our feet and scrambled in all directions. I was turbo-man and sprinted to the wall and leaped to safety, leaving a small sonic boom in my wake.

After a successful shuttle launch we often traveled to Grenada to prac-tice mountain rescue and downhill skiing. Granada is a picturesque city in southern Spain, located at the confluence of three rivers at the base of the Sierra Nevada Mountains. The city has been inhabited from the dawn of human history and currently boasts a population of 240 thousand. Muslim Moors conquered the city in 711. In the mid-fourteenth century, Moorish sultans built the Alhambra, known as the Red Fortress. The citadel is the most famous tourist attraction in Spain. The Alhambra palace is a master-piece of architecture and is the most visited historic monument in the country. In fourteen hundred and ninety two, Columbus sailed the ocean blue . . . and Sultan Boabdil surrendered Granada to Ferdinand and Isabella, the rulers of Christian Spain. Sultan Boabdil's capitulation ended the eight hundred year Muslim occupation of the Iberian Peninsula.

We did our mountain rescue training in Monochil, a short drive from Granada. The road to the rock cliffs is extremely steep and narrow with vertigo inducing drop-offs. The drive is a nail-biting, heart thumping adventure. I felt like we were in an Indiana Jones movie as we drove to the cliffs. Our passenger vans were totally unsuited for the precarious journey. When we finally arrived at the climbing area I leaped from the van and kissed the ground, thankful I hadn't tumbled down a mountain. After changing our soiled underwear, we began training on a two hundred foot rock face. Far below a long suspension bridge spanned a deep gorge. We climbed granite crags and practiced rescue procedures and systems until light failed. Then we began the dangerous descent off the mountain and back to Granada.

In addition to excellent rock climbing in Monochil, in winter there is also world class snow skiing in the Sierra Nevada Mountains. The ski area is only a short drive from Granada. PJs are adventure magnets. As if training around the world in exotic locations is not enough, there always seems to be other extravaganzas taking place, bonus adventures. At the ski slope there was a carnival celebration in full swing. Carnival in Granada takes place in February and involves masquerading in grotesque masks, much like Mardis Gras celebrations. We were training in Granada after supporting STS-75, the *Columbia* shuttle launch on 22 February1996. Also taking place on the Sierra Nevada ski slope in late February was the World Alpine Ski Championships. During the women's downhill races we positioned ourselves near a spot where racers caught some air off a small bump on the course. The women were skiing so fast you could hear air whistle off their neon bright, body suits—it was awesome! We watched American skier Picabo Street win the women's downhill title.

During ski training we arranged rescue-focused missions. We practiced cross country ski travel and hired guides and ski patrol instructors to teach us how to guide specially designed sleds down steep icy slopes. When possible we mixed in ice climbing and crevasse rescue practice. PJs constantly hone their rescue skills. When we were practicing downhill skiing, I had my hands full. Young PJs have absolutely no fear and ski the hardest, most expert slopes with breakneck speed. Sometimes they wandered off trail, ending up stuck in the middle of sheer cliffs. When crowds gathered pointing and murmuring, and women hid their faces in fear, I could be sure the object of their concern was one of my PJs. Somehow my guys always survived, although not entirely unscathed. Unlike normal humans with one guardian angel attending, God appears to assign each PJ a team of guardian angels—concrete evidence of His infinite wisdom.

CHAPTER 12

_____

YEMEN

_____

Everyone has a plan until they've been hit.
—*Joe Louis*

ALTHOUGH IT IS NOT WELL PUBLICIZED, THE AMERICAN MILITARY FRE-
quently conducts noncombatant evacuation operations (NEOs). This is
when the United States lands planes and spirits away hundreds of Americans from a dangerous political hotspot. Some NEOs are preplanned and
cocked, ready to begin if the U.S. government thinks American citizens
are in danger. Other NEOs are quickly thrown together to cope with an
emerging situation. In 1980 I deployed to Howard Air Force Base in
Panama as part of a large taskforce to support a possible NEO. The focus
of our efforts was Nicaragua. This was a huge operation with HC-130s,
HH-53 helicopters, and rescue crews from several different bases. PJs deployed from the two largest teams in the country, the 41st Rescue Squadron
at McClellan Air Force Base in California and the 55th Rescue Squadron
at Eglin Air Force Base in northwest Florida. Also included were instructors
from the PJ School at Kirtland Air Force Base, New Mexico. I deployed
with the Eglin PJs and was excited at the possibility of seeing some action.

In the years immediately leading up to 1980 the United States had
enjoyed friendly relations with Nicaragua. Ruled by the second-generation
dictator Anastasio Somoza, Nicaragua was considered an anticommunist
bastion in Central America. America gave financial aid to Somoza and
received access to Nicaragua's beef and timber industries. In return Somoza

supported U.S. policies and political agendas in the region. After a popular uprising, the Sandinistas, a communist-leaning revolutionary group, overthrew the Somoza regime and installed a five-member ruling junta. Because the United States had propped up Somoza and worked to thwart the revolution—the contra side of Ollie North's Iran-Contra operation—the Sandinistas were hostile to America. Our State Department planned to announce changes in U.S. policy regarding Nicaragua that the diplomats thought had the potential to provoke retaliation against Americans in the country. If Nicaragua reacted belligerently and became hostile towards American citizens our task force was positioned to fly into the capital city, Managua, and evacuate U.S. embassy personnel and their families. Our nation did not want another debacle like the recent Iranian hostage situation and was being proactive to ensure our citizen's safety.

The task force commander kept this operation low-key. When we arrived in Panama he ordered everyone restricted to the base for the duration of the mission. I was extremely disappointed about the restriction. I had never been to this tropical part of the world and wanted to explore the nearby city and its cultural curiosities. Another unusual aspect of this trip was our accommodations. We moved into vacant houses on base normally reserved for families. Our folks were scattered around the base housing area, four or five people to a house.

Once we settled in the tactics and plans were set and all of our planes were loaded and ready to launch into the sky at a moment's notice. We were on a short leash: in addition to being confined to base we were prohibited from drinking alcohol because we could get the word to go at any time and had to be fit to fly. We were all incredibly jazzed-up to perform the mission, but the days and weeks dragged on and on and still we never received the go-ahead. The worst-case political scenario never developed and eventually our powers on high cancelled the mission. I felt very disappointed and letdown. My dreams of combat action would not be realized on this trip. Without explanation, however, we were n't allowed to return home, and all the stifling restrictions remained in effect.

Although I was resigned to the fact that I would not see any action, I resolved that I would not return to the states without experiencing the tantalizing world outside the base gate. After we learned we were standing down I confided to a fellow PJ named Ralph that I intended to sneak off base and explore the nightlife of Panama City. He immediately insisted on coming with me. We didn't tell anyone of our plans for fear of getting in trouble. That evening we made our move. Using ninja-like stealth we easily escaped the base without being detected.

Free at last! Of course, once we escaped we quickly hailed a cab and made a beeline for the nightclub district. The transition from placid air force base to bustling metropolis was stunning. Panama City mounted an exquisite assault on our senses. The city was vibrant and alive, pulsing with energy. Delicious and exotic smells filled the air, wafting from the many curbside food vendors. Skewers of mystery meat lathered in spicy sauces sizzled and smoked on small charcoal grills. Others sold roasted plantains and other fragrant delicacies. The city was candy to our eyes with neon signs and flashing lights proclaiming the entrances to popular nightclubs. The sidewalks were human rivers flowing with crowds of colorfully dressed people jostling for space. A motley assortment of cars and trucks and bicycles plied the main thoroughfares and choked the narrow alleyways. The night was thick with sound. The noise of clanking cars and whining motorcycles, blaring horns and hawkers shouting their sales pitches, beggars pleading for money and music drifting from bars, all blended together and saturated the air with the satisfying hum of life being lived.

Ralph and I began barhopping through all the most prominent nightclubs. Although the city streets were endlessly fascinating, inside the clubs the entertainment had its own exotic appeal with an entirely different vibe from American bars. This is what I had craved, culture shock and new experiences. We were on sensory overdrive and our fun meters were pegged. I felt a tap on my shoulder and turned to see who it was. My jaw dropped! Ralph and I exchanged looks of dismay and resignation. Standing behind us were our three top PJ bosses. Somehow they had tracked us down. We were caught red-handed and there was no escape. The air went out of my emotional sails, and I felt deflated. I didn't even begin to try to talk my way out of this. I said, "OK. You got us. What can I say?"

The PJ bosses looked at me funny and started to laugh. Then a long line of PJs streamed into the bar. The bosses were just the vanguard of a boisterous posse of PJs. Cabin fever had become unbearable and apparently almost every single PJ had decided to sneak off base! Everyone was loud, animated, and ready to do some serious drinking. Thus began a spontaneous and epic night of partying. Somehow, everyone made it back onto base afterwards without incident. A few days later our entire force returned to the states and split off to their home units.

That deployment to Panama was a good example of a planned operation to carry out a NEO. Although in the end our task force was not needed, we would have had a huge positive impact on many lives if the situation had put our citizens in danger. And, as is always the case, every deployment and mission has a primary purpose, but there are always interesting side adventures and memorable experiences attached to any endeavor. Years later I would get to participate in an emergency NEO and, of course, there would be unexpected twists. Sometimes these twists are memorable adventures in their own right. During my deployments to southwest Asia I hoped to have some rescues, but I never expected I would get to participate in a NEO.

When we began deploying to Saudi Arabia in 1993 we set the routine and established the infrastructure to support follow-on deployments and rescue operations. When a new PJ team arrived, the departing team had at least a week of overlap with the new team. This allowed the new team to acclimatize, configure gear, and learn how best to carry out missions. To be effective everyone also had to be familiar with the current intelligence situation, enemy threats, and escape and evasion procedures. Although our unit was in place primarily to support rescues in the southern no-fly zone we were also available for unrelated missions that might come up, targets of opportunity, so to speak. Military commanders like PJs because we are an extremely flexible force. PJs possess such a diverse palette of rescue skills, so we never know what kind of unusual missions we may be called upon to tackle. One such mission occurred in Yemen in May 1994.

The Republic of Yemen is a small country at the southern tip of the Arabian Peninsula bordering Saudi Arabia. Yemen has a mountainous interior and flat coastal plains. Rain is scarce and only a small portion of the country is suitable for farming. Yemen has a long coastline and sits near one of the most important shipping lanes in the world. It has been a center of civilization for thousands of years. In recent centuries, the country coalesced into northern and southern factions and became a political and military battleground for foreign powers. North and South Yemen were locked in almost continual conflict as various countries in the region struggled to exert control and influence. In the nineteenth century northern Yemen was dominated by the Turkish Ottoman Empire, while Great Britain ruled southern Yemen as part of their Indian Empire. After many years of continuous strife, in 1990 North and South Yemen finally unified into the Republic of Yemen. The North dominated the new country, and the South resented the North's heavy-handed methods and policies. As a result, South Yemen tried to secede, and in late April 1994 civil war erupted between North and South Yemen.

On 4 May 1994 the North bombed the Aden Airport—Aden had been the capital of the South—and the Southern Yemini air force retaliated by attacking the Republic's capital city of Sana'a with bombs and Scud missiles, killing dozens of civilians. The situation in Sana'a was dangerous and unpredictable, and the violence had the potential to escalate. The United States decided to evacuate American civilians, embassy workers, and their families from the capital, which had an international airport nearby. The Joint Task Force Commander, Southwest Asia, assigned PJs a key role in the NEO. The operation was dubbed Tiger Rescue.

The Yemen NEO was an emergency response to an emerging situation. The commander picked PJs to act as primary airfield coordinators on the ground and as liaisons with embassy officials. At the airfield PJs would direct and position C-130 and C-141 transport aircraft and organize the loading of hundreds of evacuees. These PJs would use their portable satellite radios to establish communications with commanders back in Saudi Arabia. During the evacuation flights PJs could also provide medical care to those evacuees who needed it. If all went well during this operation PJs would once again solidify their reputations as "Jacks of all Trades." American fighter jets and AWACS prowled the edges of Saudi airspace in case they needed to provide combat air support to the transports. Ominously, South Yemen probed the operation with their fighter jets and attack helicopters, posing an unpredictable and very real danger.

Operation Tiger Rescue took place over three days. Master Sergeant Dan Inch and I acted as the PJ team leaders and took turns running the PJ portion of the evacuation. During the mission, we dressed in civilian clothes to emphasize the humanitarian nature of the evacuation. One disturbing aspect of the operation were our orders not to carry weapons. This went against my instincts as an operator, especially since we were working on an airfield pockmarked with bomb craters and surrounded by Yemini soldiers carrying AK-47 assault rifles. I chose to interpret our instructions to mean we could not *openly* carry weapons. I carried my 9mm pistol in a fanny pack around my waist and, just in case, we had some rifles broken down and stored in backpacks. I think it's unwise to walk around unarmed in a combat zone.

When I landed with my team, Amn. Rob Marks immediately set up the radio and established a communications link with our headquarters back in Saudi Arabia. Now that we were on scene I began organizing planes and load plans until an embassy official found me. He wanted me to meet with another official to receive special instructions. I followed him across the airfield and into the airport proper. We weaved around checkpoints and metal detectors eventually ending up outside the entrance to the airport. An embassy official got out of an official looking black car and introduced himself. After explaining the mission goals for the day we shook hands and he drove off.

I turned and entered the airport with my escort. Suddenly, I had a horrible realization: in order to return to the flight line I needed to move through a modern international airport complete with metal detectors and X-ray machines and I had a loaded pistol in my fanny pack. And, because of the ongoing civil war, security was beefed up and the guards were extra wary. Before we reached the first checkpoint, I pretended that I needed to use the restroom and told my escort to go on ahead. I needed to think. One option was to drop my pistol in a trash can and exit the airport, later claiming I lost the gun somehow. The lost-gun option had serious flaws. I couldn't ditch my pistol because I had signed it out by serial number. Police could easily trace the gun back to me. My personal interpretation of the, "no weapons" order would probably not be an effective defense at my court marshal. My other option was to try and sneak through the airport onto the flight line, somehow avoiding a gauntlet of security checkpoints. This was the ninja option. This daunting course of action was fraught with serious danger. If guards confronted me and caught me with a loaded pistol I knew I would not have a pleasant day. There was no telling where that situation would lead; there was a real possibility I could spend time in a Yemeni prison.

Despite the risks I decided on the ninja option. I figured I might have one slim advantage. Maybe the guards would remember me coming through the airport from the flight-line side with the embassy official and not pay me much attention. I was sweating bullets as I approached the first checkpoint. I tried to act casual and confident, not furtive and suspicious like a criminal. I waited until the guard looked away, his attention elsewhere and boldly walked behind him past the checkpoint. When I approached the X-ray and metal detectors I strode right past the line of people, bypassing the machines. I had to play it that way. I could not hang out near the detectors waiting for guards to look the other way and then sneak past; there were just too many. As I brazenly strode around each checkpoint I feared to hear a sudden barked command, rushing feet behind me, and hands spinning me around to face angry guards with drawn weapons.

The last part of my mission to get on the airfield was tricky and nerve-racking. Imagine being at an American airport in the gate area where people board the airplanes. Then imagine trying to sneak out a Jetway or access door without being stopped. I remembered the door I had used to enter the terminal and luckily it was unlocked. I picked my moment and quickly slipped out the door onto the airfield. I boldly strode across the airfield, never looking behind me until I reached my plane. Finally, I turned and looked back the way I came and saw . . . nothing. No one was pursuing me. I was in the midst of an ongoing civil war, surrounded by fresh bomb craters and soldiers carrying soviet rifles, but as scary situations go, so far Tiger Rescue was a relaxing walk in the park compared to Operation Ninja Escape.

I needed to refocus back on the mission. I quickly put my airport terminal ordeal behind me and got down to work. On the first day our PJ contingent successfully assisted in the evacuation of approximately four hundred civilians. The pilots and crews worked nonstop to bring our evacuees to safety as quickly as possible, and it wasn't easy. Our special passengers were very fearful, and we found ourselves using our medical skills and equipment more than we expected. I empathized with our unsettled passengers. I could imagine having to gather up my family and leave my home under dangerous circumstances with only a few hours to pack and prepare. To quickly evacuate as many people as possible we stuffed them into the passenger compartments of our planes like sardines. Even on a good day the stark interior of a military cargo plane is a far cry from the relative comfort of a passenger jet. A military transport is designed to move unfeeling cargo, not people. Passenger seats are made from an uncomfortable net of red webbing attached to the cold bare walls of the aluminum fuselage and appear to be a mere afterthought in the plane's design. The comfort differential between traveling on a military cargo plane versus a passenger jet equates to the degree of change one would experience moving from a lavishly furnished home with modern amenities to a house with unpainted drywall, furniture made from stacked plastic milk crates, and an outhouse. The close confines combined with the stress of the situation caused numerous bouts of airsickness. It was a puke fest, and the PJs were busy nonstop. Despite the many challenges, when the dust settled Operation Tiger Rescue had evacuated more than six hundred people in only a few days.

By July of that year the North had militarily defeated the South. The Southern rebels fled to Oman and the civil war officially ended. In the following years the South faced the daunting task of rebuilding their infrastructure and society. The North continued to dominate policy and the South remained disaffected. Conflict, strife, and instability continued to plague the country. Terrorist factions and other disaffected elements gradually gained a foothold in Yemen. The United States established relatively friendly relations with the country and after 9/11 their government worked with the America to fight terrorism. The United States even used predator drones to take out elements of Al-Qaida in Yemen.

During the Arab Spring of 2011, protests wracked Yemen and the people called for the resignation of President Ali Abdullah Saleh, who had ruled for thirty-three years. After intense political machinations Salaweh reluctantly set the stage to relinquish power. Despite the turmoil of these times, America continued to pursue its antiterror agenda in Yemen and successfully killed the infamous American citizen turned Al-Qaida terrorist, Anwar al-Awlaki, with a drone strike on 30 Sept 2011. The situation in Yemen is extremely complex and their ultimate political destiny is uncertain.

CHAPTER 13

WARRIOR DOWN

Nothing is so exhilarating in life as to be shot at with no result.
—*Winston Churchill*

I TEACH A PJ AND CRO HISTORY CLASS ON THE FIRST DAY OF THE PJ
apprentice course. When I enter the classroom twenty men dressed in impeccable uniforms snap to attention. Their class leader barks out, "Stand-
by," and I reply, "Carry on." The students take their seats and I can see
they are excited and eager to begin. I'm not teaching to academic hostages
or apathetic teenagers. These men want to be here and have struggled and
fought and suffered for the privilege to sit in these chairs—they are America's finest. To get to this point, these candidates have shed blood, sweat,
and tears for more than a year. They have completed a grueling battery of
elite military courses and six months of intensive medical training. Most
military members would consider any one of these courses an end in itself.
But for these candidates, Airborne, Halo, Combat Diver School, Survival
and all the rest of these premier schools are merely waypoints on the road
to their real goal: the PJ and CRO Apprentice Course and, ultimately, the
pararescue maroon beret.

I think it's important to know the history, standards, and milestones
of your chosen profession, especially when that profession is the unique
and storied brotherhood of pararescue. Knowledge for knowledge's sake is
certainly justified, but when I teach the history class I have other more
important goals. In order to understand what is expected of them these

candidates must know the deeds and accomplishments of the PJs who came before them. This is also an introduction to the PJ mindset and philosophy. Past PJs wrote their legacy large in the annals of military history. Colorful characters and legends, they were pioneers who set the standard. They live on in their medal citations and in stories told around PJ campfires. PJ history is a litany of heroes, awe inspiring and humbling. It seems almost impossible, given what has gone before, that anyone new can leave their own mark,the standard is so high. But I know that some of these men can and will leave their mark; I have seen it firsthand. This is the new generation and it is their turn to write the next chapters of PJ history. I start my presentation with a simple observation. "Look around the room at your teammates. Your rescue missions still lie in the future, but some of you in this room will be heroes!"

I like to follow the exploits of young PJs and CROs who I helped train. Like all instructors I hope that my teaching will have some special impact. We graduate five four classes a year, about a hundred new pararescue jumpers and ten combat rescue officers per year. Sadly, some of my former students have already died in combat. Some have suffered physical injuries such as gunshot wounds while others suffer wounds to their psyche after experiencing the loss of comrades, the stress of combat missions, and prolonged separation from family and loved ones. Some of my former students have distinguished themselves during high profile combat rescue missions. It is very satisfying to hear of their heroic exploits. Like those who have gone before this new breed of PJ warriors is writing their legacy with bold brush strokes.

Zachary Alan Kline was born 8 March 1980 in Hartford, Connecticut. His father Barry was a CPA and his mother Doreen was a stay-at-home housewife. They divorced when Zack was young and Doreen took Zack to Philadelphia. When Zack was a teenager he moved to Harrisburg and lived with his father. During high school Zack did not participate in organized sports, but he did enjoy the outdoors and became an Eagle Scout. After he graduated from Cumberland Valley High School he loaded his pickup truck and drove to Alaska.

Zack settled in Anchorage to pursue a degree in environmental planning and policy at Alaska Pacific University. To pay his way he took a job at the university and the Alaska Rock Gym. After receiving his degree he took a job with Alaska Mountaineering and Hiking. This job inspired Zack to become even more involved in outdoor pursuits and he took up sea kayaking, backcountry hiking, white water rafting, and rock climbing. Along the way he met Nick Parker. Nick was older than Zack and was an expert on Denali (Mt. McKinley) and the numerous rugged Alaskan mountain ranges. Nick was well known for his knowledge of Alaskan geography and would occasionally guide PJs from the 71st Rescue Squadron on their mountain rescue missions. It was from Nick that Zack first heard about pararescue. After a bit of online research Zack decided he wanted to become a PJ. The Alaskan PJ team is part of the Alaska Air National Guard and has evolved over time from the 71st Air Rescue Squadron to the 212th Rescue Squadron. The team consists of twenty-two full-time PJs, nine full-time CROs, and fifteen traditional part-time guardsmen, a mixture of PJs and CROs.

Zack contacted the PJ team at Kulis Air Force Base and arranged to take the Physical Ability and Stamina Test (PAST). The PAST consists of running, swimming, and calisthenics. A candidate must pass the test before he will be allowed to attempt PJ training. The test is difficult because a PJ prospect needs to have a high level of fitness to have even a slim chance at completing training. The Alaskan PJ team makes their PAST even harder than the standard, with longer run and swim distances. Zack lacked an organized athletic background, and he failed the test. That failure opened Zack's eyes, and he resolved to beat the test the next time around. He trained for nine months, running, swimming and doing calisthenics. When he took the test again, he crushed it.

With brown hair and hazel eyes, Zack is six feet one inches tall with a slim, athletic build. He was twenty-four years old when he started Air Force Basic Training in November 2004. After basic, he started the PJ indoctrination course with one hundred and nine other candidates. Zack was among the twenty PJ wannabes who completed the training, statistically finishing in the middle of his class. After completing all the required pipeline commando courses he began paramedic school in Albuquerque, New Mexico, the last hurdle before the apprentice course. During paramedic school he met a pretty emergency room technician named Naomi and they married. After he passed the Paramedic National Registry exam, Zack began the actual PJ apprentice course in January 2007 along with twenty-two other pipeline survivors, and graduating in June of that year.

After he received his maroon PJ beret, SAmn. Zack Kline reported to his unit in Alaska and worked as a part-time guardsman. In the months that followed, he participated in routine rescue missions until he was placed on full-time status to prepare for a deployment to Afghanistan. In February 2008 Zack left for Bagram Air Base, part of an Alaskan contingent of PJs and CROs. He flew on HH-60 Pave Hawk helicopters, call sign Pedro. The Pedro call sign is a throwback to the early days of Vietnam when PJs flew on HH-43 Husky helicopters and rescued hundreds of shot-down pilots. For seventy days in Afghanistan Zack flew numerous medical evacuation missions, transporting injured Americans and local Afghans to hospitals.

Zack completed his deployment and returned to Alaska in June 2008 to work full time in the unit's mission equipment section and continued to gain experience during local rescue missions. During this time, Zack's wife Naomi decided to pursue a degree and was accepted into the University of New Mexico's medical program. To stay near his wife, Zack worked a special deal between his unit and the PJ and CRO school in Albuquerque. In October 2009 Zack became a full-time PJ instructor at the school, temporarily on loan from his Alaskan unit. For the next year Zack taught PJ Medicine in the apprentice course and worked harder than he ever had in his life.

During his time as an instructor Zack perfected his medical skills and increased his general knowledge to become a well-rounded and solid PJ. In October 2010 he returned to Alaska to begin to train up for another deployment to Afghanistan. On 26 December SSgt. Zack Kline deployed to a combat theater for the second time in his fledgling career. Unlike his first uneventful deployment, however, this trip would be marked by plenty of action. In the coming days Zack would need all his skills and training just to survive.

This time Zack arrives at Bagram as part of a team of ten PJs and two CROs. Major Jesse Peterson, a recent CRO graduate, is in overall command of the PJs and MSgt. Chad Moore is the ranking NCO. The helicopter pilots and flight crews are deployed from U.S. rescue squadrons based at Royal Air Force Lakenheath, United Kingdom, and Kadena Air Base, Okinawa. All the deployed rescue forces are assigned to the 83rd Expeditionary Rescue Squadron.

The west side of Bagram Air Base is called Camp Cunningham. The camp is named after PJ Jason Cunningham, Air Force Cross recipient who lost his life on a rescue mission during the Battle of Robert's Ridge in 2002. Zack and the other rescue flyers stay on the east side of the base. Zack shares a camping-style trailer with three other PJs. The trailer sits on the edge of the flight line where the HH-60 helicopters are parked. The trailer is furnished with beds and a space heater. During the day, the mercury hovers in the fifties, but at night the temperature plunges and it often snows.

As far as rescue missions go, the deployment starts out slowly. For the first part of the deployment Zack flies as a basic PJ team member. After two months of in-flight training and experience on actual combat missions Zack is promoted to element leader. This is a significant accomplishment and means that during rescue missions Zack will be in charge of PJ operations in the helicopter. He will determine PJ tactics and be the final decision maker in the back of the Pave Hawk. Whenever possible the HH-60 Pave Hawks, call sign Pedro, are kept close to the action. Typically two rescue helicopters will locate near a forward operating base (FOB) where the army is launching ground patrols and attacks. When combat action is sporadic, crews will be on-call for twenty-four hours and then have a down day. When fighting is heavy, crews will stand alert for twelve hours and have twelve hours off.

There are different categories of rescue alert based on how fast the helicopters need to respond to a call. During Category B alert the Pedros have to be able to take off within one hour after they're scrambled. During Category A alert the helicopters and PJs have to be airborne in less than fifteen minutes. When there is a rescue mission Pedros always work in pairs and always fly in an organized formation, oftentimes in single file. They use specialized tactics and strategies that have been developed over the years. The lead helicopter carries a pilot, copilot, left-door gunner, and a flight engineer (FE) in the right door to operate the rescue hoist. The gunner and FE control .50-caliber machine guns mounted in each door. They use the fifties to protect the aircraft while it's in a hover. A CRO team commander, a PJ team leader, and a PJ team member ride in the back of the aircraft. The second helicopter is designated as trail. It follows behind the lead Pedro and has a standard flight crew plus a PJ element leader and PJ team member.

As springtime nears and the tenacious Afghan winter loosens its grip on the mountain passes, the Taliban begin to step up their attacks. Decades of fighting have hardened the Taliban, forging them into formidable adversaries. Taliban often fight in three-man fire teams. One guerilla carries a rocket propelled grenade launcher (RPG), a second man acts as a light machine gunner or mortarman, and the third man loads up with extra ammo, rockets, and supplies. They all carry the ubiquitous AK-47 assault rifles. The enemy is a master of the local terrain and geography and knows all the secret paths and hiding places. They have caches of food and supplies, and use handheld radios and cell phones to communicate and coordinate attacks. Using up to fifty fighters they attack even well-fortified positions. The Taliban are an incongruous mix of Isalmic fundamentalism, tribal primitivism, and sophisticated technology.

Coalition forces are supremely confident and set up camps in the midst of enemy territory. A typical FOB can shelter hundreds of soldiers and is reminiscent of an ancient Roman fort. Combat engineers fortify the defense perimeter with Hesco barriers. Hercules Engineering Solutions Consortium is the British company that invented and manufactures these collapsible steel mesh containers lined with heavy duty synthetic fabric. Natural disaster experts originally designed these barriers to serve as emergency dikes to guard against floods. Soldiers can quickly erect Hesco barriers and use front loaders to fill them with sand and rocks. In their final form they are giant sand-filled cubes. Some barriers are seven feet tall, one hundred feet long, and five feet thick. These barriers can protect against rocket propelled grenades and most car bombs. The army tops the Hescos with a tangle of razor wire and strategically placed heavy machine guns to protect the camp. Soldiers inside the fort live in prefabricated buildings and fortified bunkers. Some FOBs even have small airfields and field hospitals.

Army units aggressively mount operations to clear valleys of enemy fighters, secure territory, or go after important terrorist leaders. Operations can involve hundreds of soldiers with support from Apache and Kiowa attack helicopters and sometimes even A-10 Thunderbolts. F-15s and F-16s can also use guns and laser-guided bombs to support the ground operations. There is a lot of daytime fighting. The Taliban and Al Qaeda have learned the hard way that coalition forces have a huge advantage when it's dark. With night vision goggles (NVGs), forward looking infrared cameras, and thermal imaging devices, the U.S. Air Force owns the night.

BAGRAM AIR BASE & ALASAY VALLEY, KAPISA PROVINCE AFGHANISTAN, 23 APRIL 2011

THE PLAYERS:

Lead HH-60G Pave Hawk helicopter, call sign Pedro 83:

    Pilot Capt. Joshua Hallada

    Copilot 1st Lt. Elliott Milliken

    Flight engineer SAmn. Michael Price

    Left-door gunner SAmn. Justin Tite

    CRO Maj. Jesse Peterson

    PJ team leader TSgt. Chris "Uri" Uriarte

    PJ team member TSgt. Shane Hargis

Trail HH-60G Pave Hawk helicopter, call sign Pedro 84:

    Pilot Maj. Philip Bryant

    Copilot Capt. Louis Nolting

    Flight engineer TSgt. James Davis

    Flight engineer TSgt. Heath "Scuba" Culbertson

    Left-door gunner SSgt. William "Gonzo" Gonzalez

    PJ element leader SSgt. Zack Kline

    PJ team member SSgt. Bill Cenna

Crashed helicopter's wingman, OH-58 Kiowa Warrior attack helicopter, call sign Pest

AH-64 Apache attack helicopters, call sign Apache Warrior

A-10 Thunderbolt II "Warthog" close-air support aircraft, call sign Sandy

------

Sergeants Zack Kline and Bill Cenna are on Category A alert. They are part of a two-ship rescue task force and will ride on the trail aircraft. Major Peterson and Sergeants Chris Uriarte and Shane Hargis will fly on the lead helicopter. When the squadron scrambles the alert crews at four o'clock in the morning, the airfield is cloaked in darkness and the cold is brittle. They are told there is a Fallen Angel, code words for a downed aircraft and crew. The rescue pilot, CRO, and PJ team leader get mission details from the tactical operations center (TOC) while the rest of the crews get the Pedros ready for takeoff. It's assholes and elbows and everyone moves with a purpose. Engines whine, rotors turn, and both helicopters lift off in only nine minutes.

The two rescue Pave Hawks speed through the night, flying less than one hundred feet above the ground. They fly towards the crash site of an OH-58D Kiowa Warrior attack and reconnaissance helicopter. The Kiowa got off a quick Mayday call before crashing east of Bagram in a large field of boulders five thousand feet up the side of a mountain. The crash site is only twenty miles away, a short flight for the Pedros. The PJs don't know the reason for the crash, but it is possible that Taliban insurgents brought down the Kiowa. The downed helicopter was part of a two-ship formation. The word is that one of the crashed Kiowa's pilots is not doing so well.

When the stricken Kiowa went down his wingman immediately passed the coordinates of the crash site to the TOC and remained on scene, circling overhead. The recovery of shot-down pilots is always a high priority and American combat rescue forces are the best in the world. Within minutes F-15 Strike Eagles and two AH-64 Apache attack helicopters arrive on scene. The Kiowa carries a crew of two, but communications with the crashed pilots is extremely broken and for the most part unreadable. During its flight pattern, one of the Apaches spots a firefly three hundred meters from the crash site. The firefly is a small infra red signaling light that is invisible to the naked eye but shows as a bright green light when viewed through night vision goggles (NVGs). The presence of the firefly confirms there is at least one survivor and provides a tangible target for the rescuers. An Apache highlights the survivor's location for the Pave Hawks by "painting" the crewman's position with its infrared laser target designator. The pilots flying the Pave Hawks can see the laser light through their goggles.

The Pedros arrive and link up with the attack aircraft and take up an orbit a few miles from the crash site while they devise a plan and coordinate their actions. The Pave Hawks are lean, mean, and stripped for action. Over the past few years rescue crews have changed the Pave hawk's configuration to adapt to enemy attack schemes and to compensate for the high altitude Afghan geography. The Pave Hawk is a relatively small helicopter and has limited space for patients. Heavily loaded with fuel and rescue gear, it can't hover at higher altitudes where the air is thin. Because of these limitations, the crew scrutinizes every piece of equipment on the chopper with an eye towards trimming off useless weight. Crews forego using most of the available helicopter armor because it's too heavy. The benefit of discarding the armor is a lighter aircraft and more speed and hovering power; the risk is greater crew vulnerability to enemy fire. Without armor, rifle bullets can easily penetrate the thin aluminum skin of the helicopter and kill crewmembers inside.

Helicopter mechanics long ago removed the extra internal fuel tanks. Full of fuel, the gas tanks were heavy and took up a lot of room in the cramped cargo compartment. Now the choppers have a shorter flight range, but they have more power, maneuverability, and space to hold wounded soldiers. Mechanics even stripped the helicopter of the heavy steel support framework on the ceiling used to anchor rappel and fast ropes. Also gone are the bulky fast ropes that PJs normally use to slide to the ground. Instead, the PJs use the Pedro's rescue hoist to infiltrate—it's light and fast. However, some items are worth their weight and stay onboard. The left door gunner and the FE in the right door each carry twelve hundred rounds for their .50-caliber machine guns. They use the fifties to protect the aircraft from enemy attack while the helicopter floats motionless and vulnerable in a hover, trying to hoist PJs and their patients to safety. Without its guns the helicopter would be a sitting duck. Even with the fifties it is still crazy dangerous and super courageous for a pilot to hold a hover and attempt a pickup in a hail of bullets.

The PJs also configure their gear to be bare-bones light but combat effective. Since they conduct so many missions during the day, good camouflage is supremely important. PJs wear state-of the-art multi-cam uniforms that make them nearly invisible on the ground. They paint every piece of gear to blend with their surroundings, including their rifles. They wear body armor and carry short, collapsible M-4 rifles mounted with advanced optics and 40mm grenade launchers. And they carry plenty of hand grenades and thirty-round magazines full of rifle ammunition. When you enter the shadow of the valley of death you need to be able to fight your way back into the light. PJs don't skimp on guns and bullets.

To save weight the PJs scrap their standard forty pound medical rucksacks. They position the bulk of their medical supplies in a roll-down bag attached to helicopter's aft bulkhead. In the back of the chopper they also stow body bags and American flags. In the event they recover a fallen hero, they transport him in dignity in a body bag carefully draped with the Stars and Stripes. Sergeant Cenna carries a streamlined ten pound medical kit with only the most useful gear, time-tested on numerous combat missions. Sergeant Kline carries a bag containing extrication tools, including a Sawzall, grinder and crash axe in case he needs to free a pilot trapped in metal wreckage. The PJs wear bullet-resistant ballistic helmets and noise-cancelling headsets. They configure their headsets and radios so they can hear the helicopter pilots' talk in their left ear while they can talk privately with each other on a different frequency and listen with their right ears. For them, multitasking is second nature.

It's still dark when the rescue attempt begins. Pedro 83, the lead helicopter, flies to what the crew thinks is the crash site. The Pedro pulls into a hover and the Guardian Angel team consisting of Maj. Jesse Peterson, and Tech Sergeants Chris Uriarte and Shane Hargis quickly hoist to the ground. Once down, they free themselves from the cable and move to the survivor. The rescue team gets hands-on the surviving copilot, takes cover, and establishes security. They perform a quick medical assessment and discover the army aviator has a broken jaw and some scrapes and bruises, but is otherwise uninjured. The copilot tells his rescuers that after the crash he moved about three hundred meters upslope away from the wreckage, dodging bullets as he fled the scene. He reports that the other pilot is still at the crash site, dead or unconscious. The rescue team passes on the information about the other pilot and Pedro 84 speeds into action.

Sergeants Zack Kline and Bill Cenna are on Pedro 84 readying to deploy to the actual crash site. It is one minute from insert and dawn is just beginning to break. Sergeant Kline flips up his helmet-mounted NVGs and uses his naked eyes. Sergeant Cenna does the same; they have much better depth perception without the goggles and the rapidly changing light conditions make the NVGs a liability. Because of the steep slope and the boulder field the Pedro will have to hold a high hover and lower the PJs from 160 feet above ground. This is an unusually high hover and will add time and danger to the insert. Sergeant Kline clips the Jaws of Life extraction device onto the hook at the end of the rescue hoist cable. He also connects the titanium basket litter to the hook and positions the litter between himself and Sergeant Cenna. The two PJs stand in the open door with the litter between them. Their hip harnesses are connected to the hook with unbreakable, two foot long lanyards that will suspend them from the cable: they are ready to go.

Pedro 84's flight engineer, Tech Sergeant Davis, uses the rescue hoist to rapidly lower Sergeants Kline and Cenna, and the litter and Jaws of Life, to the ground. Once they reach the ground and disconnect themselves and the litter and Jaws from the hook they take a knee and scan for the other rescue team. As they assess the situation they see that Pedro 84 is taking fire and is quickly departing the area. The PJs are only fifty meters from the crashed Kiowa but are separated from the other team by three hundred meters and an intervening boulder-strewn ridge. They can't see the other team so they begin to pick their way down to the crash site.

Frustratingly, despite being separated by only a few hundred meters the two PJ rescue teams cannot talk to each other because there is a large ridge of jumbled granite boulders between them that blocks their radio signals. Both teams have to glean their information from the helicopters, which can talk to everyone from their vantage on high.

It's time to press on with their mission and Sergeants Kline and Cenna carefully pick their way fifty feet down the boulder strewn hill to the man-gled Kiowa. The ground slopes steeply downward at thirty degrees. The bleak boulder field is occasionally slashed by pea-gravel washes and dirt ravines. They realize they are stranded, but stay focused on the immediate task at hand. The twisted helicopter is mashed into the ground with its left side facing up. There is debris scattered around the area, including the heli-copter's two Hydra rocket pods. Each seven-tube pod has live rockets still inside. There is no evidence of a fire: a good thing! The high explosive, 70mm Hydra rockets, called ten pounders, have a kill radius of over 150 feet. The rockets do not discriminate between good and evil; if they deto-nate Sergeants Kline and Cenna could be killed.

While Pedro 83 and the PJs at the high site cope with their situation, Sergeants Kline and Cenna have their own circumstances to deal with. It only takes a cursory search to find the pilot. He is lying next to the crashed chopper. Mysteriously, it looks like someone has dragged him from the wreckage and arranged his body. He is apparently deceased and lies with his helmet still on and his eyes closed. His legs are straight and his feet are placed together with his arms are at his side. Sergeant Cenna carefully checks for vital signs and does a medical assessment while Sergeant Kline scours the area for sensitive items. The pilot is twenty-nine-year-old CWO Terry L. Varnadore. As the pilot he sat in the right seat and it's apparent that his Kiowa impacted the ground on its right side. He has no pulse, blood pressure, or respiration. In anticipation of their extraction, the PJs carefully place the fallen hero's body into the basket litter and securely strap him in. Kline also places the pilot's weapon and various documents in the litter. When the helicopter returns they will hoist everyone into the chopper in two iterations. As the PJs take cover about ten feet from the wreckage and wait for their ride home, they will guard and watch over the pilot.

When the PJs unclipped from the hook, Sergeant Davis reversed the hoist and retrieved the cable back into the chopper where it wound onto its spool. As the helicopter transitioned into forward flight, the crew heard the pop, pop, pop of hostile gunfire. Sergeant Davis had barely finished retrieving the cable when the attack began. As he moved away from the open door he took an AK-47 round through his right calf. The bullet shattered both bones in his lower leg and the flight engineer screamed, "I'm hit!" Pedro 84's pilot immediately accelerated the chopper away from the fire zone and radioed that his FE has been shot. Sergeant Davis tells his crew he's not doing too well and is bleeding profusely. The pilot decides to quickly return to Bagram to get him definitive medical care and to pick up a replacement flight engineer.

Soon after Sergeant Davis is shot, the gunner, SSgt. William Gonzalez scrambles over to provide first aid. He sees a pool of blood on the floor by his friend, but remarkably Davis is still conscious and breathing. Sergeant Gonzalez quickly applies a tourniquet to stop the bleeding and scavenges the PJ medical kit for gauze and bandages to sop up the blood. During the flight, Sergeant Gonzalez does what he can to care for the wounded flight engineer. Sergeant Davis is lucky. If he had lingered in the open door for only a second longer, the bullet would have hit him dead center. After a short flight Pedro 84 lands and the crew transfers Sergeant Davis into the care of the Craig Joint Theater Hospital emergency room.

During the flight to Bagram Pedro 84 radioed the base to coordinate a replacement for Sergeant Davis. After landing and dropping their flight engineer off at the hospital, they taxi from the refueling point to pick up their new FE, TSgt. Heath Culbertson. When Sergeant Culbertson climbs aboard, he is shocked to see the blood soaked interior of the helicopter. He has seen blood before, but this is different. It's not the blood of a stranger he has picked up on a rescue mission; it's the blood of a friend. Only minutes earlier he had been awakened from a deep sleep by frantic banging on his door. When he tumbled from his rack and opened his door, he was quickly briefed on the situation. In only a few hectic minutes Culbertson suited up and raced to the aircraft. And now here he is, stepping in blood and hooking into the intercom system, getting ready to fly on a dangerous rescue mission. The whole situation seems unreal.

Meanwhile, three hundred meters upslope from the crash site and Staff Sergeant Kline's PJ team, Major Peterson works the radios, coordinating with Pedro 83 for pickup and relaying information about the situation on the ground. The Pedro 83 PJ team leader, Tech Sergeant Uriarte, decides against moving down slope to link up with the other PJ team, which is at the crash site. The two Guardian Angel teams are separated by a steep ridge with insurgents in between. They decide to stay in place and wait for extraction. A few moments later Pedro 83 swoops in to pick up their rescue team and the surviving copilot. The helicopter immediately takes enemy fire from the vicinity of a large tree midway between the two PJ teams. The left gunner, SAmn. Justin Tite, sees the bullets coming up and returns fire with his .50-caliber machine gun.

The situation is getting dicey. Pedro 83 pilot, Capt. Joshua Hallada, decides to pullout his PJ team now! The chopper has been flying and burning fuel for some time and is much lighter and more maneuverable. Captain Hallada comes in low and powers into a twenty foot hover. Senior Airman Michael Price, the flight engineer, lowers the cable and strop to the ground. Tech Sergeant Shane Hargis, who has been acting as the primary medic prepares to take the copilot up on the hoist. He quickly connects himself and the copilot to the cable and gives a thumbs-up signal for the FE to begin retrieval. At that moment insurgents open fire on the hovering helicopter. The Pedro is a stationary target and can't survive for long in the fierce swarm of bullets. Someone calls a go-around, an emergency command to immediately abandon the operation and fly free of the fire zone. Since the PJ and survivor are already connected to the cable, Senior Airman Price has no choice but to cut the hoist cable to prevent dragging

Sergeant Hargis and the co-pilot through a boulder field. The drag through boulders will almost certainly kill Sergeant Hargis and his patient, and if the steel cable tangles on a rock it will endanger the whole helicopter.

Sergeant Hargis is looking up at the FE in the door expecting to be hoisted into the air with the copilot in tow when suddenly twenty feet of quarter-inch thick steel cable falls from the sky. After the FE triggered an explosive guillotine device to chop through the twisted steel strands of the hoist cable it fell free. Sergeant Hargis is fortunate he is still on the ground when Airman Price shears the cable. If he had been thirty or more feet above ground the fall would likely dash him and his patient onto jagged rocks and almost certainly kill them. All Pave Hawks have a device that can chop through the hoist cable. The crew only uses this explosive guillotine as a last resort when there is a danger to the aircraft, such as the cable getting jammed among large boulders. In this case, the FE knows the PJ is still on the ground and he needs to chop the cable and leave now! In the back of their minds all PJs know that during a hoist there is always a possibility the crew will cut the cable. It makes sense to shear the cable and sacrifice one PJ if it means saving five other souls onboard the helicopter. The result of this emergency is that Pedro 83s recovery attempt fails and for the moment the rescue team and their survivor are stranded in extremely hostile territory.

After shearing the hoist cable and bugging out, the lead helicopter takes up an orbit a safe distance away, while the crew brain-storms a plan to retrieve their rescue team. A short time later they notify their PJs that since they no longer have a hoist, they will come in and attempt a one wheel hover. This means they will descend as if they were going to land, but only the right wheel will touch the steep slope. If they were to let the helicopter settle until the left wheel also touched the ground, the aircraft would list to the left, tip over and tumble down the hill. So, they plan to keep power in their hover, balance the right wheel on the slope, and keep the chopper level with the left wheel five feet off the ground. The helicopter makes its final approach, and everyone is laser focused and on the lookout for hostile fire. The pilot skillfully executes the one wheel hover, and the rescue team and their patient scramble in through the right door in less than ten seconds. The pilot pulls power and Pedro 84 quickly departs the area—a successful rescue! However, as they leave they again take enemy fire and damage to the aircraft. Despite all this, Captain Hallada wants to try to extract the second team of PJs and radios Staff Sergeant Kline to look for suitable landing areas. Damaged and running low on fuel, Pedro 83 is relieved to hear that Pedro 84 has dropped off their wounded FE and is on its way back to rejoin the fight. In the meantime, Captain Hallada plans to try another one wheel hover to recover Sergeants Kline and Cenna along with the fallen hero. Pedro 84's PJs have now been on the ground for two hours.

Pedro 83 calls Sergeant Kline on the radio and tells him they are ready to try a one wheel hover pick up. The PJs search, but they can't find a good area nearby for the helicopter to attempt the recovery. With no place to land, Captain Hallada decides to make for FOB Morales-Frazier to get gas and ammo. A minute later, any further search for a landing site is abruptly terminated when the Pedro 84 PJs come under intense automatic weapons fire. They scramble for cover and dive behind some large boulders. The enemy fire tapers off after a few minutes, and the PJs finally get some good news over the radio. Their helicopter, Pedro 84, has dropped off the wounded FE at the hospital and is on its way back to the crash site.

All during this rescue operation the Apache and Kiowa attack helicopters fly circles in the distance. Their specialty is killing and neutralizing enemy threats with rockets and machine guns, but so far no one can pinpoint exactly where the bad guys are hiding. The gunships stay out of the rescuers way, but are immediately available if needed. A four-ship flight of A-10 Thunderbolts has also arrived on scene. Affectionately nicknamed Warthogs because of their toughness and ungainly appearance, their call sign Sandy harkens back to the propeller-driven A-1 Skyraiders of the Vietnam era and was the standard call sign for air-to-ground attack aircraft that provided protection and fire support to rescue helicopters.

Pedro 84 finally arrives and is determined to reclaim its rescue team. On the ground the PJs move cautiously about the area and prepare for the helicopter's pickup attempt. They give the chopper an update on the situation and report the recent attack on their position. The pilot says he will fly the helicopter straight to the PJs location and hoist them out. To help the chopper spot them from the air, Zack marks his position by spreading a VS-17 signal panel on the ground. The panel is two feet by six feet and is a bright fluorescent pink designed to be easily seen from the air. Even though the rescue team has experienced hostile fire they still plan to take the time needed to recover the pilot's body. The pilot remains their focus and they position him in a protected area. The initial plan is for one PJ to accompany the litter and hoist into the helicopter with the deceased pilot; then, the second PJ will hoist into the aircraft.

On Pedro 84 Flight Engineer Heath Culbertson will operate the hoist during this pickup attempt. As the helicopter descends on its approach it comes under intense enemy fire. Sergeant Culbertson can feel rounds slamming into the helicopter and hears bullets hissing around him as he searches for the origin of the attack. Suddenly, a bullet hammers into the side of his helmet and slams him into a control panel and onto the floor. Incredibly, the bullet penetrates his helmet but careens around the inside contour and miraculously misses his skull by a small fraction of an inch. The bullet blasts out the opposite side of the helmet and punches through the windshield, about a foot above the pilot's head. From his vantage point on the floor of the helicopter Sergeant Culbertson is able to look out under his .50-caliber machine gun and can finally see the muzzle flashes of the enemy attackers. He quickly calls for a go-around. Enraged, he focuses his gun on the enemy and unleashes a blistering barrage of heavy .50-caliber bullets. Sergeant Culbertson's quick response in returning fire suppresses the threat and probably saves the helicopter. On the left side of the chopper an enemy bullet comes up through the floor directly under the gunner's seat. The round rips a hole through Sergeant Gonzalez's kneepad and tears it off his leg but miraculously misses his kneecap. The Pedro suffers at least seven solid bullet impacts during the attack and the pilot reluctantly decides to head for FOB Morales-Frazier to refuel and check the helicopter for potentially damage.

For the moment, both rescue helicopters are gone, but there are still plenty of attack planes in the air. Sergeants Kline and Cenna take cover behind some large stones. They are having trouble getting radio reception and try to move to a better area, but as soon as they move back near the wreckage enemy Taliban fighters open fire, forcing them to dive behind a boulder to take cover. They both huddle behind a granite rock the size of a tombstone; they are practically stacked on top of each other. Zack still wears his noise-canceling headset, so he hears the loud reports of gunshots as strange staccato bursts of silence. Bullets chew up the earth on either side of the PJs sending gouts of dirt into the air. Rounds thwack into the wreckage behind them sounding like dull, muted bells. As bullets streak past them the PJs' conversation mostly consists of short, disjointed exclamations like, "Holy Shit!" and "Can you fucking believe this?" Their situation is very unnerving and they squish against the rock, trying to get small.

Sergeant Kline spies a ravine twenty meters away that looks like a possible escape route. He tells Sergeant Cenna, "If things get too bad, that's our back door out of here." Zack gets on the radio to request fire support from the Apaches and Warthogs. Like small explosions, enemy bullets are churning up dirt all around him. In the heat of the moment he abandons all radio and close-air-support protocols and yells into his radio, "We're getting shot at from the tree up on the hill. Shoot the fucking tree!" His instructions are actually better than they sound. The tree in question is about one hundred meters upslope. It's a huge, forty-foot tall tree and stands alone, the only tree for miles. The Apaches and Warthogs take turns making gun and rocket runs. Explosions rock the hillside and blow all the leaves off the tree, but the tree still stands. Aerial destruction rains down on the Taliban's hiding spots and temporarily silences their rifles.

The lull in the attack is brief and soon bullets are again impacting around the PJs' position. The planes in the sky do their best to protect the beleaguered PJs. Sergeant Kline listens to their radio chatter. They call out the position of some insurgents and seconds later the PJs are rocked by the concussion of exploding rockets. Despite the air support the Taliban's attack intensifies and the PJs start taking even more concentrated fire. Bullets rip up the landscape and tear into the wrecked Kiowa. Luckily the pilot's body is sheltered from the mayhem. The two PJs are only a few feet away from the ruined helicopter when the sheer volume of bullets becomes so intense it sets the wrecked Kiowa on fire. The high-tech alloys burn with an eerie blue flame that crawls over the twisted metal. Zack sees that the rocket pods lying nearby on the ground will soon ignite and yells, "Let's get the hell out of here!" The PJs make a dash for the backdoor ravine they spotted earlier. Dodging bullets during their sprint to the ravine they barely have time to dive behind some boulders before the rocket pods explode, throwing huge columns of roiling black smoke into the clear mountain air. The explosion sends chunks of blazing hot metal and debris screaming through the air, snapping into the rocks that shelter the PJs. It's a close call.

Some of the molten metal from the explosion spatters onto to Zack's equipment, melting into the fabric.

After the PJs ran up the ravine the gunships are no longer sure where they are and are reluctant to fire for fear of hitting them. Sergeant Kline has smoke grenades that he carries in his gear. He tells the gunships to watch for red smoke and pops the canister right on his own position. Thick red smoke sparks and hisses from the can and billows thickly into the sky. Now the Apaches and Warthogs can see exactly where the PJs are. Heavy rifle fire is still coming from the vicinity of the tree as the gunships dive to the attack. The sky swarms with American aircraft: Apaches, Kiowas, Pave Hawks, and Warthogs. Zack has read accounts of past high-profile rescue missions where our military committed every available aircraft to rescue a high-value target, such as a pilot with important military secrets. Looking around he's amazed; it seems like the whole world is in on this mission. As they hunker down a helicopter flies over their position carrying members of an army quick reaction force (QRF). The helicopter is low enough for them to see the soldiers sitting inside. The PJs look on helplessly as insurgents try to shoot down the army chopper with a rocket propelled grenade. Originally designed as antitank weapons, insurgents often use rocket propelled grenades as makeshift antiaircraft missiles, sometimes with success. This time their aim is off and the grenade whizzes by overhead, missing the helicopter, and, exploding on a nearby hillside, causes a small avalanche. Responding to Sergeant Kline's call for fire the gunships roll in and carpet the area with rockets and bombs. Their chain guns and 30mm cannons create a deafening roar as they spit out thousands of rounds per minute. The Apaches and Sandys smother the insurgents under a devastating blanket of lethal explosives.

Back at FOB Morales-Frazier, Pedro 83 lands and the PJs hand-off the rescued army aviator to the surgical team. Their helicopter has taken a lot of battle damage and its transmission is bone dry. The crew arranges for a ride back to Bagram to get another helicopter. They are anxious to get back in the fight. At Bagram they fire up another Pave Hawk, load on another team of PJs and a maintenance team, and head back to the FOB. Pedro 84 has also taken battle damage, but despite the numerous bullet holes the crew decides the chopper is still flyable. Pedro 83 loads a fresh team of PJs, which is led by Lt. Aaron Hunter and includes MSgt. Matt Schrader and

SSgt. Jason Ruiz. These fresh PJs replace Major Peterson's crew and allow for extended operations. Pedro 84 also gets fresh PJs when SSgt. Nate Greene and Tech Sergeants Joshua Vandenbrink and Angel Santana get onboard. In short order the two helicopters takeoff together and return to the crash site.

To take the pressure off the rescue force the 113th Cavalry Regiment from the Iowa Army National Guard inserts sixteen soldiers between Sadigan village and the crash site. This QRF redirects the attention of the Taliban away from the rescuers and probably saves the lives of PJs Kline and Cenna. But, there is a high price to pay. The army helicopters take heavy fire during the insertion and barely escape unscathed. The soldiers on the ground soon engage in a fierce firefight to the point where they are running low on ammunition. Army SSgt. James A. Justice, is killed in the fighting and Spec. Zachary Durham is wounded. The QRF radios the Pedros and requests an immediate medical evacuation for their wounded soldier.

The PJs can see their helicopter flying in the distance, sometimes dipping into valleys then reappearing. Sergeant Cenna has turned off his radio to conserve batteries and team leader Kline does all the talking. Despite all that has happened, they still have control of the fallen pilot's remains. The Pedro 84 pilot occasionally radios Sergeant Kline, saying things like, "Hang on Zack!" Zack still has his sense of humor and replies, "We're just catching a tan and waiting for our ride home." Over the radio, Sergeant Kline hears the QRF request medical evacuation for a wounded soldier. The PJs will have to hold out a while longer while the Pedros pick up the casualty.

The two Pedros fly towards the QRF along with an escort of two Apaches. The airspace is saturated with coalition aircraft. In addition to the Pave Hawks, Kiowas, Warthogs and Apaches there are now French helicopters in the sky. But, the enemy has a lot of firepower on the ground. On the first rescue attempt of the wounded QRF soldier Pedro 84's pilots, Major Bryant and Captain Nolting, fly down to thirty feet while the other three helicopters provide cover fire. However, before they can complete the rescue insurgents attack the chopper from the shelter of a building three hundred meters away. Pedro 84 has to abort, but on its way out the PJ and FE focus their guns on the building and fire it up. Dodging hostile fire and steel cables strung along the valley, the Pedros quickly form up for another rescue attempt.

This time Pedro 83 tries to make the pickup, but as Captain Hallada is about to land his Pedro once again comes under intense fire. All the Pave Hawks and Apaches return fire, but the attack still forces Pedro 83 to go around. Pedro 84 makes the next attempt to land, but three times is not a charm. Only a few feet above ground the Pave Hawk takes fire and has to abort the landing. This time the Apaches have a definite tally ho on the enemy location and roll in on it, their muzzle flashes unleashing hellfire missiles and chain-gun fire. This destroys the threat and on the fourth try Pedro 83 is finally able to land and pickup the wounded soldier. Now, it's finally time to recover PJs Zack Kline and Bill Cenna who have now spent more than five hours on the ground.

The pilots radio their intentions and Pedro 84 moves into position to extract the PJs. The FE, Sergeant Culbertson, knows this is the best and maybe last opportunity to hoist out the rescue team, but when he preps the hoist he discovers it's broken. Sergeant Culbertson tries the hoist in backup mode and luckily it works, but the cable will only lower and raise at the dangerously slow speed of fifty feet per minute. Dangerously slow because this means the helicopter will have to spend more time in a hover as a stationary target for insurgents. Culbertson lowers the cable and the PJs hook it to the litter containing the Kiowa pilot's body. When the FE raises the litter, the PJs on the ground are nervous at the slow rate of ascent. Captain Nolting is struck by the PJs' bravery in sending up the pilot first. This after they have been stranded on the ground under hostile fire for going on six hours. Nolting is also nervous about the slow speed of the recovery. The hovering helicopter is an easy target and as Pedro 84 finally retrieves its PJs during the second hoist he expects to be shot down at any moment. But, for the first time that day the helicopter does not come under attack. With the PJs and fallen hero safely onboard Pedro 84 finally leaves the crash site for good—mission completed!

CHAPTER 14

_____

LIFE AFTER PARARESCUE

_____

The memories of a man in his old age
Are the deeds of a man in his prime.
—*Roger Waters, Pink Floyd, "Free Four"*

If you would not be forgotten as soon as you are dead, either
write something worth reading or do things worth writing.
—*Benjamin Franklin*

I RETIRED FROM THE U.S. AIR FORCE IN JULY 2003; I WAS FORTY-SIX
years old. My final assignment was with the 38th Rescue Squadron at
Moody Air Force Base outside Valdosta, Georgia. I retired at the pinnacle
of my career and was blessed to be able to make enduring contributions
during a major transitional time in PJ history. I witnessed the beginning
of the combat rescue officer (CRO) career field and had a small part in
shaping its character and success. I was the first operations superintendent
at the very first rescue squadron commanded by a CRO. After the terrorist
attacks on 9/11, I helped prepare our squadron for war and led the first PJ
combat rescue jump in history, which set a precedent. That jump broke
the ice and since then there have been many other PJ combat rescue jumps.
I also had the honor of being the project officer for designing the 38th's
unit emblem.

   During my last year on active duty my son Billy graduated from Valdosta High School. I had raised Billy as a single parent since he was two

years old. When he graduated from high school I considered it one of the greatest achievements in my life. Although Billy was very smart and gifted, I struggled to get him to apply himself. He seemed to delight in skipping school and blowing off homework assignments. My frequent military deployments for months at a time didn't help. Billy viewed my absences as good opportunities to skip school; he was a record-setting truant. Although he was very talented, his attitude towards school gave new meaning to the word lackadaisical. With much wringing of hands and gnashing of teeth I somehow managed to shepherd Billy through high school. My military career and Billy's high school ordeal both concluded successfully and almost simultaneously. Both of us were ready to begin a fresh chapter in our lives.

After I retired I planned to take some time off before deciding on a new career. Billy planned to join the air force to be a PJ. The 123rd Air National Guard Special Tactics Squadron (STS) is located in Louisville, Kentucky, only a six hour drive from my hometown Warren, Ohio, where my mother still lives. I have many friends in the STS and they agreed to consider Billy for a spot on their team if he could meet the requirements. I also had other close friends who lived in the Louisville area. A month before my actual retirement, Billy and I drove to Louisville, found an apartment, bought cell phones and joined a gym: we were prepared. The day after I retired from the air force we drove to Kentucky and immediately moved into our new apartment.

In Louisville I trained Billy for pararescue, coaching him on running, swimming, and lifting weights. I spent most of my personal time working out and enjoying retirement. However, I made a serious mistake when I bought Billy a car. Suddenly his focus shifted from training to chasing girls and partying. After a time he finally admitted he didn't want to join the air force. I didn't really care what profession Billy chose to pursue, I just wanted him to be successful in life. For the time being, I didn't have a problem with him just having fun. I reasoned he would have the rest of his life to work.

After taking six months off I decided it was time to get a job and ended up applying at the gym where I worked out. Premier Health and Fitness had five gyms in the Louisville area and I landed a position as a manager at their club across the Ohio River in nearby Clarksville, Indiana. I didn't make a lot of money, but liked the atmosphere and energy. I had plenty of time to work out and was mostly surrounded by folks I could relate too: gym rats. This club was a big operation with lots of moving parts. I was in charge of personal fitness trainers, front desk personnel, sales staff, aerobics instructors, and a cleaning crew. I found that managing a large, complex fitness club is definitely a challenge.

After spending twenty-eight years in the military where my ultimate goal was saving lives, I suddenly found myself managing a business where my goal was making a profit. In the air force I had worked in positions of great responsibility and was an expert in my field. In my new job I was a manager but not a real expert in the gym business. One thing I had not fully appreciated while I was in the military was the systematic and continuous leadership training I had received. I took my leadership and management skills for granted, considering them common sense. I assumed that those in positions of power in the private sector would know and apply the basics tenets of leadership and management. But, I soon discovered that this is not always the case and most supervisors I met had no formal leadership training. Some of the top gym managers naively thought that reading a few self-help books equated to formal leadership training. I could not help comparing this civilian business run by self-taught managers to a military unit led by professionally-trained leaders. I was the new guy and tried to stay low key, but it was hard. I viewed it as a test from God and I only snapped a couple of times. However, I did take advantage of opportunities to broaden my horizons. I took up step aerobics and became certified as a group fitness instructor and personal trainer.

In January of 2005 I took the helm of Premier's flagship gym in Louisville. This complex gym was the largest in the franchise and even had a swimming pool. During this time I was also becoming frustrated with my stay-at-home son. Billy was getting speeding tickets and not making any real progress on choosing a career. Finally, I gave him an ultimatum. On the first day of June he would have to move out of my apartment and get a place of his own. To help with deposits and moving expenses I offered to match any money he saved during the six months leading up to his June deadline.

Billy had tried his hand at several different jobs and for a time even worked for me at the gym, but he was not very enthusiastic. One day he announced he had finally decided on a career. Like many in his generation,

Billy had grown up playing first-person-shooter video games. He decided to take that experience a few steps further and resolved to join a SWAT team and shoot bad guys for real. He visited the local police station to find out what requirements and training were necessary to become a SWAT team member. He found out that the process was a lot more involved than he expected. He first needed to attend a police academy and become a police officer. Afterwards he would have to work his way onto a SWAT team over time. There were no guarantees. During his visit to the police station he learned that many SWAT members were former Marine Corps snipers. During that same visit the cops ran Billy's plates through their criminal database and learned that he had outstanding warrants for speeding tickets. They unceremoniously arrested him and tossed him into jail. After seriously considering the pros and cons of letting Billy rot in a cell, I reluctantly paid off his fines and sprung him from the hoosegow.

Ultimately, Billy decided to join the U.S. Marine Corps to become a sniper. I had my doubts about his sincerity, but when I visited a Marine recruiter with him I realized he was serious. I always thought the Marine Corps was special. If anyone could transform my son into a contributing member of society it would be The Corps. Billy shipped out on 31 May 2005 and as I saw him off he said, "Made it by one day." He was referring to the 1 June deadline I had set for him to flee the nest. "Amazing, I forgot all about that!" I said.

Billy successfully completed Marine Corps Basic Training and infantry school. Afterwards, instead of sniper school he chose to try his hand at amphibious reconnaissance. Even average marines are bad asses, and recon selection and training is the among the most difficult and demanding specialties in the Marines Corps. Recon marines are among the Corp's elite. Billy successfully completed the grueling training and became a recon marine. I attended his graduation and the ceremony was in keeping with the Marine Corps's hard-core image. I was very emotional and proud of my son. Why recon and not pararescue? Billy wanted to make his own mark as a warrior completely independent of my influence, and he succeeded. My son is on his second enlistment and continues to adventure around the world. I am also blessed with a marine daughter-in-law Lindsey and a beautiful granddaughter Maddison. Billy has a fantastic family and is thriving in the Marines Corps. I'm an unbelievably proud father!

During my time in Kentucky I also met my future wife Debra. She was the star salesperson of the gym franchise and everywhere else she has ever worked. She is a sales and marketing savant. She is blond, beautiful, and talented. People often underestimate her. She takes advantage of other people's misconceptions and is good at thriving under the radar. Debbie used to be a regional account coordinator for a major cosmetic company. During that time she developed ground-breaking marketing strategies that were implemented nationally and industry wide. She made tons of money for her company. For reasons of her own she eventually moved on to pursue work in other areas.

Debbie worked with me in the gym and we got to know each other well. I discovered she was smarter and more capable than many of the consultants the gym brought in to increase business. I could not pursue her romantically as long as I was her manager, so I stepped down and transitioned to teaching aerobics and working as a personal trainer. Even though I had been single for eighteen years we had a special chemistry, and she finally put an end to my barbaric bachelor ways. Debbie has a wonderful personality and is a lifelong fitness buff. She also accepts my PJ brothers and views my sometimes checkered past with amusement. We are both a little eccentric.

As smart as she is Debbie has occasional moments that are so amazing they keep life interesting. Debbie was a bit inexperienced with social media and internet subtleties and conventions. One Christmas my son was visiting and our family was relaxing and talking. During the course of our conversation we started discussing internet lingo and acronyms. Billy made an off handed remark about LOL meaning "laugh out loud." Debbie said, "You're not serious are you?" We all looked at her wondering where this was going. "Of course he's serious. LOL means laugh out loud." I said. I watched in surprise as the blood drained from her face, and she became white as a sheet. I could tell by the expression on her face that her mind was racing. I didn't know what was going on, but her distress was almost palpable. You could hear a pin drop as we all waited for her next words. "I thought it meant "lots of love." Her pale skin and panic were the result of thinking back over all the occasions she improperly used LOL. The implications were staggering. Imagine that a good friend's mother dies and you offer condolences on Face Book, "I'm so sorry for your loss. LOL." Or, "I was so saddened to learn you have cancer. LOL." We laughed for hours! Debbie is definitely unique. Debbie jokes that my twenty-eight years as a PJ dealing with life and death situations was merely God's way of training me to handle life with her.

Overall I enjoyed the time I spent in the gym business and met many good and interesting people, but it was becoming increasingly clear to me that it was time to move on. When Debbie and I decided to marry I realized I needed to get serious about a second career. And as always seems to happen, at exactly the perfect time God provided the perfect opportunity. For the first time in history the Guardian Angel Training Center at Kirtland Air Force Base in Albuquerque, New Mexico, advertised for civilian PJ instructors. I immediately applied, was immediately accepted, and just like that I stepped into a new reality.

In September 2005 I married Debbie and adopted her dog Rosie, an ornery Lhasa Apso. In October we drove to Albuquerque to begin our new life. After a short two-year absence I was once again in the familiar environs of a PJ team. The Guardian Angel Training Center is an impressive facility. This multi-million dollar campus complex was specially built to train PJs and CROs. The school puts through five classes of about twenty-five students per year. This is barely enough PJs and CROs to replace those leaving the profession due to normal attrition, but you absolutely can't mass produce special operators. The PJ and CRO professions are very selective, choosing only those candidates who are the most likely to make it through the two years of training. Potential PJs and CROs must first pass a physical ability and stamina test (PAST) that helps predict their chances of making it through rigorous PJ training. The PAST is to pararescue selection what the SAT is to college admissions offices. The quality of the final product, in this case PJs and CROs, depends on the quality of the men entering training. If you don't begin with top quality raw material, you will be disappointed—garbage in garbage out.

The Guardian Angel Training Center is at the forefront of producing American warriors. I'm not just saying that because I'm connected to the school. I went through the PJ School in 1976 and followed its evolution during the twenty-eight years I served on active duty. I also attended many PJ graduations over the years in my capacity as a pararescue leader. The PJ and CRO School represents the pinnacle of combat rescue training.

In 2001 the PJ profession realized an important milestone. The PJ career field and CMSgt. Paul Miller, the PJ career-field manager at the time, had aggressively pushed for the creation of the combat rescue officer program. I was present at the inception of the CRO program and the creation of the first CRO-led PJ unit, the 38th Rescue Squadron. At that time there were only three CROs in the entire U.S. Air Force. At Moody Air Force Base, I helped stand-up the 38th Rescue Squadron. Our commander Maj. Vincent "Vinnie" Savino and our operations director Maj. Terry Johnson were our squadron's first CROs. Under their leadership, and with the help of our senior NCOs, our squadron flourished and distinguished itself in combat. Today there are nearly a hundred CROs in the air force and the program is strongly entrenched. Around the globe PJs and CROs accomplish hundreds of lifesaving missions per year. Put on your shades; the future of PJs and CROs is bright!

I wrote this book to tell of my missions and adventures and those of some PJ brothers to whom I'm connected. I enjoyed an unbelievably satisfying and exciting career. Despite a long history of amazing contributions to the United States and humanity, most Americans have never heard of pararescue. I want to shine a brilliant spotlight on the PJ and CRO professions as premier special operations assets. As operators go I have made a modest mark on PJ history, but I am not by any stretch of the imagination the most extraordinary or famous pararescueman. Some PJs have lost their lives serving our country and others have been prisoners of war. Many PJs have earned many more and higher medals for heroism than I have. Airman First Class William H. Pitsenbarger gave his life for his country and received the Medal of Honor; twelve PJs have earned the Air Force Cross, our nation's second highest honor, and a hundred and thirty five PJs have earned Silver Stars. Many PJs have had more missions than I have had, and many PJs have saved more lives than I have saved. However, I'm willing to bet not too many PJs have had more fun and adventure than I have had. But there are many PJs who would even take me up on that bet. I am known among PJs, but I'm not unique. There are a lot of spectacular PJs out there, it's enough just to belong to the brotherhood.

During my life I have lost many PJ brothers to aircraft crashes, parachute and scuba diving accidents, enemy gunfire, old age and disease, and other acts of God. At PJ get-togethers and reunions we remember our lost comrades with unbearable compassion. At the Guardian Angel Training Center I work to mold our next generation of PJ warriors. Like the other instructors I teach our rich PJ traditions and pass on lessons learned to help fledgling PJs and CROs survive in combat. Like all PJ instructors past and present I share our special brand of PJ humor with our students and teach them to spit in the grim reaper's eye. Pararescue is a dangerous profession. We use technology, constant training, experience, and strong leadership to survive. But ultimately, when it's your time to go, it's your time to go.

I have been intimately involved with pararescue for more than three decades. I have seen smooth-faced youngsters right out of PJ School, as green as the Jolly Green footprints tattooed on my backside, grow into amazing and accomplished PJs. Many of the rowdy young airmen I served with are now accomplished chief master sergeants and combat rescue officers. They are today's leaders, role models, mentors, heroes, and the guardians of our pararescue heritage and traditions.

I took the road less traveled by and it led to a pararescue career. As a result, I was privileged to travel the world and have incredible adventures. I also had the opportunity to serve my country and to make a difference by saving lives. When I get together with old PJ buddies someone will invariably say, "Do you remember that time when . . . ?" Like an electric shock, I experience a momentary jolt in my cerebral cortex, "Damn! I haven't thought about that for years!" Memories come flooding back and for the next few minutes we relive those distant events in time, laughing, spilling beer, and gesturing wildly as we tell our amazing, improbable, and sometimes embellished war stories. And, every PJ within earshot understands and can relate because they have all had similar experiences.

Once PJs retire and move on to a different profession they all say the same thing. What they miss the most is not the parachuting or scuba diving or flying, it's their PJ brothers. There are so many unique and eccentric PJ personalities! That's why PJs hold a reunion every two years. We miss the company of others who have had the same types of experiences and share the same sense of humor and world view. I spent most of my PJ career laughing, partying, and having adrenaline rushes. It was so much fun! I have literally forgotten more adventures than a lot of people ever experience. Marco Polo, a Venetian merchant, embarked on an epic journey of exploration and wonder that dramatically expanded the frontiers of Europe's knowledge of Central Asia and China. His subsequent book of adventures was so astounding, that many people remained skeptical of his claims until the day he died. When he was on his deathbed, a priest offered him a final chance to recant his story. Marco Polo replied, "I have not told half of what I saw." In a sense each PJ and CRO is a modern-day Marco Polo, exploring the word and having unbelievable adventures. I feel a certain kinship to the spirit of Marco Polo, because I have told only a small fraction of what I experienced.

Bad ass Samurai warriors used to write poems before going into battle, so I thought it would not be too unmanly to write a PJ poem. This short verse sums up my thoughts on my life in pararescue:

Lives entwine, friendships shine, variety is the spice
If I could relive my life, I would do it twice
WFS